MW00850160

To Sing with Pigs Is Human

The Concept of Person in Papua New Guinea

To Sing with Pigs Is Human

The Concept of Person in Papua New Guinea

JANE C. GOODALE

University of Washington Press

Seattle and London

Copyright © 1995 by the University of Washington Press
Printed in the United States of America

All rights reserved. No portion of this publication may be reproduced or
transmitted in any form or by any means, electronic or mechanical, including
photocopy, recording, or any information storage or retrieval system, without
permission in writing from the publisher.

Library of Congress Cataloging-in-Publication Data
Goodale, Jane C. (Jane Carter), 1926–
To sing with pigs is human : the concept of person
in Papua New Guinea / Jane C. Goodale.
p.   cm.
Includes bibliographical references (p.   ) and index.
ISBN 0-295-97454-0 (cl.)
ISBN 0-295-97436-2 (pbk.)
1. Kaulong (Papua New Guinea people)—Psychology.
2. Kaulong (Papua New Guinea people)—Social life and customs.
3. Identity (Psychology)—Papua New Guinea—New Britain Island.
4. Gender identity—Papua New Guinea—New Britain Island.
5. Self-perception—Papua New Guinea—New Britain Island.
6. Big man (Melanesia)—Papua New Guinea—New Britain Island.
7. New Britain Island (Papua New Guinea)—Social life and customs.
I. Title.
DU740.42.G66   1995   94-40671
306'.089'9912—dc20   CIP

The paper used in this publication meets the minimum requirements of American
National Standard for Information Sciences—Permanence of Paper for Printed
Library Materials, ANSI Z39.48—1984. ∞

Contents

Illustrations

MUSIC TRANSCRIPTIONS

Preface

While in Australia engaged in fieldwork during the 1950s, I became fascinated by the flood of ethnographic information coming out of the (then) Territory of Papua New Guinea. Ethnographers had worked in and written about many coastal regions of Papua New Guinea, but it was not until the years of the Second World War that the interior of New Guinea, and of some of the smaller islands, became known. Ann Chowning, who had already worked on the north coast of New Britain (Chowning 1958), suggested to me in 1960 that we might venture together into an as yet little-known region, the interior of southwestern New Britain. With the exception of a brief, published account of an expedition through this area by an ornithologist (Gilliard 1961), brief accounts of coastal peoples by Lewis (1945) and Todd (1934–35, 1935–36), and unpublished Patrol Reports, almost nothing was known of this region, its people, their language, or their culture.

Because our ethnographic interests are very similar and because we did not want to impose an awkward division of labor on our research topics and focuses, Ann and I planned to find two communities, linguistically (and we hoped culturally) distinct, where we could work independently but be close enough for periodic visits. We wanted to be able to compare notes and keep each other "sane and happy" and intellectually stimulated.

Our first trip in the summer of 1962 was an exploratory one. With a week's trek in and another similar trek out, our village stays lasted six weeks. I chose the Kaulong-speaking community of Umbi, located about four hours' walk away from the Sengseng-speaking community of Dulago in which Ann settled. Both communities were approximately twenty miles, and three days' walk, inland from the government post at Kandrian on the south coast. In 1963–64, we both returned to our respective communities for a research period of thirteen months in the interior.

We had expected to find significant cultural and social differences between the two communities, reflecting the distinctiveness of their languages, but we did not. Much of what is said here about Kaulong-speakers is also true for Sengseng-speakers, at least as far as our interpretations of these cultures can be said to reflect their reality. What we did find in this first short trip was quite provocative: unlike other Melanesian peoples of whom we had knowledge, and to cite the most obvious, the Kaulong and Sengseng hunt with twenty-foot blowguns, strangle widows on the death of their husbands, bind the heads of newborn infants, and consider marriage (and sexual activity) extremely dangerous for men. These traits are unusual for Melanesians.

Culturally constituted ideas of the nature of gender difference and gender relations were a major focus of our first extended study in Umbi and Dulago in 1963–64. In addition, and of necessity, both of us were obliged to study the languages. My own language study had only the practical aim of gaining fluency in Kaulong and initially (and to a limited extent) in *tok pisin*, a Melanesian lingua franca that few in Umbi spoke.

I chose to move to Angelek, a Kaulong community located closer to the coast, for my third and fourth visits (1967–68 and 1974) in order to gather comparative data for Kaulong-speakers. Here, and not surprisingly, I found that there were some significant differences *within* the Kaulong-speaking region. The meaning of these differences and when and how they came about are part of my analysis, and I will make reference to them in this work when I consider them to be significant and, of course, when I have the pertinent data.

In Angelek, I focused my study even more closely on gender differentiation and attitudes toward sexuality and marriage, on politics, on attaining humanity, and on the ritual of death and accompanying songs and performances. During my last, two-month visit in 1974, I worked almost solely on obtaining translations of more than three hundred recorded songs then in my possession.

It seemed to me, as I struggled to comprehend the underlying cultural themes and values of life in Kaulong, that the people were singularly concerned with self-definition as human beings. And so, in this monograph I have organized the discussion and description to present a comprehensive and inclusive analysis of the meaning and definition of *humanity*—what they call *potunus*—in Kaulong society and culture. How does one become human and, equally important, how does one maintain this human condition? And, finally, how does one exhibit—and thereby validate—one's humanity through public performances and activities?

The word *potunus* is a noun form that I gloss as "human," or humanity, collectively. Literally, the word may be broken down as follows: *po-*, "all"; *-tunus*, "good" or "complete." In its combined form, *potunus* is applied only to people and denotes their condition on a conceptual continuum of nonhuman (animal-like) to human.

Becoming *potunus* is a personal achievement for both men and women. Much has been written about individuality in Melanesian culture, but I know of no other society in which so much is focused on the individual to the detriment of community. The Kaulong said to me, "If a person wants to live in peace, he or she lives in the bush alone." Since living in the bush alone is not human behavior (neither is fighting), the basic life problem is set: to be "human" one must live with others and one must do this without fighting, which is itself natural, expected, and animal-like.

Clifford Geertz has written: "Man is an animal suspended in webs of significance he himself has spun. I take culture to be those webs and the analysis of it to be . . . a search for meaning" (1973a:51). The meaning for which I searched among the Kaulong was the meaning of the culturally constructed category of being human.

Following an introduction to locate the Kaulong geographically and historically and describe the ethnographer's experience among them, I begin, in chapter 2, a discussion of Kaulong humanity. How do Kaulong perceive their own physical bodies, minds, and selves or souls? I show that knowledge is acquired through the interaction of body, self, and mind, but is stored in the self—the *enu*. This leads to a discussion (chapters 3 and 4) of a wide variety of details of Kaulong daily life, including production of resources and the system of exchange. In chapter 5, I discuss the differentiation between people as they become politically active and acquire, through human activities, variable quantities of fame as *potunus*, big men and big women, the Kaulong elite.

In chapters 6 and 7, through the major differentiating characteristics of women and men, I show that the former exhibit certain natural qualities that are considered to be dangerous to men. The asexual (and human) cross-sex relationship of the brother-sister dyad is then contrasted with the sexual (and not human) relationship of husband and wife. I argue that the fundamental and culturally constructed problem of maintaining one's humanity is that the act of sexually reproducing one's self is seen to be inhuman. Yet immortality is achieved only through the replacement of one's self with a child. How the Kaulong meet this challenge concludes this section.

In the final chapters (8 through 10), the most human of activities—the performance of song with pigs in a ritual context—is described, discussed, and analyzed. The meanings of song and song performances are illustrated with examples selected to show the various types of song and the poetry imbedded within. The most serious of all song performances is the one having to do with the skull of a deceased human being, a *potunus* of significant fame. I show what it means to have achieved and retained the culturally constituted status of *potunus*, and conclude with a discussion of what I believe are the key symbols of Kaulong humanity: pigs, teeth, bones, fire, sex, and song. With this discussion I give voice to the meaning of the web strung by the Kaulong between the (human) clearing and the (animal) forest.

My primary purpose in this study has been to describe the Kaulong culture through their concept of the place of humanity in the world they have constructed. From my experience with two pieces of long-term repeated fieldwork, first among the Tiwi of North Australia and second among the Kaulong, I have found that most of the "imponderables" (Malinowski 1929) and contradictions that I observed or heard expressed by informants will eventually make sense when the right questions have been asked, both in the field and afterwards in analyses. Understanding is achieved, I believe, in the completeness of the data; but, of course, there is always more to gather, more to learn, to see, and to hear. When most of the loose ends become attached, when

most of the seemingly irrelevant information or behavior becomes relevant, then I believe there is validity to the explanation offered by the
ethnographer.

Finding validity in an explanation is similar to the pleasure one feels
when, in unravelling a skirt hem, the right thread is cut and pulled. As
those who sew know, there is only *one* thread that allows a smooth and
complete undoing in one pull. When you don't find that one right
thread, the unravelling is both tedious and tiring—a snippet here, a
snippet there. When I have found that sought-for explanation, the
interlocking connections between a host of previously unrelated facts
literally flow from my thinking and are seemingly unforced, natural,
real, and, moreover, compellingly right.

Ideally, these ethnographic explanations should be delivered back to
one's informants to see if they make sense to them. I had such an
opportunity to check some grand insights with the Tiwi of North Australia, who then remarked, "that's what we've been trying to tell you
all along." Among the Kaulong, I had a number of opportunities to do
the same, although not on such a grand scale because I have not
returned to the area since completing some of my analyses that have
led to the understanding that has shaped this book. Even though what
I report on here is of the period of 1962–74, I hope that the Kaulong
also would agree that "that's what they had been trying to teach me all
along." For, while some of the details of their lives have certainly
changed, I believe that their concept of humanness is so fundamental
an aspect of their being that it is not subject to quick change.

As I have tried to make my description understandable to contemporary Kaulong, I have also had other readers in mind. Much excellent
ethnography is being written on Melanesian cultures and societies, but
little of this comes from one of the major islands in the modern nation of
Papua New Guinea, New Britain. The region of New Britain is one
where a considerable amount of ethnography has been carried out by
scholars, but only a few of these have chosen the monograph form in
which to present their data: Harding (1967) and Pomponio (1991) have
written about the Vitiaz Strait region at the western end of New Britain;
Salisbury (1970), T. S. Epstein (1968), A. L. Epstein (1969), and Errington
(1974) have covered the eastern region around Rabaul. With the excep-

tion of Valentine's work, *Masks and Men in Melanesian Society* (1961), on the north coastal region of the Lakalai, most of the ethnography has found its way into journal articles and book chapters or rests in as yet unpublished dissertations (see, for example, Chowning and the Countses' many journal publications). Perhaps because of this, New Britain peoples and cultures have been largely left out of the many debates concerning such common Papua New Guinea themes as gender, politics, religion, ritual, exchange, and social organization.

I believe that there are some significant comparisons to be made that will enlarge our understanding of the variations as well as similarities in Melanesian culture and society. Although these comparisons are not a part of this monograph, I had them in mind while presenting these data. To this end I have used a minimum of jargon and anthropological terminology, feeling that these more often cloud than clear the communication between the observer and the observed, the author and the reader.

A Kaulong once asked me, "Why should anyone care to understand us?" I replied, "With the knowing of others there are no strangers to fear." He seemed satisfied.

Acknowledgments

With fieldwork extending over twelve years, there are many whose support I want to acknowledge. First and foremost, Ann Chowning has assisted my understanding both in the field and subsequently. While we have published little jointly, our mutual support, while in shadow, is no less important. Secondly, I must acknowledge the many fellow participants in the Association for Social Anthropology in Oceania who over the years have commented individually and collectively on various earlier versions of much of the discussions included here. In particular I single out David and Dorothy Counts, Mac Marshall, and Mike Lieber. To the latter I owe an additional debt of gratitude for his close editorial reading of the manuscript and for forcing me to think more deeply about some of the concepts.

I have drawn extensively from three previously published papers and to the editors, C. MacCormack and M. Strathern, M. Marshall, and S. Lindenbaum, and to unknown reviewers of these manuscripts, I also extend my thanks. In addition, I am very grateful to A. Weidman and S. Glickman for assistance with the music, and in particular to Inants Mezzaraups for his fine transcriptions.

Members of the Australian administration and expatriates in private enterprise aided me in many official and personal ways. In the administrative headquarters at Kandrian, D. Stevens, D. Goodger, Frank Empin, John and Eddie Yun, J. R. Snashall, Algie Bessasperis, Bruce McLean, C. P. Campbell, E. Dallamor, Mark Jeram, and Fr. Hoffman all gave generously of their hospitality, logistical support, and paperback books, for which mere thanks seem inadequate.

To all Kaulong men and women, old and young, in Umbi, Angelek, and neighboring communities, who helped me intellectually, emotionally, and physically; who so willingly answered my questions and accompanied me on the many excursions through the forests; and who risked their own lives to give me a supporting hand as we inched together across the slippery logs above raging waters—to all these Kaulong friends I give my sincere and heartfelt thanks, for their enormous contribution to this work.

Residents of Umbi—Kahamei, Liem, Kasli, Iangmei, Ulengmei, Sakhun, Utwungin, Panpan, Lepli, Debli, Ningbi, Ihime, Sekiali, Sutli, Kaliam, Gospo, Blakli, Nelulu, Ligiok, Dangit, Slabli, Pahinbo, Soksili, Utsili, Laulu, Hingmei, Isu, Utkunut, Korepo, Imutmei, Yingme, Gaho, Maulme, Kongli, Utkiwo, Tuntunio, Hugut, Debe, Kilengmei, Longpapa, Molme, Idaso, Lusmei, and their children.

Residents of Angelek—Lemli, Koros, Kamil, Wiame, Mikail, Molio, Peinwhal, Pangel, Papolio, Yangin, Sergit, Tehigit, Lengme, Gaspat, Nakling, Lipok, Posin, Kinegit, Yielo, Peiying, Kalingio, Siame, Kusuk, Sukulme, Lata, Warkorok, Palak, Galap, Wilwil, Mili, Irep, Iskit, Sambet, Linga, Tihimis, Rihelik, Yiakas, Mulungio, Pamonme, Tomli, and Maria.

I hope that some of my Kaulong friends or their descendants may read these words. I hope, too, that I have not misinterpreted what they told me in explanation. Any errors of interpretation are, of course, entirely mine.

This study was supported by grants from the National Institute of Mental Health (M6484-A); National Science Foundation (GS77, GS-1470); National Geographic Society; American Council of Learned Societies; and Bryn Mawr College Faculty Research Funds—for all of which I am most grateful.

To Sing with Pigs Is Human

The Concept of Person in Papua New Guinea

1/ The Kaulong and "Others":
An Interpretive History

Early in the course of my ethnographic fieldwork among the Tiwi of North Australia during the 1950s (Goodale 1971), I found that I often debated with myself as to how to deal with my own involvement in events that I observed. Since I was part of the observed event, I reasoned that my field notes should contain my participation, including thoughts and feelings along with those observed activities and related information.

As my note-taking evolved during the four Kaulong trips in the sixties and seventies, I gave up keeping a separate diary and began including all kinds of information in my field notebooks: the weather, the goings and comings of people, and my own mood and activities not related directly to the recording of information. Often when it seemed that "nothing was going on" I recorded that, too; at the least it explained the thinness of some of the daily entries. I remember my colleague Frederica de Laguna telling me that "an ethnographer should record everything that she would need in order to write a novel in addition to a monograph." Consequently, in otherwise idle moments I recorded detailed physical and psychological descriptions of the main and minor characters, the different smells that particular kinds of firewood gave as they burned, the particular pitch of a voice that might indicate that someone was angry and wanted an audience to gather to hear the complaint, air temperatures, bird calls, the sound of light and heavy rain pelting on the thatched roof, and the sound of the small rats having a domestic quarrel in the thatch during their nightly stirrings while I tried to sleep, how it felt to fall asleep to the drumming and singing of a hamlet's all-night ceremony (*singsing*), the bone-chill of the hour before the *kauk* (a small

Kandrian Region of Southern West New Britain Province

bird) sang out to herald the rise of the sun, the agonizing human quality of the cry of a sacrificial pig being speared, and the moment of fear as I was nearly pulled under the turbulent waters of the flooded Ason River while returning home after visiting in Dulago. In my notebooks, I separated what I had seen and heard from what I thought or interpreted with brackets around the latter. I kept my notes running in chronological order, reasoning that no event is ever entirely "out of place."

My own approach to the reality of the interpretive nature of ethnographic fieldwork has been to consider that cultural interpretation is to be found imbedded in that central cross-cultural dialogue between informant and anthropologist. I learned early in my professional life that my informants are testing their own theories of the cultural concepts underlying *my* behavior even as I am struggling to interpret theirs. I believe both parties to the cross-cultural encounter have a mutual aim: to learn the underlying culturally constructed concepts of humanness and social order by which others express rules and strategies, beliefs and understandings of the world in which they live. Why this endeavor to understand the "other" takes place at all within a meaningful relationship may be explained at the simplest level: so that each can learn to predict moods and motivations of the other in a variety of situations. This was extremely difficult for both the Kaulong and their ethnographer particularly in the remote community of Umbi. I believe this difficulty was partly because our basic underlying cultural concepts were so very different. However, a major factor was that the Kaulong of Umbi had had so little contact with Europeans, or, indeed, any "others," that they lacked experience in assessing cultural differences. Initially, the dialogue I had with informants seemed to be very one-sided; I was making all the effort to understand them while it seemed that they made little or no effort to understand me. Inevitably we grew to understand each other better, and out of this comes my interpretation of their life—and in particular their ideas of humanity.

And so in this introductory chapter, I include myself in the discussion of the setting, in order to provide an adequate account of my field experiences, even while describing the background information necessary for a reader's comprehension of the particulars of my interpretation of individual personhood among the Kaulong.

THE SETTING

The Passismanua region of southwestern New Britain includes two major language families: (1) the people of the offshore islands who are linguistically related to other Arawe-speakers who live along the coast from west of Kandrian to the Arawe Islands; and (2) people speaking one of the four closely related languages (Kaulong, Sengseng, Karore, and Miu) of the Whiteman language family (Chowning 1969b), who live inland and extend into the foothills of the Whiteman Mountains.

This inland region receives more than 250 inches of annual rainfall. Five major rivers, rising in the Whiteman Mountains, drain south and roughly form the boundaries of the four Whiteman linguistic groups. From west to east: the Alimbit River forms the western boundary of the approximately one thousand Kaulong-speakers. The Kaulong extend along both sides of the river designated on maps as the Apaon but called Ason by the Kaulong living in the foothills of the Whiteman mountain range. The very small numbers (fewer than three hundred) of Miu-speakers live near the headwaters of the Alimbit River and by 1974 were still largely uncontacted. Sengseng-speakers (numbering about three hundred) live on both sides of the Andru River, and to their east are the Karore-speakers. These four language groups are Austronesian (although utilizing a somewhat aberrant vocabulary) in contrast to many other interior peoples of New Britain whose language is non-Austronesian. It was because Chowning expected these heretofore unstudied languages to be Austronesian that we chose this region in which to work. Chowning already spoke two Austronesian languages, Lakalai and Molima, and had an interest in comparative Austronesian. I was encouraged that Austronesian languages were generally considered much easier for a European to learn than the non-Austronesian languages spoken in many other parts of Papua New Guinea.

In July 1962, Ann Chowning and I flew from Rabaul to Kandrian, the administrative post for southwestern New Britain. This small settlement was perched on a narrow strip of flat ground, beside a body of water named Moewehafen by the Germans in the early twentieth century. On the other side of the bay lay three offshore islands, each rising to about five hundred feet above sea level. On one of these—Apugi—the Church of England had a mission. These islands were matched by an escarpment rising to an equal height inland just behind Kandrian.

The European community at Kandrian consisted of Assistant District Officer Dave Stevens, his wife Mary, and children; a patrol officer, David Goodger, and his wife and child; Frank Empin, a malaria control officer; John Snashall, a European medical assistant who manned a small aid post; and a school teacher in charge of an elementary school. A small trade store was run by John, then Eddie, Yun. On the bluff above Kandrian, a Catholic mission housed a European priest and several nuns who ran an elementary school. Below the bluff, squeezed into the flat area, there was a small jail with a detachment of native police billeted nearby.

The personnel at Kandrian changed throughout the twelve-year span of my work. All were enormously helpful to those of us living and working in the bush. They opened their houses to us, fed us, kept us happy with a constant supply of reading matter, and were, in fact, the only outside visitors to our field sites.

Prior to our 1962 trip, Ann and I arranged, through the Department of Native Affairs in Port Moresby, Rabaul, and Kandrian, to be escorted into the interior of the Passismanua region on an exploratory expedition in search of two communities that would be distinct in language and culture but adjacent enough to allow us to visit each other occasionally. We also wished to check the nature of the languages and the degree of acculturation from contact with government and missions. Our interests lay in religion, gender relations, and political organization, and we hoped to study groups minimally affected by contact with non-Melanesians. We had chosen this region because Gilliard (1961) had reported the recency of contact, particularly in the foothills of the Whiteman Mountains, and also had described three rare, even unique, aspects of these societies: twenty-foot-long blowguns, head binding, and the strangling of widows.

We found that, except for the immediate coast and perhaps ten miles inland, this region had never been mapped. Behind the coast was a vast blank on which the words "unmapped—gently undulating" were hardly informative. David Goodger, the Kandrian patrol officer, had spent a week preparing for us a sketch map of the region from his own patrols into the interior. No map gave us any true indication of the nature of the terrain that was to confront us in our "exploratory expedition." And although we knew that this was the height of the rainy season, we had at that time no conception of what an annual rainfall of 250 inches meant to human life.

On Tuesday, July 17, our expedition left Kandrian. Dave Goodger asked another member of the administrative staff of Kandrian, Malaria Control Officer Frank Empin, to help him in accompanying the two of us. He had also gathered six native policemen and forty-five local carriers to transport our collective gear—tents and camping equipment, clothes, and food. For the initial hour of our journey we all rode on top of a tractor-drawn wagon. The first escarpment was easily climbed, and we rode past the grass airstrip and past the cutoff to the Catholic mission station at Turuk. The road then became muddy and eroded. After we had barely escaped sliding off several log bridges into ditches, we reached the village of Seilwa. From here we began the real journey inland, following wide footpaths leading into the heavily forested interior on the way to our first day's destination of Aka. The procession was always the same. First were the local carriers loaded down with our gear, some of it packed into aluminum patrol boxes and slung on stout poles carried on the shoulders of two men. Other smaller containers were balanced on the top of the head, the position favored by women carriers. Some of the police went with the first carriers and some followed behind. We almost never saw the carriers from the moment they went ahead to when at last we caught up with them at the end of our daily trek. Dave, Frank, Ann, and I brought up the rear, with perhaps one or two young men or women carrying our travel gear and guiding us over the hazards, holding our hands and encouraging us to advance.

The forest was incredibly beautiful in the sunlight. Huge trees with enormous, buttressing roots rose into the sky and their branches splattered the rays of the sun on the almost bare forest floor. Many of the trees trailed lengthy veils of vines from their tops to secondary trees and eventually to the ground. And there was a pleasing damp earth smell and a lovely coolness out of the intense sunlight of the open road.

The paths we found were treacherous, slippery with packed moist clay, and crisscrossed in every direction by numerous roots to trip one up. It could be fatal to remove one's eyes from the next foot placement. Very quickly the path began to climb over a continuous series of steep ridges providing slopes on which we slid both going down and climbing up. At the bottom of the slopes were gullies, some with and others without flowing water and often spanned by a single slippery felled log for travelers to inch across above a raging torrent. There were swamps with hungry clinging mud that threatened to consume our shoes, if not our entire bodies. At the top of each slope, painfully reached, there was not a vista by which to measure one's progress, only the same brown and green forest and the slippery path leading down to the next stream or swamp with its own uniquely frightening excuse for a bridge. I can truthfully say that of all the dreamed-of hazards of life in the deep and uncharted forests of southwestern New Britain, it was only the inevitable challenge of stream- or river-crossings by log that, to the very end, petrified me so that I often had cause to rue the day that I had decided to become an anthropologist.

By the time I reached Aka, I had the beginning of blisters on both heels. Aka was a small village of about eight rectangular houses built in a circle around a central clearing, itself bare of vegetation. The houses were made of rough-hewn planks and the roofs were thatched with lawyer-vine leaves. Aka had a government rest house that Ann and I were offered for the night; Dave and Frank shared a tent. It was here that Ann collected enough of the vocabulary to determine that Kaulong was indeed Austronesian, so that one of our criteria was met.

The following day after breakfast we set off on the next leg of our journey, which took us about five hours of painful progress as I nursed my taped heels. Shortly after we left Aka the true nature of a limestone karst environment became apparent as we climbed the next escarpment; from there on, the way grew increasingly steep, slippery, and dangerous. The narrow footpath negotiated edges of open potholes of undetermined depth, some with underground rivers roaring below, or took the dangerous route on top of slippery fallen logs. Infrequently the path led over broken log fences to make its way through the entangling dense patches of secondary growth in gardens long abandoned.

As we neared a small settlement we walked outside strongly bound log fences rising four to five feet high, which protected a growing garden from domestic and wild pigs. We passed through a number of small communities, each under a dozen houses, in which we paused only long enough to drink from a green coconut for refreshment before we reached Arihi.

Dave Goodger had told us that Arihi might be a good place for one of us as it was beyond mission influence. It was, he added incidentally, where a European who was recruiting labor for a plantation on the coast had been murdered in the late 1950s. The convicted murderers had only recently returned from their imprisonment. Arihi was a larger village than those we had previously seen, but we were dismayed to find that two lay brothers of the Church of England, recruited from the Solomon Islands, were also in residence. As we hoped to locate our research in groups that had not yet had mission influence in order to study the precontact religion, we made plans to continue our search for the first "ideal" community farther on into Kaulong country. However, our departure was delayed by the rain.

At the height of the rainy season, we had been very lucky not to have had much rain during the first two days. It now caught up with us and we spent all the next day experiencing our first drenching rain as it turned the central village clearing into a lake. Ann and I sat in the rest house most of the day, imprisoned by the rain and not seeing a living soul, although smoke rising through the thatch of village roofs made us believe that we were not abandoned. At tea time Frank and Dave appeared and we commiserated about the situation over tea as they told us they had slept all day. We were to find out later that both Kaulong and Sengseng fall asleep at the beginning of a drenching rainfall and may sleep for days, rising only to eat a little food and attend to nature's calls, before stretching out to sleep until the rain abates. Later I, too, found this response to heavy rain easy to make habitual.

The following day, with a destination of Umbi, we moved on over a bush track that went through a region empty of any village settlements and said to be difficult. It was a memorable day for me. Although my blistered heels were fully taped, I was forced by pain to walk entirely on my toes with the heels of my shoes folded down so that they could not further irritate my feet. I contemplated going without shoes altogether, but was persuaded not to do so because the mud was booby-trapped with sharp chert flakes ready to slice one's flesh to the bone. For nine agonizing hours I trailed behind all the others, with only Frank encouraging me to trudge onward. We followed the now very narrow and sometimes invisible bush track over streams, ridges, and bridges, through heavy forest and the tangle of the occasional over-grown former garden, and through numerous mud swamps, all of which were becoming familiar but no less difficult to negotiate.

Unlike our previous days, we passed no signs of human life or habitation, save one small hamlet with a log-type house inhabited by an old man, an hour from our destination of Umbi. Shortly after this, one of the policemen came back along the path carrying a pressure lamp to light our last mile or so. What a relief to find that a tent had been set up for Ann and me, another for Frank and Dave, and one for the police. And a steaming mug of strong tea was pressed into my hand.

With some apprehension I peeled my soggy, muddy socks off my feet to find that heels and toes and everything in between had been rubbed raw. It was clear to me that I would go no farther in the near future.

Umbi

How does any anthropologist select the particular research community in which to live for a year or more? Not many of us detail the particulars that led us to choose community x over community y, and I wonder if many like me had the choice made for them by some not-so-scientific fact (see, for example, Mead 1938). Whatever the case, I have yet to hear an anthropologist say that they chose their community wrongly or unwisely. I can now fully justify my "choice" by saying that Umbi was the ideal community for one of us to settle in. It was the largest community in the region, with a registered population of seventy-eight men, women, and children. It was Kaulong-speaking and had no missionaries. In fact, it was a fairly new community that had come into official existence only five years before, and during the five years had received very few patrols. Dave told us that just below the village was the large river Ason; and while there were a few Kaulong-speaking communities on the other side, this one was close to Sengseng territory, where Ann would be likely to find a satisfactory community.

The following day it truly poured, and poured, until the water flooded the ground in our tent. We sat crosslegged on our cots and wrote letters to be mailed eventually in Kandrian, carried by Dave, Frank, and the patrol returning from depositing Ann. In spite of the rain, Dave came to tell me that he had negotiated with the local people and I could stay here—"to learn the language," he had told them. Soon I was introduced to Kahamei, the *luluai* or government-appointed village headman, and Sekiali, a young cousin of the headman who would, I was told, work for me. This introduction and explanation was in *tok pisin*, of which I could speak or understand very little. As it turned out, very few of these villagers knew *tok pisin* either. I was told that the police were overseeing construction of a house that was being built for me, in the pouring rain.

It continued to rain hard. The Ason, the villagers told us, was completely flooded and impassable, and thus Ann could not continue her journey into the neighboring Sengseng-speaking area. I remember feeling enormously relieved that I was not going to be abandoned—today. I cautiously ventured out (with my feet loosely covered by rubber boots) and found myself in a community of about ten houses situated on a narrow shoulder of the steep mountainside. The houses were of the thatched-plank style, set in a circle around the edge of the central clearing. Behind the houses on three sides was the solid, dark green forest screen of the mountain wall. The path to the river led steeply down on the fourth side just in front of the men's house guarding the clearing. Spirals of smoke coming through the thatched roofs were of little comfort—I wondered how I was to get along in a community where no one spoke any language with which I was familiar, and where everything, including our latrine, was afloat.

I found out the next day. My house was finished and the river had subsided enough for the patrol and Ann to cross to the other side, guided through the turbulent, shoulder-high water and unsure footing by clutching a lawyer vine strung between trees on each bank. It was raining lightly. I went with them down the steep approach to the river and watched for an hour as the carriers struggled across with the cargo; then finally Dave, Frank, and Ann also reached the opposite bank, waved back at me, and disappeared into the forest to climb the mountain on the other side. I was very glad I didn't have to make the crossing, and I turned to my companions from Umbi. Language was not necessary as we easily communicated our mutual desire to climb hastily back up to the village and get warm and dry.

My first house was built on a platform of logs, with bark walls and a thatch roof. Measuring no more than eight by eight feet, it barely held a card table, a chair (on loan from the Department of Native Administration), and a canvas cot on which to put my air mattress. My supplies were in two metal "patrol boxes," especially made to be carried suspended from a strong pole set on the shoulders of two men. On the table sat my single-burner pressure-stove, my enameled plate and mug, and a hurricane lamp hung from the center ridge pole. There was a very small extension of the floor outside in the front, which could be loosely called a verandah, on which I could sit and survey the surrounding scene, weather permitting. Close by there was a plank-style house, where my assistant, Sekiali, would live. There was also another young man, whose name was Debli, who said "I work for you." Because he was busy cleaning my collection of mud-laden shoes and boots and had made my bed and because I had no way to disagree, I acknowledged that he was also working for me.

From my house, the village was hidden by a screen of dense forest, but inside of a few days, this was cleared, giving me a lovely overview of the entire village. A bark-covered, circular enclosure close by gave me privacy for my shower, which dripped from a suspended overhead bucket. I soon found that I had to wait for the rain to stop before I could both shower and change into clean and *dry* clothing.

Somehow we communicated. Much of it was with sign language. During the first days I managed to buy some bananas and taro to supplement my tinned food; and with the help of the *luluai*, I paid all the housebuilders for their labor. But one day, in frustrated boredom, I started to play with a circle of string, making a string figure I knew as "crow's feet." The girls visiting in my house exclaimed in evident delight. They rushed to find vine-string in order to have me teach it to them and to teach me some of their very extensive and complex repertory of string figures. Constant instructions involving "this one, that one, under here, over there, no, yes," and the language lessons began to take on meaning. The entire community of men, women, and children took it as a directive from the *kiap* (the government official) that they were to teach me the language, and so they uttered sounds and I repeated them and transcribed them on paper. Toward the end of the first week or so, I noticed that all the utterances ended with two sounds, *"e"* and *"di."* I wondered if this could mean something like "repeat after me." If it did, then I could leave it out of my repetition of sounds. This I did when my companions instructed me to say *"wom moh e di"* to some approaching women. Without a clue as to what it meant, *"Wom moh"* (you three come), I repeated, and was both surprised and delighted when the women responded; we all together danced our joy at found communication. Obviously a linguistic breakthrough had occurred. I had finally given them proof that I was a potentially intelligent human being; that I could be taught their language.

I wonder today at the patience of my Kaulong language tutors. Like all good teachers they went slowly but surely, instructing me endlessly in simple conversation, much as they taught their own children to understand their first words. I learned to communicate without translation, some of my speech mixed with *tok pisin,* for I had a dictionary of that language, and my two assistants and one or two others as well knew the rudiments of this *lingua franca.* But it did not seem to matter to any of us which vocabulary we used. Our sole, and mutual, desire was to understand each other. This, my major research goal in 1962, was achieved to a considerable degree by the end of my initial six-week sojourn in Umbi. After about three weeks, I found I could both question and understand most of the answers concerning everyday needs, activities, and simple ideas.

My ability to move about the vicinity depended on the healing of my feet. Since I dared not walk with shoes until my heels were completely healed, Ann came to Umbi for a visit after a month. She brought with her a beautiful chipped chert artifact she found on the path between our two communities. We were very excited, for until that find, no chipped stone tools had been reported anywhere in New Britain.[1] But we were not there to dig into the prehistory of the area, and we spent our time together comparing our two communities, situations, problems, and progress. Ann had settled in the Sengseng-speaking village of Dulago, which with only six houses was considerably smaller than Umbi. The road between our two sites passed through Silop, a linguistically mixed Kaulong and Sengseng village, and Yombon, which was Sengseng. The biggest physical hazard between us was the large Ason River, which ran in a steep-sided valley between two mountain ridges and was subject to frequent flash floods. But once one had crossed the river and climbed for an hour up the ridge on the other side, the road to Dulago was fairly gentle and forgiving to the traveler, and the entire trip usually took about four hours.

We found that our two communities, in spite of the language differences, were probably quite similar culturally, but we decided to make plans to return the following June for a major, year-long ethnographic trip. We had achieved our initial aim: we had located two communities, speaking different but related Austronesian languages, where the contact with missions and external governments had been minimal or nonexistent and where the people would be willing to have us return for a more extended stay. We made long lists of necessities for both professional and personal comfort for the next year.

Together with Debli and the *luluai*, I planned a far larger house, with a verandah on which people could sit and talk, high enough off the ground to have a fire below the house for cooking and for warmth, and with an inside shower. I arranged that once I had obtained a grant to fund the stay, I would send word to Debli, who with others of his choosing would pick up in the Kandrian trade store both building

1. Eventually our collection of more than three hundred chert artifacts was distributed as follows: two small study collections, one for each of us, and the rest eventually to the museum in Port Moresby (Chowning and Goodale 1966; Goodale 1966b). Subsequently, an archeological survey and recent excavations at Yombon (a village between Umbi and Dulago) revealed evidence of occupation dated at 35,000 BP—the oldest site in New Britain (Specht et al. 1981, 1983; Pavlides 1993).

supplies (axes, nails) and bags of rice to feed the builders, so that the house would be ready and waiting for my return the following year.

Financed by a joint grant from the National Science Foundation, and with the loan of cameras and supplies of film from the National Geographic Society, whose editors felt there might be a publishable story in our research (see Goodale 1966a), we returned in June of 1963. This time, Ann and I traveled inland with a single native policeman accompanying us whose job it was to negotiate with the succession of necessary carriers to move the greatly enlarged collection of equipment we felt necessary for our living, cooking, lighting, recording, etc., for a thirteen-month period.

We took a different route this time, crossing the Ason much further down at Ngata over a rickety bridge of loosely bundled logs, thence through two communities before reaching Pomalal. Here our roads diverged, Ann traveling the track to the northeast and Dulago, and I going to the northwest, through Akiuli and Hulem and then down the ridge to the river-crossing just below Umbi. We had fairly good weather this time, but since Ann had dislocated her knee just three weeks prior to our trek inland and I had spent the last night before departing from Kandrian cutting her free from the hip-to-ankle-length plaster cast with a small pair of nail scissors, it was a trip in its own way remarkable, as well as slow because Ann could not bend her right knee at all.

I found upon my return to Umbi that some Solomon Island lay mission-brothers had arrived a month earlier and had built themselves a house farther up the ridge on which my house was situated, overlooking the village. I was disappointed and decided to ignore them for the time being. When I asked why they were allowed to build there (the year before I was told Umbi would never allow any missionaries to come), the *luluai* told me that the community had come to realize that it was inevitable that either the Catholics or the Church of England would reach them. A delegation had gone on a fact-finding mission and learned that "Englands" like to work their own garden and not depend on donations of food from the community and indeed often helped others build gardens. Furthermore, they learned that the "Englands" did not force children to come to school or beat them if they misbehaved. All of these behaviors, they learned, were different from *"pasim bilong popi"* (the way of the Catholics). So they invited the Solomon Islands "brothers" to come.

My house had indeed been built under Debli's direction, hardly to the design I had agreed upon, but no less impressive and fitting to my needs. Constructed on a rather high platform of logs fully five feet from the ground, its floor beams were covered with split black palm trunks. The walls and partitions were of hand-hewn planks, nailed to supporting poles and beams in a design remarkable because it seemed to defy the laws of physics. Inside there was one open front room with an adjoining closed room—respectively, my living room and the assistants' bedroom. Across the entire center of the house was our kitchen and storage room. Across the back were two small rooms with a passageway between them; these became my bedroom and my *inside* shower room. All of this was accommodated in a rectangular space of about twelve by twenty feet. The usual cane-leaf thatch covered it all, and shoulder-high room partitions allowed the air to flow freely throughout the house.

A ladder of split logs nailed to risers provided entrance to the front room. The back bedroom had a window out of which I had a magnificent view of the forest, but eventually the area was cleared for planting and I had a more interesting vista to gaze upon. A magnificent latrine was dug into the ground close to the precipitous side of the ridge, entered through a mazelike passageway. The vista from this place was clear across the Ason River valley to the opposite ridge.

Here I lived from late June until August of the following year, with but one trip out—a week's rest and recuperation in Mount Hagen in early January 1964. Ann and I alternated monthly visits throughout the period, when we managed to compare notes on all matters of mutual concern, for two or three days of mental and physical stimulation. Once Ann visited me to observe a major ceremony, and toward the end of our stay in 1964 her community hosted an even bigger ceremony, which I attended and helped photograph. Other than these moments of shared knowledge (we read and discussed each other's field notes), we worked independently, focusing on topics of personal interest and on the fortuitous events that occur—and stir the ethnographer's interest—in any community, such as births, deaths, marriages, fights, exchanges, rituals, sickness, floods, even an earthquake or two.

While Debli was ready and waiting to work for me again, Sekiali had left the area and another young man, Ningbi, offered himself as a replacement. Debli and Ningbi both had had experiences in the outside world. Debli had been captured by a medical patrol and sent to Rabaul to undergo the removal of his entirely cancerous lower jaw. The doctors told him that he should find work with Europeans and learn to eat their food because it would be impossible for him to return to the bush and subsist entirely on local food. He had followed our patrol into the bush in 1962, and had decided that if he worked for me he would be able to exist in the bush. In spite of his disability, I found him a patient language instructor and a loyal guide on all things Kaulong. There were moments, however, when relations between us became full of tension for multiple reasons, but although I threatened to fire him a number of times, he remained a member of my household to the end.

Ningbi was one of the few people from this remote region of the Kaulong interior to have ventured out to work on a plantation near Rabaul. He had spent about seven years away from the region and was just returning as I arrived. His *tok pisin* was excellent, and his loyalty to me throughout the many months was never in question. He said to me one day, "Isn't it remarkable that the two of us have never had any misunderstanding?" I asked him why he thought that might be, and he replied, "Because I know how Europeans think and others in Umbi have not had the experience." When I thought about it, I concluded that he had correctly sized up the situation. And I remembered his comment when I chose my second Kaulong community to return to in 1967.

One of the most difficult parts of the initial fieldwork was the prior almost total isolation of these remote inland communities. In 1958 Thomas Gilliard, an ornithologist from the New York Natural History Museum, had traveled through Arihi, Umbi, Dulago, and far into the uninhabited bush of the Whiteman Mountains, seeking in vain for evidence of birds of paradise (Gilliard 1961). Until Gilliard and his wife and accompanying patrol officers passed through, many of these interior people had had no contact with the outside world; they had never presented themselves to the few patrols that ventured inland this far. Their timidity may have been in part because of the punitive patrols into the Arihi region bent on capturing those responsible for the murder in the late 1950s of a European plantation recruiter, himself the first European most of the people had ever seen.

Umbi was a community formed about the time of Gilliard's trip.[2] Among the inhabitants were people who had fled from the punitive expeditions, others who had never been in contact with Europeans before, and others, like Debli and Ningbi, who had been listed in the government books as resident in other communities and who had had varying amounts of contact with outsiders. Without exception, none of the women of Umbi had been beyond Kandrian, and women familiar with this coastal settlement were very few in number.

Whereas my rather single-minded aim the previous year had been to learn enough of the language to begin to communicate, to question and to understand conversation, I had been somewhat puzzled as to the nature of the social group that claimed to live in Umbi. Apparently there was no one in charge (despite the existence of a *luluai* and *tultul*, primary and secondary officials, respectively, appointed by the government), and, aside from nuclear families, I could find no significant organizational structure. In 1962 I was hardly aware of the transient nature of the village population (I myself being an interesting if odd attraction), but soon after my return it became clear that only my two assistants and I really "lived" in Umbi. The single men's house, guarding the path leading up from the river Ason, might have an occasional visitor or resident sleeping there. Most of the time the other houses, one for each married couple, were empty, closed and often locked, while their owners worked and slept elsewhere in the bush.

Every Monday, the village would fill up with about half of the registered inhabitants, to carry out "government work." The government had decreed that one day a week should be put aside for this "community" work—removing grass from the center clearing, patching the

2. An official census of the community was taken in 1959. Thirty-two previously unknown names were added to the official rolls.

roof of the men's house, building a government rest house (*haus kiap*) in anticipation of the rare visit of someone from Kandrian on medical, malarial, agricultural, or administrative patrol. But on most Mondays, the time was spent in interpersonal negotiations and exchanges of many different kinds. Visitors arrived expecting locals to be in Umbi. They came to ask for payment of a debt, only to find that the debtor likely had gone visiting in other villages on a similar mission or had chosen to remain hidden in some bush locale to avoid the confrontation. Mondays were always a good day for the anthropologist—something of interest to observe and record and to raise questions about was bound to happen.

But Umbi was an unrewarding place to do ethnography most of the time. Except on Mondays, no one was at home other than one or the other of my assistants, but they were officially free to do what they wanted during the daylight hours and often went off on missions of their own. Often a small child, or two or more, was left with me while the parents went elsewhere; and as time went on, often I would be the only one in the village during the daytime.

One of my daily tasks was recording the rainfall, temperature, and humidity for the Australian Weather Service (who thought it worthwhile to get figures for the interior mountains comparable to those officially recorded in Kandrian). I was given a bucket in which to gather the rainfall, a measure to measure it out, and the necessary thermometers. Little did I realize the need for the bucket, until in the height of the rainy season, in the middle of a downpour, I would have to measure the brimming bucket (5 inches). Once when I went off to visit Ann for a few days, to my surprise I found the bucket empty when I returned, although I knew it had rained. "Sutli drank it," I was informed readily enough. When I asked Sutli whether this was true, he replied, "Yes, but I measured it before I drank it." "So, how much did it measure?" I asked this very good but illiterate friend of mine. "One glass full and this (he demonstrated) much more." I was curious but never found out what the Weather Bureau in Lae thought of my notation against that measure.

In 1963–64 we received 218.61 inches of rain. Comparable figures for

Kandrian showed that this was quite far below the average of 250 inches. The monthly fall for Umbi was as follows:

May	16.27	November	5.70
June	16.49	December	2.88
July	40.22	January	11.15
August	22.83	February	13.26
September	38.63	March	19.82
October	17.59	April	12.77

During the rainy season (approximately May through October) very little gardening was done. Kaulong worried about the shallow-rooted trees that could be dislodged easily and might fall on one. The constant flooding of small and large streams often held hostage those who would journey beyond. Typically, people slept in the rain, going to gardens only to harvest a few days' worth of taro and replant the stalks of those they have eaten. The only hunting for which heavy rains are a benefit is the hunting of wild pigs, for pigs, like humans, prefer to hole up in their sleeping dens. There dogs can easily corner them while a hunter spears them.

The good weather (December through April) brings first a maximum effort by both men and women to clear new gardens, harvest old ones, and hunt in the forest and streams. As the level of water goes down in the streams, men may dam them and then scoop out all the water to gather eels, fish, shrimp, etc. The cool forest beckons men, who hunt birds and possums with their blowguns, and brings women to the streams for frogs and shrimp. In Umbi I reckoned that approximately 60 percent of the daily diet, on an annual basis, came from hunting. In Angelek, the figure was approximately 40 percent.

To find people to talk to on days other than Mondays, I had to go to where they lived and worked throughout the bush, often four or more miles away from Umbi and typically farther up into the foothills. Wisely, they chose to live close to where they worked clearing and tending taro gardens, often making a crude, lean-to garden hut from logs felled in the clearing. But I also found some families living in natural caves located close to the garden, and one family had built a shelter into the buttressed roots of a giant ficus. To these gardens I would travel with the gardener or with Debli, Ningbi, or some other young person as guide. I spent countless hours watching the women using machetes to slash and cut away the entangling vines so that the men (today using steel not stone axes) could cut through and fell the heavy timber. We collected about two dozen polished stone adzes and ax blades. Some of the older men remember the first steel tools being traded in from the coast and what it was like before the introduction of steel. They claimed that with steel tools they could make bigger gardens more quickly (see Salisbury 1962).

The logs from the clearing were used to build the encircling fences (the logs lay horizontally between two courses of upright poles tied tightly together to form a strong, high barricade against wild and domestic pigs). I watched the planting of taro and other plants of less dietary value (manioc, yams, sweet potatoes, and various "greens"). I sat and observed the weeding and the harvesting, during which the corm and leaves were carefully cut away for eating and the stalks were saved for planting and regeneration. I sat in small leafy shelters around smoking fires, eating a great variety of insects and grubs and sometimes larger game—a fruit bat or possum—all of them the "fallout" from the clearing process. I saw many different kinds of garden magic being performed and listened to gossip and stories of events of the more distant past. These were welcome excursions not only for the information they gave me about the all-important garden activity, but because I came to know the countryside and the pattern of residence.

I learned that Umbi was in reality made up of people with loyalties to three distinct places of affiliation (bi). Each bi was a small area of under an acre that had a men's house (mang), often made of logs, and perhaps one or two women's houses (mok). Typically, planted around the small clearing were areca palm, coconut palm, bananas, breadfruit, and perhaps a ficus—a strangler fig tree—planted in the center. The bi were centers of residential affiliation, where the bones of previous affiliates were buried. The mang was also where the exhumed skulls of affiliates were kept (until the Australian kiaps forbade the practice). After the government contacted them, the people reburied these skulls in the open ground of the hamlet. Umbi was an invention of the

Australian *kiaps*, a place to meet with outsiders in order to be counted, medically treated, and talked to, but hardly a place to live, and in no way a "community."

In addition to my learning the language and gaining a working knowledge of social organization (i.e., kinship, politics, and economics), my stay in Umbi provided particular events that claimed my ethnographic interest. Here I summarize some of the most important aspects of Kaulong life that Umbi drew to my attention.

Early in 1962, I was witness to the violent pursuit of young men by courting young women and was made aware of the genuine fear of marriage (and sex) held by all men. Sekiali, Ningbi, and Debli were, in the eyes of two young Umbi women, eligible targets for courtship. Eventually in early 1964, one of the women, Ihime, managed to "catch" Ningbi when he was ill and in a weakened condition and forced a marriage on him. The incident gave me an excellent vantage point from which to gather data on gender relations, including marriage. The Kaulong regard any sexual activity between men and women as placing both permanently in the category of married persons. As is true for many other reported Melanesian societies, Kaulong have placed considerable cultural emphasis on distinctions in gender identity, including ideas of the polluting effect on men of certain kinds of contact with women. The Kaulong, however, are very different from others in how they manage this polluting characteristic and in their emphasis on marriage as a permanent condition. Because sexual contact/marriage is feared by men, it is the women who do the pursuing. The permanency of marriage is illustrated most emphatically by the expected strangulation of a wife (by her own close male kin) upon the death of her husband.

I witnessed the deaths of two married men, but only one had a living wife. She was spared strangulation, probably because of my presence. However, many of my male informants had themselves witnessed and participated in the strangulation of sisters and mothers, the latest incidence occurring five years prior to my arrival. I had a very cranky Butoba tape recorder and I remember well what happened after I got it working again by kicking it. I asked for stories from my visitors—and, as the word spread, for the next three days I was visited by a stream of men telling me of killings they had done. One father related how he had tracked down a son and daughter and speared them both because of incest between them. This story turned up in Angelek, far removed from Umbi, where it was told as a myth, something that had happened long ago. Much of the data reported on and interpreted concerning gender, marriage, and sexuality (see chapters 6 and 7) were gathered throughout my investigations in Umbi and were corroborated by comparative data from Angelek.

Umbi also provided extensive information concerning sorcery, death, and medicine. Early in 1963, the first of the eventual four deaths to occur during my stay was determined to be the result of sorcery. I soon learned that Umbi itself had a number of known and feared sorcerers and that others lived in other Kaulong communities on both sides of the Ason; indeed, there were sorcerers in Arihi and on down to the coast. In contrast, Ann found that few in Sengseng were recognized as having the knowledge to practice this trade. Close to the end of 1963 an epidemic of dysentery hit the inland regions. While no one in Umbi was afflicted, deaths occurring in another Kaulong community—Womilo— were attributed to revenge for the earlier Umbi death; and throughout the remainder of my stay, we in Umbi found ourselves in the middle of an ongoing sorcery war with Womilo. The situation was perfect for data gathering, and I fully experienced the dilemma of the anthropologist: how to remain sympathetic to the plight of one's friends while inwardly rejoicing at the rich harvest of information.

The epidemic itself gave both Ann and me a period of personal hardship, together with information of a different nature. Each of our communities totally abandoned the village clearing and, taking us with them, went to hide from the spirit thought to be causing this illness. For four weeks I lived in the bush with a very small group and gained a firsthand feel for the more traditional residential patterns and an intensified understanding of the balance of garden and forest as food resources (as this was at the beginning of the good season when full exploitation of the forest begins to take place).

The men use very long blowguns to impale aboreal game and birds; they use dogs to corner wild pigs, and traps to entangle cassowaries. Small game abounds; streams are habitats for shrimp (prawns), frogs, eels, and, in the case of rivers, succulent fish and very large eels. Wild nuts and fruits are abundant at this time of year. Women frequently brought me a packet of a frog and half a dozen shrimp, wrapped in the leaf in which they had been cooked. In exchange for a stick of tobacco I had a delicious afternoon snack. Women did not go on pig or cassowary hunts, but I spent many warm days with the women in the stream collecting shellfish. The children learned that I had a craving for wild fruit and provided me amply in exchange for a piece or two of candy.

We brought shillings and stick tobacco (one stick of tobacco equalled a shilling) into the bush to pay for food and services, but some of the people did not want (or have any use for) shillings, and often an intermediate transaction took place, with a third person exchanging our shillings for a gold-lip pearl shell (the major medium of exchange in this region). It was in Umbi that I began my own instruction in shell evaluation, although I never felt that I could rely entirely on using shells myself and continued to use shillings or tobacco almost exclusively to buy goods and pay for services. By the time I moved to Angelek, I trusted myself enough to accept shells for my goods (primarily rice and canned mackerel), which were offered to the community at cost. And it was in Angelek where I focused more intensely on trade and transaction. What the people of Umbi taught me were the fundamental lessons of Melanesian economics: balance of export/import, managing the money supply, credit lending and debt collecting, interest building, and the like. Most of this knowledge came to me through my own participation in exchange. For example, I tried to buy as much local food as possible in order to keep the imports from Kandrian at a minimum.

One day, the young man entrusted with carrying in a new supply of shillings had tried to swim a flooded stream and had sunk to the bottom with their weight. Fortunately he had been able to walk out to the bank. After this incident, I was told not to buy food from other communities. Why not? I asked, seeing no connection. "Because your money will be lost (if you buy outside Umbi). If you only buy from Umbi your money won't be lost, and you won't have to bring in more." When I asked for further clarification, feeling that my money would be lost in either case, my informant said, "But we will buy things from you with your shillings, and you can buy things from us with shillings, but they will be the same shillings." So ended my first lesson in balance of payments and international monetary principles. There were many more such lessons.

Mail and shillings were unavoidable necessities, as were such culturally significant items as peanut butter, coffee, tea, chocolates, sardines, cookies, canned meat, and fruit. So we hired carriers to make a trip to Kandrian for us once a month or if possible at longer intervals. I eventually found that the teenagers of both genders were delighted to make the trip. I paid them in advance and they spent their shillings in the trade store for things they never had had an opportunity to own (or want) before. Many of the women and young girls made their first trip to the coast on a cargo-carrying trip for me.

Finally, it was early in my stay that I became aware of the importance of song performance in ceremony and in daily life. People were always singing, in the morning as they left for the gardens, during idle moments in the day, and at night before turning in. Children and adults of both sexes were delighted to sing for my tape recorder. The first song performance I saw was at a memorial mortuary ritual for the man who died in early 1963. I arranged for Ann to join me at the small hamlet of Angus for the *lut a yu* ("to sing with pigs"), a type of song performance or "singsing" involving the sacrifice of pigs. Not knowing what to expect, I went to Angus for an all-night singsing prior to the final performance. With Debli and Ningbi and two other young men and two girls, I sat all night near the log house where Kinegit had been buried and listened to the singsing of these six people from before dusk to dawn.

The following day, others arrived carrying three live pigs slung by their legs from stout poles. The pigs were made comfortable in a slight depression, their weight eased by the support of the poles on uprights in such a way that they could sleep but not struggle. Taro was also carried in and cooked and consumed. Ann arrived in late afternoon, and for this second night the much larger group of about forty people sang throughout the darkness until dawn. I taped the singing until I ran out of tape sometime before morning. Exhausted by lack of sleep for more than thirty-six hours, I found two free poles supported on horizontal logs, and, balancing my body on this sparse bed, I fell asleep. At dawn the singing stopped, but the activity picked up as the pigs were displayed, killed, butchered, and distributed to those coming from other communities who carried off their portions to cook and eat. This was but the first of many such singsings that I recorded throughout my field research in Umbi and later in Angelek.

The topics I have outlined became the major foci of my research interests at Umbi. Interspersed with these issues, I also raised two puppies in Kaulong-style to become hunting dogs; I witnessed the noninvolvement of Umbi in the first national elections (see Chowning and Goodale 1965); and continued making a surface collection of a rather extensive chipped stone industry located in a site between our two villages (see Chowning and Goodale 1966; Goodale 1966b). I was present at the birth of the first twins "ever born to us bush people," which afforded me a fascinating look into the world of child care. And I had ample opportunity to record local spirits of major and minor importance.

Angelek

My choice of Angelek for a comparative and continuing study of the Kaulong was made with a bit more control and considered thought than I had been able to exercise in the choice of Umbi. For this period of work, 1967–68 and 1972, I gave careful thought to the difficulties of the previous location, principally the isolation, and to problems of supply and communication with the coast. I also remembered Ningbi's assessment of why we had gotten along so well—that he knew how I thought—and I concluded that a community that had had more extensive European contact would allow me to avoid both isolation and mutual understanding problems, as well as provide an excellent contrast for my study of Kaulong culture and society.

Thus, I decided to select a Kaulong-speaking community within a day's walk of the coast. After arriving in Kandrian and consulting with both missions and the assistant district officer and patrol officers, I took a preliminary drive one Monday (the "work" day) to the end of the one road leading from the airstrip into the interior, stopping at three likely communities to make known my intent and my three requirements: a house, a steady water supply, and their willingness to play host to me. Where the road came to an end at an unbridged stream, we met a middleaged man who persuaded me to walk a mile further to have a look at the village called Angelek.

As my driver and I sat in the rest house, sipping tea and eating some cooked pork offered to us for purchase, I gave my speech, repeating what I had told people in the other villages. I asked the community to discuss my proposal among themselves and if everyone was willing for me to come live with them for twelve months, they should send a representative to Kandrian on a Saturday to let me know.

I was a little taken aback when representatives of all three villages arrived the following morning (Tuesday), each with an invitation to live in *their* village. I chose the third one, Angelek, off the end of the road, because the rest house (which I could immediately occupy) was in the very center of the village clearing, because it was the largest of the three, and, finally, because it was close to a fairly large river providing excellent water year round.

There were approximately a hundred residents listed in the census book for Angelek and seventeen houses. Tall coconuts planted here during the time of the Germans before World War I gave evidence of a fairly long history.[3] The many flowering and fruit-bearing trees around the houses were pleasant to look at, and there was a giant ficus growing just in front of the rest house. All gave the impression of a firmly established community with considerable experience with outsiders. In retrospect, I feel I could not have chosen a better community. All my personal and ethnographic requirements were met here, and my understanding of Kaulong society and culture was greatly enhanced through the numerous contrasts with the isolated Umbi community I had known previously.

In the course of the next twelve months I pieced together some of the history of contact of this community. I was told a story of the first visit by the Germans:

3. Patrol records report that the village was established in 1954; however, it was on the site of an older hamlet.

My grandfathers heard the sound of the ships and hid their children in the bush, saying "the ships are ghost ships, the smoke from the engines come from their cooking fires." Then a young, unmarried man named Karenge made magic, and stood his ground and his magic drew the ships to the shore.

The Germans went ashore and asked Karenge, "Are you human?" and Karenge replied, "yes." Then Karenge went with the Germans and worked for two or three years and when he returned he brought with him shells, knives, axes and a laplap [a long strip of calico worn by male laborers] as long as from here [demonstrated] to there [about 150 to 200 yards]. Then all the young men decided to go and work so as to bring back these things. After a while a leader, Kaklal, told the Germans they must "buy" the young men, saying, "These young men aren't rubbish. They are our children, and are our kinsmen."

My informant went on to explain that the payment of shells, axes, knives, and cloth to the parents of the recruited laborers was in case the workers died on the plantations. I was told that being killed by falling trees or being kicked to death in a soccer match are two causes of work-related deaths today and in the past.

The Germans did not have an outpost of control on the southwest coast, I was told. About once a year they did patrol inland regions within a day's walk from the coast, including many of the communities surrounding Angelek. They heard "trouble cases" (complaints) and hanged murderers in front of as many witnesses as they could round up. They also distributed coconuts for planting.

A solitary coconut plantation was established at Ablingi, farther east up the coast and outside of the Kaulong area. As of the period of my fieldwork, it was still in operation, recruiting workers from coastal as well as these inland communities.

The Australian administration, which followed the Germans after their defeat in World War I, established a coastal base at Gasmata to the east of Kandrian and followed the German pattern of annual patrols into the interior, but penetrated only as far as Pomalal (see map) in the

Kaulong/Sengseng area. A former patrol officer Horace Niall told me that in 1930 he had established the first Australian Patrol Post at Kandrian with a few native police, and he said, "We really tamed those bush people."[4] His police sergeant, now old and nearly blind, traveled from his coastal home community west of Kandrian in order to meet me in 1967 and confirmed the story. The Catholic Church was also established at Turuk in the 1930s.

The coastal region, but not the interior, came under anthropological study during this early period of post-German contact. The government anthropologist E. W. P. Chinnery (1928) made a brief survey along the coast in 1925; and in 1933 and 1935, a postgraduate student from the University of Sydney made an extended study of the people and culture of Moewehafen, one of the offshore islands, but published only three papers on his findings (Todd 1934–35, 1935–36).

Europeans abandoned Kandrian during the Japanese invasion of northern and eastern New Britain in the early years of World War II, but the southwest region saw little action. Some men from Angelek, however, were caught by the Japanese while working on plantations in Rabaul and on New Ireland and told me some vivid accounts of their firsthand experiences. They described bombing and fighting first by Japanese and later by Americans, and they compared their life under the Japanese and then Americans before they were sent back home.

Following World War II, the Australian government and the Catholic Church of England missions had reestablished themselves in Kandrian. The Catholic Church concentrated efforts among the inland "bush" people, while the Church of England mainly sought converts among the linguistically distinct coastal peoples, until both of them began to explore the remote interior for converts just at the time Ann Chowning and I began to work in Umbi and Dulago. On the day of my initial contact, the people of Angelek told me they had gotten rid of all their local spirits—the priest had come and "blessed" all the streams, rock

---

4. Australians perpetuated the labor-driven colonial attitude of the Germans who preceded them, showing little of the paternalistic style characteristic of their administration of the Territory of Papua. Niall made frequent patrols, none penetrating the remote interior, using armed police escorts to make sure his interpretations of Pax Australiana laws were obeyed.

holes, and other places made dangerous by inhabiting spirits. I found this to be patently false, as I began to bump into local spirits soon after my arrival in Angelek.

Having made my choice to work in Angelek, I and my supplies were quickly and easily transported by tractor-wagon to the end of the road, in a three-hour journey. The entire village—men, women, and children—waited for me on the other side of the yet-unbridged stream and made quick time carrying my possessions the remaining distance. I was soon settled in. Two days later the community was involved in an extensive marriage exchange, and I remember struggling to record who was giving what to whom, when I knew no one's name or kinship relation to the principals nor whether they were locals or visitors. I fell back on the not so accurate designation: "the man in blue shirt, the extremely old and withered woman, the child with a running nose," etcetera, all of which was of no help later when I tried to attach names to these descriptions. But the event gave a good indication of the greatly increased amount of activity I could expect in this community and of the size of the intercommunity exchange relationships of this entire region. The larger population density in these communities is probably due to what an early mapmaker characterized as the "gentle undulations" of the limestone base to the land, which allowed more extensive cultivation of gardens planted in a contiguous, rather than scattered, pattern. This landscape also permitted greater ease of travel between communities, and thus an expanded network of trade relationships and intercommunity ritual activity involving pigs and song.

It was in Angelek that I began to understand the dynamics of political life, the nature of the Kaulong *midan* ("big man") and his counterpart, the *polamit* ("big woman"). Angelek was within the sphere of influence of one of the truly big men of the entire Passismanua region: Maklun was a man of impressive physical stature, who wore his hair long and in red clayed dreadlocks. Ann and I first met Maklun briefly in 1962 on our way through his village. At that time he and other community leaders were overseeing the building of an aid post in Lapalam, Maklun's village, and the patrol officer in charge, David Goodger, asked them all to don their "valuables" so we could see them. Maklun and the others lined up, their loins girded with long strips of painted bark cloth, over which strings of dogs' teeth and strings of cassowary pinion interspersed with nassa shells were many times wrapped. Around their necks hung double spirals of boars' tusks bound together and suspended on a braided hair rope on which small nassa shells were sewn. They showed us small disks of polished stone strung at intervals along the ropes of the dogs' teeth, and other larger disks strung on a rope that they held in their hands. These are the stone valuables known in *tok pisin* as *mokmok*, and in Kaulong as *niglak* or *singa*.

Of all these regional big men, I remember Maklun held by far the most impressive and numerous *mokmoks*. Little did I realize then that this man would become a most important person in my continued study of Kaulong. Maklun eventually honored me by initiating a significant pork exchange with me during the initiation rituals for his sister's son. I was able to be present at other exchanges in which he and his immediate following held important positions. Angelek was not his hamlet, but the mother of my assistant Gaspat was his niece so I was in a position to come to know him fairly well and learn from him appropriate political behavior.

In Angelek, I again hired two young men to work for me. After some experimenting, I settled on two who had no experience of working for Europeans, but whose families wished them to receive some training by being my cooks and assistants. I fear I failed in this mission miserably. I remember tuning in on a conversation in which young and middleaged men were comparing notes on European women for whom they had worked and their demands, and I heard Gaspat remark that "Jane doesn't ask us to do any of those things, and she never gets cross at us," referring to my almost nonexistent standards of table-setting, dish-washing, and house-cleaning. Ah well, these young men were far more valuable to me as informants, guides, and companions than as household help. While neither Gaspat nor Nakling had any work experience away from the bush, Nakling had gone to mission school at Lakung-kung, six miles away, for long enough to learn minimal English and how to write in English and *tok pisin*. He spoke English to me only once, when he was quite drunk, but he carried on a correspondence with my nephew of the same age in the United States, a relationship I arranged for them.

In Angelek I continued my study of the language, but while my understanding increased, my speaking ability grew less because nearly everyone was fluent in *tok pisin*. I continued observing and questioning many of the same aspects that had held my interest before, such as gender identity, cross-sex relations, marriage and courtship. I had a much greater chance to travel to communities near and far on trading trips, frequent singsings, and pork exchanges, as well as simply to visit relations and friends. I met and talked to a wider range of informants, male and female of all ages, as I gathered extensive genealogies and made notes and tapes of many different kinds of rituals involving singsing, with and without pig sacrifice. I raised an orphaned wild piglet and thus learned much about this significant activity and came to understand the very human nature of pigs (see chapter 3). Once as I was mixing a dinner of milk and rice for "Gudeo," a man commented that I was raising her the right way—the way his grandmother raised pigs. "How's that?" "Because you are giving her milk." And there followed a discussion of the close kinship between a pig and a baby who have both been nursed by the same woman.

Angelek built a church down by the river while I was there, which was nominally under the influence of the Catholic Church located at Turuk, above Kandrian. There was no resident catechist at Angelek; the priest visited a few times, but those who wished to participate in Church activities either traveled the ten miles or so cross country to Turuk, or the six miles to Lakungkung, where a catechist was in residence and maintained a small bush school.

I was told by the resident priest at Turuk that the bush people were the hardest people he ever knew to convert to Christianity. He believed that only a few who had forsaken their own beliefs could be considered true Christians. In 1967, I attended the first Christmas mass in the bush at Lakungkung.

In 1974, on the eve of independence of the Papua New Guinea nation, I returned to Angelek for three months in order to work on translations of the more than three hundred songs I had recorded previously at all-night rituals or at the house. I found Angelek nearly deserted except for the small hamlet section that contained the rest house, two married people's houses, and the men's house. The majority of former residents had gone back to the pattern of affiliating in far smaller units, focused on a clearing (*bi*) or hamlet containing its own men's house and one or two women's lean-tos. As I traveled to other sites of former villages, I found these, too, were greatly reduced in size, with only one or two houses still occupied. When the Kaulong discovered that they were no longer required by a colonial government to live in large groups in villages, they reverted quickly to their traditional pattern of small, dispersed residential groupings.

I discovered that the important big man, Maklun, had died, as had Kamil, Angelek's own resident *midan*. Mikail, Maklun's son, and Molio, former government-appointed second headman (*tultul*), were competing for prestige. I found myself being used by both as local foil, a person of political importance, apparently to fill the void that the death of the previous leader had created and to mask their own political maneuvers. My being forced into playing a political role, however ineptly, gave me an opportunity to test my knowledge of political behavior, and I gained much insight.

In describing my experiences among the Kaulong, I have tried to give some sense of how I acquired the data on which my interpretations are based and a sense of the contrast between the two communities, emphasizing the very different contact histories of Umbi and Angelek, and the different amount of intergroup activity that characterized them.

I had many informants, but grew to rely on some to a greater extent than others, chiefly because they were around more often and had proven to be interested in helping me understand what was going on. Some became significant for certain kinds of knowledge as their own skill was revealed; others were informants of a more general nature and confidants, sharing with me their emotions, problems, and worries as I found I could share mine with them.

I used informal interview techniques for almost all kinds of information, with the exception of genealogies and song translations. Gathering the exacting data for the latter two required great patience on the part of both informant and recorder, and after a couple of hours of intense work, we would share a meal or tobacco and often a laugh of relief. I paid for no information directly. Only for cargo-carrying did I pay shillings, and my household help received a weekly wage and ate all their meals with me. My shillings were readily and consistently distributed throughout the wider community as I bought food of all kinds. In Angelek, I became a safe repository for other peoples' shillings, learning in the process a great deal more about the shell/shilling game.

I kept my own thoughts, observations, and interviews recorded on consecutive pages of spiral stenopads. I confess that I rarely took the time away from recording to make a second copy of these notes, only typing them after returning from the field (and I gave daily pleas and eventually thanks to the Powers, temporal and spiritual, who kept them safe from harm). However, frequent rereading of my notes allowed me to summarize and speculate, to pose questions, to add additional data or eventual results of a situation left unresolved at the time, and so on. I was blessed with excellent informants most of the time. I remember one coming to me before he left for the gardens one morning, saying, "Has anyone told you about digging up and preparing the skull of a man deceased? No? Well, let me tell you all about it," and proceeding to give me an account, which in its fullness and organization was a model of descriptive ethnography. And there were others, named and unnamed in the following discussion, whose reflections on their own culture greatly aided me in my task.

In the following chapters, I draw from both Umbi and Angelek experiences and studies and have also had the benefit of Ann's notes for the Sengseng. There were significant differences between the groups, but much was also the same. Where I feel the differences need to be made known and perhaps explained, I have done so; otherwise, I believe the interpretation represents the Kaulong of both regions.

Finally, the ethnographic present is the twelve years between 1962 and 1974. I present this study as an intensive, long-range interpretive ethnography, representing the Kaulong during a mere slice of time in the total history of this region.

2/ The Management of Knowledge

In Melanesian ethnographic literature knowledge has been discussed mainly in terms of the contexts for different categories of knowledge— for example, childhood acquisition of language, kinship, and social responsibilities (Whiting 1946; Schieffelin 1976; Read 1965); the revelation of gender-specific knowledge within male/female initiation ceremonies (Barth 1975; Bateson 1958; Herdt 1980, 1987; Poole 1982); inheritance of specialized knowledge such as magic formulae, craft skills, and the like (Malinowski 1984; Fortune 1932, 1935). In this chapter, I first examine the nature of knowledge as a concept among the Kaulong, and then look at how the Kaulong manage and use knowledge in the everyday game of social life. I show that for the Kaulong the game is one where bluff, ambiguity, coolness, and control are all used to demonstrate one's power and ability to acquire and manage large amounts of diverse sorts of knowledge, a goal that is the ultimate in personal and political life because it validates self-identity and self-worth. To be renowned is to be reputed to have substantial amounts of knowledge, and it is only through skillful management of knowledge that one becomes renowned.

I could not elicit a generic Kaulong word for knowledge. People specify things known and the means by which they can be said to have learned each entity. Learning may be through seeing (*yiong*), experiencing (*huwang* or *poldan*) or, in rarer cases, hearing (*hul*). Knowledge must be acquired through contact, experience, and internalization, and as I shall discuss below, in most cases this contact must be direct, the result of personal action. Knowledge is potentially available to all persons regardless of birth place in the social order and with few exceptions without regard to gender. There is, however, considerable differential in individual acquisition, both in quantity and quality, but as knowledge appears to be infinite, no one is ever considered to have acquired all knowledge, nor is everything known. While much knowledge is common and shared, each person is considered to acquire a unique collection of knowledge which accounts for his or her individuality.

KNOWLEDGE AS AN ATTRIBUTE OF SELF

In the following discussion I sometimes use the words "soul" and "self" interchangeably. I believe that the Kaulong concepts of the soul and self are quite similar to those so elegantly discussed by M. Panoff (1966) for the Maenge of southeast New Britain. I shall not here be concerned with the double self (reported for the Maenge), for I am unsure whether it is a characteristic of the Kaulong belief. Rather, I am concerned with the self as the locus of knowledge, and in this a double nature is not relevant.

The Kaulong consider the human body (*wo*) to be composed of skin, flesh, bone, and blood as well as numerous organs, which taken all together form a container for both the self (*enu*) and the mind (*mi*). When the body, self, and mind are all intact, one can refer to the person as "being human"—*potunus*. The self and mind are in one sense independent of the body, and in another sense independent of each other. Before proceeding to the discussion of their role in the acquisition and management of knowledge, the characteristics of each and their interrelationship with the body and each other must be considered.

One essential distinction to be made between self and mind is that the mind never leaves the body, while the self frequently departs from the entire body which it permeates. It is appropriate therefore to speak of a contained self and a detached self. Control of self (contained or detached) and control of mind are essential parts of one's social learning throughout life. A person may gain control over another's self or mind; such situations have disastrous but quite different effects on the controlled person's physical and social existence.

The Self

The word *enu* is most frequently glossed as soul, self, spirit, or shadow, and is used only in connection with a *potunus* (living whole person). This word contrasts with *iwun*, commonly glossed as ghost, that part of a deceased person that departs from the dead body and eventually reaches designated mountain tops, where all ghosts reside.

It is apparent that the *enu*, which permeates the entire skin, flesh, bone, and blood of the body, is the part of one's being that experiences knowledge and in which knowledge is internalized. The self apparently also grows in volume, but not in direct parallel with its container. While one's body grows and develops over time with the necessary input of food, the self increases in volume only with increased internalization of experience—a process in which time is not relevant, but activity is. As the self grows, it will fill the body container, causing rounded body contours, the skin to shine in its tightness, and, above all, the robust self to be seen reflected outward from one's eyes as they appear to others to sparkle with vitality.

The self frequently leaves the body, and when so detached, it may manifest itself in the exact image of the body quite apart from the true physical container. Detached selves usually act in all ways similar to their person's normal behavior when the self is contained. Once when nearly the entire community of Angelek went to the mission house on the coast for Easter services, I remained with half a dozen others in the village. Toward dusk as one man returned to the village from his garden he stopped by my house and told me that he had met K and her young son on the path and they had told him that they were returning home from the mission because the young boy was ill. My informant said, "we must be quiet now so that we don't disturb them." (As I discuss below, sudden loud noise that awakens a sleeper while his self is detached [dreaming] may cause great harm, even death, to the sleeper.) Shortly after I heard this, another returning resident asked me if I had seen K and her son. He, too, had met the woman and her son and heard the same explanation for their unexpected appearance. In the morning when we went to check on K and her sick son we found their door locked on the outside and the house empty.

When the mission-goers returned that afternoon, K, her son, and her husband were with them. We told them what had occurred the previous evening and residents gathered to discuss the event. K's husband related that the previous afternoon he had left his wife and son at the airstrip shelter while he went ahead to determine whether there was a place for them to sleep at the Kandrian mission establishment. As he was returning to take them to the mission he was caught in a great cloudburst and took shelter. Suddenly, he related, he felt that his wife and son were in grave danger and he left the shelter to go to the aid of his family. When he arrived at the airstrip he found his wife and son were, in fact, perfectly safe and well so the three went to the mission for the night and stayed for morning mass. By my records, the same cloudburst hit us back in the village approximately the same time as the husband and father felt his wife and son to be in "terrible danger." One explanation was therefore that at this same time the *enu* of his wife and son, frightened by the fury of the storm, detached themselves and traveled, in the likeness of their physical appearance, back home and were seen by the two witnesses. An alternate explanation (Kaulong rarely will rest on only one explanation) was that before he left to go to the mission, the husband locked the padlock on his Angelek house and then spat sung-over (bespelled) ginger root on the doorstep, calling into existence a protective spirit to guard the house and its contents while the owners were absent. This protective spirit can also take the likeness of those it is asked to protect.

A detached self may manifest itself in the shape/appearance of a moth called *enuhi*, as I learned when I went to slap a moth disturbing me as I read. I was stopped from doing so in the nick of time and told in most serious tones that I would have caused great illness, if not death, to the individual whose soul it was.

The most frequent detachment happens during sleep: *enu-ngo yol ma enu-ngo li*, "my self goes out, and my spirit goes" to dream. During such detached travels, the self can be involved in new experiences and can internalize new knowledge, thus adding to its growth. Normally, among adults such a detached self remains under some degree of control, returning to its usual container at the conclusion of sleep. Certain individuals develop unusual powers of self-control and are able to direct their wandering self in deliberate fashion in order to seek out, discover, see, or hear that which is desired by the person. Such individuals are often hired to find lost possessions, including lost *enu*, or to spy on the activities of enemies. Some men are known to send their detached selves out to seek and destroy the spirit form of some illnesses. For most individuals, however, the self, while detached, is considered vulnerable. In detachment the *enu* is far more likely to be captured and perhaps even killed by a sorcerer, who may wrap it in a banana leaf and alternately smoke and beat it for a number of days, while reciting appropriate empowering formulae that cause the victim's empty body to grow ever weaker and eventually to die.

The most frequent cause of soul loss among both adults and children is sudden awakening from sleep before the soul is able to reenter the body. The result of such soul loss among adults is usually immediate and severe hysteria, often leading to death within a few hours. If soul loss can be attributed to another's action, intentional or not, and death results, the action is considered to be and is treated as murder.

My assistant, Gaspat, experienced such soul loss just prior to going on a trip. He came into my house looking miserable and as he slumped down on a bench he appeared to me as a loose bundle of skin, bones, and flesh.

"What's wrong?" I asked.

"I'm not going. I'm sick."

"What kind of sickness?"

He replied that someone had awakened him from a sound sleep and his soul was still out there in the bush somewhere.

"Had anyone worked a cure on you?" I asked.

He told me two people had done so using bespelled ginger root. As I looked at him, a vision came to my mind of a then current television ad for the cure of a sickness called the blahs. The victims of the blahs looked as empty of life as Gaspat now appeared to me. With the simple administration of Alka-Seltzer in a glass of water, the loose bundle of bones, flesh, and skin almost instantaneously regained the contours of an intact person.

"Would you like to try some of my medicine?" I asked Gaspat, who readily agreed to add one more cure to those already administered in the hopes that one, any one, would work to restore his soul. After drinking the medicine, he returned to his house to sleep. Within the hour he surprised me by running up the ladder into my house, grabbing his belongings, and saying, "I'm off to catch up with the others."

"You're cured?" I asked, although there was little need for me to verbalize it, as his appearance clearly demonstrated recovery of his *enu*. Throughout the rest of my stay in Angelek, people from this and other communities frequently came to request my miraculous cure for soul loss, which I dispensed willingly.

Sudden accident, fear, injury, or severe illness will also cause loss of self, which may become permanent if the self cannot be found and induced to return. While descending from a coconut palm a village man missed his grip and had fallen to the ground with such force that he was winded and disoriented. As he was being carried into a nearby house I noticed an elderly man with a broom, sweeping the ground from the place where the man had fallen along the path over which they carried his body. I asked him later why he had done this. "To make sure the self [jarred loose from the body] keeps in touch with the man's body so he can recover."

Sickly children almost always were known to be children with lost souls, which may have been lost for some years after a specific accident. One boy was nearly killed by a large stalk of ripening bananas that fell from the roof beam of my house where it had been hung. I was concerned for the lad's close encounter and also for my liability for his probable loss of soul. When I voiced my concern to his father later that evening, he told me not to worry, that his son's soul had been jarred loose several years earlier when he ran from the safety of his mother's side to his father just as a tree being cleared from the garden began to fall. The tree narrowly missed the young boy as it crashed to the ground. "That is why L is always sickly," the father concluded. I asked him what he was doing or would do to find his son's soul. He said that most often a child's soul returns of its own accord, but that if it didn't he might pay for someone (a specialist) to find it and send it back.

Thus, the self can be considered to lead a somewhat independent existence from the body and to remain related to the body only under favorable, attractive conditions. Should the body not be maintained in an attractive state, the self may decide to leave and not wish to return after its normal nocturnal stroll. It is difficult and perhaps unwise to try to determine a cause and effect relationship between soul loss and health: together they mean well-being; separated they mean illness.

Health Knowledge

How to keep healthy and how to cure illness are extremely important kinds of knowledge not only so that one may maintain a most attractive body for the self, but so that the person may be so physically conditioned to be able to travel extensively throughout the countryside in order to engage in and expose one's self to an ever increasing variety of learning experiences. The most common phrases heard relating to someone's good health were that the person had good wind (breath) and/or strong legs. Either together or separately, wind and legs refer to the ease, frequency, and speed by which one can travel through the rugged and difficult terrain.

A clear, firm, and shiny skin is also visual evidence of good health, and anything affecting it also affects one's attractiveness. Individuals with *tinea* (ringworm) were said to be at a disadvantage particularly in the outside world, but were also "unable to find as many shells" as those with clear skin. I was able to provide everyone in Angelek who wished it with the medicine to cure ringworm. They endured and followed my and the community's prohibitions (burning all their clothes [my prescription], not eating coconut [theirs]) with great determination. Gaspat discovered with great joy that he had freckles when he saw his own skin for the first time in his memory.

Accident and disease will affect one's ability to travel and one's ability to attract not only relationships with others, but with one's own *enu* itself. Burns are the most common accident resulting in significant deformities and physical restrictions. I know of no severely burned individual considered to have acquired more than the adequate knowledge of most adults. Young children and babies who have been severely burned are thought to have lost their souls because of this disabling accident. Burns are frequent and there is special knowledge directed toward removing the pain and scarring of burns that involves both magic formula and the application of juice of a plant, followed by an application of powdered charcoal as a dressing.

Accidents in the garden or on the trail are quite frequent and if severe may frighten a soul into leaving permanently. The most frequent are those caused by falling trees, the sudden opening up of an

underground cavern, near or actual drowning in flooded streams, falling from trees in the pursuit of game or fruit, or severe lacerations from
a knife or ax, either one's own or when engaged in a brawl or fight
with another. The major focus of all cures is to retrieve the frightened
soul concurrently with any practical treatment of open wounds or
broken bones. While techniques of both aspects of the treatment may
be of general knowledge, some individuals are known to have especially effective formulae in addition.

Prevention of accidents is important, and the knowledge of how,
when, and under what circumstances any particular endeavor should
or should not be undertaken is necessary to personal success and
survival. Significantly, innovation in any technique or in behavior relating to the natural environment is considered to be extremely dangerous. There is a rather narrow range of correct behavior, beyond which
there is the distinct and oft-stated danger of the sudden opening of the
ground under one's feet, the falling of a tree as one walks underneath,
or the sudden rise of flood waters while one is attempting to cross over
to the other bank. For example, I was told to stop skipping stones on
the surface of our river: "a flood will come up"; not to play with fire:
"the ground will open up" (or equally frequently heard: "the fire will
burn you, and not cook your food"); not to call the name of cave bats
while hunting them: "the cave will collapse"; and many other "don'ts"
with similar sanctions carried out by the natural environment. After a
youth had badly cut his hand while gathering bamboo (*kaut*) to use in
making a panpipe, everyone in the community was told to gather no
more bamboo. When I asked why, I was told that *kaut* was angry
because so many panpipes and flutes were being made. In the days
before steel, my informant continued, *kaut* was used for knives.

The most common illness is upper respiratory distress. In men this
is frequently said to be caused by contamination by women (see chapter 6), but among women and in the population in general it may have
other causes, including sorcery and improper behavior in relation to
certain types of plants. The danger of respiratory illness is its effect on
one's "wind" (lung capacity), thereby restricting one's endurance and
speed, hence, ability to travel, as well as to engage in other activities.
Cures for common and uncommon colds are all formulaic and may

involve bespelled ginger root, breast milk, the sap of certain leaves, and ashes. Although most adults know one or more cures, women are considered to have the best cures for those illnesses caused by their contamination. Most colds are considered avoidable if one is knowledgeable enough.

Only those illnesses caused by sorcery are unavoidable. For these illnesses the sorcerer must be identified and the cure bought from him. Sorcery was very much part of daily life in both Umbi and Angelek.[1] During the period of my fieldwork in Umbi, there were four deaths attributed to sorcery administered by known sorcerers in another community. The victims—one man and three women—were all middleaged, healthy up to a week before their death, sick with an illness quickly affecting their body and their minds so that near the end "all they can do is lie there and cry." A sorcery trial was held for the first death, involving the use of special water carried in bamboo tubes to the bereaved community where all people known to have knowledge of sorcery were invited to gather. Each person swore innocence while washing hands in the poured water, or while drinking it. It is believed that the water itself will punish those who speak falsely, by causing their death. It was interesting to see the reaction of men when a number of women made the request that they be permitted to take the oath. The request was vehemently opposed by all the assembled men in almost one unified and horrified voice. It seemed to me that the men found it inconceivable that women might have sorcery knowledge, but they protested almost too loudly, which suggested to me that it might not be long before women were likely to gain this knowledge. In Angelek a woman was refused permission to swear her innocence on the special water, not because she was a woman, but because she was pregnant and the water could harm her child.

Sorcery was also a problem in Angelek, where a number of known sorcerers were resident both in the community and nearby. I was told that sorcery (the knowledge) began "on top," a phrase that generally

1. Ann Chowning reports that the Sengseng of Dulago and other communities in which she worked were generally free of sorcerers in their own communities and were justifiably afraid of unknown sorcerers in Kaulong communities.

designated the interior region, of which Umbi was a part. Knowledge of sorcery technique and spells was, at the very time of my study, being transmitted to even more individuals in the Angelek region. Men bought the knowledge from kin trade-partners, and one was caught attempting to test his new knowledge on people of his own place (as was the custom for such a trial run) and a special water trial was called for. The accused was last seen as he fled by the first plane out of the region rather than face the special water.

Cures for sorcery illness require that the sorcerer be identified and then persuaded to effect the cure. Posin became very ill while working in Manus and was eventually hospitalized and had many tests to determine his illness. None of the conventional Western medicines worked and he grew weaker. Finally the doctor sent him home, saying that this illness was not one that Europeans could cure. At home it was determined that a big man was causing his illness and Posin went to him and paid him for the cure; Posin recovered. Later this man became ill and accused Posin of causing it. After being paid, Posin made him well.

I was told that some in the Angelek region acquired sorcery from other Papua New Guinea regions where they went to work and where they came in contact with many other peoples. A Tolai teacher bespelled with a protective charm the coconuts growing near the local school at Lakungkung that Nakling attended. Nakling climbed one of the trees and as a result of the spell acquired an enormous tropical ulcer on his leg. When his relatives took Nakling to the teacher for him to work his cure, the teacher said he had not learned the cure, only the enabling spell. Nakling's relatives were enraged at the teacher's irresponsibility and took Nakling out of the school. Fortunately, my antibiotics proved more powerful than the spell, and a cured Nakling stayed in Angelek as one of my assistants. It is the irresponsibility of some of the new breed of sorcerers in using incomplete knowledge that causes the Kaulong to worry.

Most illnesses are said to be caused by the ill person him- or herself, through oversight or commission of an act against nature to cause loss of soul, even if only temporarily. Persons who remain without a soul for long are particularly vulnerable to illnesses, which debilitate the body and make it unattractive, so that the soul may be repelled forever. Significantly, permanent loss of self results in social death, whether or not the body ceases physiological function, or whether or not the mind continues to be capable of rational thought. The body and mind may linger for a considerable time after the departure of the self, but loss of the self will lead to a powerless life as a social nonperson, most frequently ignored by all. Although the mind remains, knowledge contained in the *enu* can no longer be controlled by the mind.

The Mind

The word *mi*, which I gloss here as "mind" may also be used for emotions or desires (*wami-ngo*, "I desire," "I choose," or "I think of." The word also means "inside" or "interior," as in *mi mang* [in the house]). Thoughts, desires, and intent are located in the head (*miheng*) and appear to remain there. Just as one must work to control the self, one must work to maintain personal control over one's *mi* and guard it from external forces that can override one's own control.

The mind appears to be the locus of control over both the body and the self, directing each to put into action the intentions, thoughts, and desires of the mind. A person's mind is considered to be completely private—no one can ever know another's intent, thought, or desire of the past, present, or future. The consistent and frustrating answer to my question, "Why did so-and-so hit his child?" (or some other act), was, "How should I know? No one knows [another's] mind." Thus, while it is possible to know of another's talent, power, potential, ability, etc., through the public display of these attributes of the self, whether a person desires to exercise their power, or may in the future, with regard to some event, person, or thing can never be known or predicted. Nor can it usually be determined that something has specifically caused something to occur. As I shall discuss later, there are certain means by which such prediction or determination is attempted in some very restricted and specific situations, but it is generally acknowledged that no one can predict another's intent, nor know what is in his mind.

Loss of control of one's own mind through control by external forces (both human and spirit) causes lack of rational thought in directing and controlling both the self and the body. It does not lead necessarily or directly to loss of self and social death, but it does lead to uncontrolled and therefore (in my usage), irrational behavior of both body and self (the latter being either contained or detached). A fairly frequent means of control is through love magic, whereby a courting girl is able to control the mind of her desired lover and cause the boy to lose control over his mind and therefore behave irrationally by having a premarital affair, in spite of the fact that such an affair is punishable by death (or instant marriage, if carried out intentionally, i.e., by a boy in full control of his own mind). Both males and females may use love magic to overcome traditional and legal restraints on extramarital sexual affairs (see chapter 7).

Spirits can frequently gain control over a person's mind, causing the person to act irrationally. One such class of spirits called *esusu* are female spirits who are known to entice men, causing the men to follow them eternally, forever forsaking human ties of any kind. I was told of a man so bespelled who was told by his *esusu* captor to kill his wife and cook and eat her. He returned home and slaughtered his wife and cooked her on the fire and began to eat her. However, with the first taste of human blood he regained his senses. Full of remorse when he saw what he had done, he hung himself from his house beam. Although I could find no eyewitness, my informants insisted that this had happened.

Interestingly enough, to a certain extent some types of uncontrolled mental states (mental illness, *menge, ulu*) appear to result in more predictable behavior than controlled, rational thought. *Menge* is a very common condition. Like the "common cold" to which everyone is susceptible in Western countries, so is "everyone" liable to become *menge* at some point in their lives, and some experience frequent reoccurrence of the condition. In the five cases of *menge* I witnessed, the people lost touch with reality, their manner of walking became exaggerated and was often the first clue to the affliction. For the duration of the episode, the patient may become violent and aggressive toward others, often causing harm to him- or herself. Therefore, the first action others must take is to remove to safe-keeping all objects that the victim of *menge* might use to cause harm. Those present maintain constant awareness of the afflicted person, standing ready to prevent any kind of damage or injury to others and most particularly to that person.

In one case, the *menge* person went to the men's house and set one huge fire burning from the front of the house to the back. Several men went into the house with the man, did not interfere with his building the fire nor his lighting it, but waited long enough for the man to fall asleep, out of harm's way, before leaving him alone. "When he wakes up, he'll be all right," we were told.

In extreme cases where the afflicted one does not seem to be able to recover normally, I was told that several people catch him and tie him to a tree. Then they make a small cut in one of his fingers and force him to drink his own blood and he will instantly recover his senses. Just as in the case of the bewitched cannibalistic husband (in the story above), the instant that human blood or flesh is consumed senses return. The Kaulong are vehemently anticannibalistic. Animals and nonhuman spirits and monsters will eat their own kind, but humans in full control of their minds do not.

Adult women and men are most likely to become *menge*, but I was told that children can also be afflicted. While it is not considered a laughing matter, a grandmother one day kept the village children amused for hours by acting as if she were *menge*. This condition appears most similar to the erratic behavior, labeled *amok,* found elsewhere in the southwest Pacific region.

Kaulong distinguish m*enge* from the illness they call *ulu* (literally, spinning or running around). Only one man I knew experienced *ulu*, but I was told of another one known to the community but resident elsewhere. Gospo, a young man in his mid to late twenties, lived mostly in the bush with his mother and looked after his gardens and pigs. But he turned up in Umbi approximately once every two weeks and would tell me stories that he had heard from his mother. He would parcel them out one at a time in return for a meal—a bargain well worth the price to me. But one day when he arrived he marched militantly into the center of my house, an area normally restricted to my assistants and myself, and announced loudly and in *tok pisin* (which almost no one in Umbi spoke fluently or frequently) that everything in the house belonged to him, the pots were his, the stoves were his, the beds, the food, the money, the tobacco, the books, the bananas—everything was his. I was to leave immediately. It was early enough in my fieldwork (in 1963) that I was shocked by this onslaught and truly afraid. What really concerned me was that no one was rushing to my rescue, no one was doing anything but watching the two of us. Eventually, however, they got Gospo out of my house. I remember that it was some little time later that Gospo himself returned and casually asked me for a razor blade, a request that did nothing to reassure me that things were under control. Then someone said, "It's okay, Jane, give him the razor." So I did.

After he left I was told that Gospo is the only one here who goes *ulu*. When he does, he is entirely harmless to others and people merely look after him to see that he does not hurt himself. He uses only *tok pisin* when *ulu*. When he was young and did not know *tok pisin*, he did not speak at all when *ulu*. He has been subject to these fits since he was about fourteen years old. Gospo had another attack of *ulu* while I was there. I was able to record this one as it occurred:

> August 26, 9:30 P.M., Gospo went *ulu*. Sitting by the fire underneath my house are Gospo myself and Ningbi, Debli, Ligiok, Naingli and girls. Ningbi says, "Gospo is sick." Gospo sits with his head bowed, arms loose and motionless, with only occasional slight shake of his head, hardly noticeable. Ningbi says, "When he sleeps like that he cannot hear us." He calls to him softly by name, "Gospo!" "Gospo!" There is no answer. After fifteen minutes Gospo makes an attempt to get up but falls down into a sleeping position again and breathes heavily. After twenty minutes he awakes and sits up. "Gospo," calls Ningbi. "Yes?" he replies. The rest of the conversation was carried out completely in *tok pisin*.
>
> Ningbi: "Let us two go down to the men's house."
> Gospo: "Where is the men's house?"
> Ningbi: "Down below in the village."
> Gospo (looking out from the fire): "What is that here?"

Ningbi: "Where?"

Gospo (looking at a banana plant): "This here?"

Gospo gets up and strides to the banana plant and picks about six small and unripe bananas from the stalk.

Ningbi: "What's that?"

Gospo: "Food for me."

Ningbi: "What kind of food?"

Gospo: "Pig's feces. I like to eat all kinds of feces: dog's and pig's feces and man's as well. Who is that coming? A man or woman?"

Ningbi: "A man." (as Naingli approaches).

Gospo (repeats): "A man or woman?"

Ningbi: "A man."

Gospo now chews a banana with exaggerated motion and then puts the others in his basket.

Gospo: "Where is my tobacco?"

He finds it in his hand, lights it, and puts the burning end into his mouth as if to eat it.

Ningbi: "Hey, you can't eat fire!"

Gospo: "I've lost my cigarette."

Ningbi: "Your tobacco is in the men's house below, let's go together down there."

Gospo: "No way! I sleep here close to my food."

Ningbi: "There are plenty feces in the men's house, and betel, and tobacco."

Debli goes and gets tobacco for Gospo who tries to fold rather than roll it into a cigarette. Debli makes a cigarette for Gospo, and Gospo tries to light it by pushing against a glowing ember that slides away from him.

Gospo (to the fire): "Hey, you can't run away from me."

He finally gets the cigarette lighted and says to Debli: "Hey you mixed water with the tobacco."

Debli: "No, I didn't."

Gospo continues to smoke, occasionally nibbling at the glowing end. He then puts his foot on the glowing coals and says:

"What's this here?"
Ningbi shouts: "Hey, fire is burning you!"

Gospo removes his foot from the fire but appears insensitive to heat. He goes to get more bananas.

Ningbi: "Hey, you can't eat Jane's bananas."
Gospo (to me): "True?"
Jane: "Yes, I bought them."
Gospo: "All right, I will pay you."
Ningbi (tries again): "Let's both go to the men's house."
Gospo: "No. I will sleep here. Where does Jane sleep?"
Ningbi: "Up above."
Gospo: "All right, I will sleep down here. It's all right."
Ningbi: "No, it isn't all right. This is Jane's house. The men's house has plenty feces and tobacco."
Gospo: "This house belongs to both Jane and me."
Jane: "No, it doesn't. I paid for this house."
Gospo: "I paid for it also."
Debli: "Let's all of us go to the men's house—Jane also."
Gospo (after a pause): "All right. We will all go together." Ningbi, Debli, and Ligiok take him down to the men's house. Naingli remains with me. Gospo walks with a swagger, swinging his shoulders and taking deliberate steps.

Whatever else may be said about *menge* and *ulu*, the striking aspect of it appears to be the utter unpredictability of behavior when one's mind is afflicted, which is in sharp contrast to the predictability of a person in full control of his mind and body. The Kaulong believed that *menge* and *ulu* have no known cause. There was no way to prevent an attack, and as the affliction was self-limiting there was no cure, other than the extreme "shock" treatment of forcing the afflicted one to drink his or her own blood.

THE MIND AND THE SELF TOGETHER

The mind as controller of self makes decisions concerning the display of the knowledge contained by the self. A healthy, ever-increasing self must be publicly displayed in order to be acknowledged and thereby validated. One displays one's self by using its contained knowledge in the production of such objects as garden products, pigs, trade items (chapter 5), and in creating events, such as interhamlet song ceremonies or *singsings* (chapter 8), and perhaps also in creating children (replications of one's self; chapter 7). There is some evidence that a display of self in such a fashion also involves some partial displacement of self into the event, object, or child, as M. Panoff has described for the Maenge.[2]

One who has an enlarged self, and the ability continually to acquire more, can maintain a higher frequency of display and displacement of self into a large number of objects (e.g., plants, animals, children, shells, trade items), and has the power to bring about many events without significantly depleting one's *enu* (self).

Things that contain displaced portions of a self remain in contact with the parent self, however physically separated. For example, upon death of the body, there is some attempt, by the kinsmen of the de-

2. Panoff writes of the Maenge (1966:276-77), "*kanu* appears . . . to connote those inner attributes which constitute the self of a given object. . . . Thus, if we turn to the process of canoe-making, we perceive a stage at which the general shape of the hull is emerging from the rough mass of wood. From this time on it is said that the *kanu* of the craftsman is being embodied in the log, that is, that his mental plan is taking concrete form and is becoming definitely recognizable."

ceased, to collect all detached portions of the self to help the completely intact self go with the *iwun* (ghost) to the mountain where *iwun*
reside, so that no part of a self remains to cause unwanted events to
happen. Before the custom was outlawed by the colonial powers, a
man's wife was strangled by her closest male relatives and buried with
her husband in order that the two, forever united in marriage, could
travel together to the place of ghosts. The majority of a person's pigs
and taro was also destroyed (often as part of mortuary rituals) so that
the ghost would have taro and pigs in the afterworld. And finally, the
deceased's personal belongings were broken and destroyed, or, along
with some of his bones, were used in subsequent mortuary rituals as
"reminders" of the person. The ritually exhumed and treated skulls of
important individuals were used in the mortuary rituals (see chapter
9). This final ritual treatment is designed to detach any lingering, and
therefore potent, portion of the *enu*.

ACQUISITION OF KNOWLEDGE

In Kaulong, to know something is to have heard it (*hul*) or to have
come upon it (*pol*), and/or to have seen it (*yiong*), by which means one
can internalize the experience and be said to know it, to have learned
it, to have possession of it, and to control it completely: *huwang gut, pol
dan koho, yiong gut*—all may be glossed as "to know it well."

The word *hul* (to hear, to understand, to know) appears to be related
to types of knowledge that are transmitted by word alone, such as
language, spells, songs, esoteric vocabulary, and other verbal valuables. *Pol* (to come upon, to find, and to know through physical contact) refers to knowledge of persons, places, techniques, skills, and
physical features of the world, such as types of animals, vegetables,
minerals, chemicals, and intangible aspects of the physical and social
environment. *Yiong i* (to see it) appears to be less frequently used and
often in the context of the immediate present, as in *na yiong gut*, "I see
it completely, I know it now."

Kaulong knowledge thus may be acquired directly by the *enu*
through participation and observation alone, or may include the passing on of verbal formulae, as in the case of learning magic spells,

formal genealogy, songs, etc. As with other valuable possessions, such as shells (see chapter 4), transmission of verbal knowledge must involve another person. The instructing self may be either contained or detached from its own body, although the most commonly attributed source of verbal knowledge is a living whole person. Magic formulae are usually taught by father to son, by mother to daughter (never spouse to spouse), each child being given specific formulae. The great majority of formulae are directed toward success in the maintenance of health, in the production of taro and pigs, and in the management of wealth (as I discuss more fully in following chapters). In all three areas men and women acquire significant and valued verbal knowledge. Both songs and foreign languages are acquired through direct experience and practice, although some songs are transmitted privately to individuals by intact persons or detached souls.

All knowledge, however acquired, contributes to the expansion of the self, to one's fullness of body, vitality, and power to cause things to occur. Some types of knowledge are more sought-after because of their greater contribution to personal power, and some types of knowledge have little or no positive value. The most highly valued types are those that lead directly to one's social and political success.

All normal Kaulong adults (those with intact and controlled selves and minds) are considered to have acquired the necessary basic knowledge to achieve adequate success in the areas of personal health, wealth and attractiveness. The terms *pomidan* and *polamit* are used to refer to all adult males and females, respectively, as well as to those who have gained great respect and power—the highly regarded hamlet leaders, the "big men" and "big women" (see chapter 5). What distinguishes the "normal" from the "big" *pomidan, polamit* is that the latter are considered to have more effective verbal formulae, with a greater range. For example, while every normal adult will have formulae affecting positively his or her own health and wealth, it is not common for everyone to have those spells that will adversely affect another person's health, wealth, and well-being. A spell by which one may affect another person, or another's possessions, is a spell that has tangible value (it may be purchased), whereas most other verbal formulae are apparently never sold or shared. Thus, politically significant individuals (*pomidan, polamit*) have experienced and internalized not only more knowledge, but also qualitatively more potent, powerful kinds of knowledge to achieve these common ends.

In the following chapters I discuss some of the most common and therefore significant displays of knowledge having to do with production of garden and pig resources (chapter 3), management of shell valuables as a display of self (chapter 4); knowledge of songs and their display of collective and individual selves in competitive public ceremonies (chapters 8 and 9).

CONTROL AND MANAGEMENT OF KNOWLEDGE: THE POKER GAME OF LIFE

The control and management of knowledge among the Kaulong is considered to be an entirely individual problem, rather than a collective or societal concern. Knowlege as an attribute of the self is a power to be used to enable the intentions and thoughts of the controlling mind to come into being and thus to animate one's social identity. Only a young pre-adult soul is considered to be the responsibility of another. However, even a parent's responsibility—keeping the child's soul from loss and exposing it to the required minimum of experience for survival—is somewhat limited.

Individuals gradually learn self-control and become personally responsible for the growth, development, and display of the self. Acquiring knowledge is lifelong. There appears to be no "prime" time for learning, thought to be a constant process of intake and output. As old age and physical disability prohibit or restrict travel and constant involvement in activities and public events, the skin of the body begins to show the gradual depletion of self. The self grows in youth as knowledge is gained; now there is a shrinking of self with greater output of knowledge and fewer opportunities for input. The skin becomes wrinkled and slack, and the eyes lose their glow and reflection of vitality. Eventually the gradual slow depletion of self will lead to a natural death at the completion of what is called "one's time." Without exception, individuals who live up to or beyond their "time" are acknowledged to have been "internationally" famous men or women, remembered long after their death. If still living, they are accorded extreme respect. as I show in the case of *Lipok*, a big woman (chapter 5).

In a sense, knowledge is like a possession that has value only if displayed. One displays knowledge by using it, but, if mismanaged, the display itself may lead to permanent loss of self or loss of control over the self. As mentioned earlier, permanent loss of self will cause social death even before an untimely physical death takes place. A soulless person is powerless, is without social identity, and is largely ignored by others and considered "rubbish." Such people are capable of rational thought, but their minds are considered lazy, for they cannot put their thoughts into action when there is no soul to activate. I knew one person identified as soulless, a man with a wife and six children, who, as I was often told, had never been able to garden with any success. His children were always hungry and were fed by others; he was considered by everyone to be a poor relation, a man of no account, and often a troublemaker with his habitual stealing of food to feed his family.

In the evaluation of others as social persons, what is important is not only the estimation of potential (quantity and quality of knowledge), but also reputation for self-control. Where, when, and how much to display at any given time is an important part of developing of one's style of social interaction. In any display, it is very important that one never gives the impression that all of one's knowledge in any particular category, or all of one's valuables, has been revealed in the display. Once someone has revealed any part of his or her knowledge, some measure of control over that part is lost, since it is up for challenge and perhaps acquisition by others. Display of knowledge is, I conclude, like a poker game in which hands are partially revealed to demonstrate a player's potential: evaluation of each partially revealed hand is made on the basis of the player's reputation and known previous achievements as a skilled, cool, determined, patient, and completely controlled player. To lose control (or temper) is to reveal too much or perhaps all of one's knowledge and self, and the expected result is complete loss of respect and power. Kaulong is a society in which men known to be quick to show anger and to be skilled at physical combat are common and feared, but not usually respected. Men who talk of peace are rare and are the respected leaders. Examples of both extremes are given in chapter 5.

To learn to display knowledge through stylized control requires considerable practice to gain minimal competence. Extraordinary concentration of a well-nourished, healthy, and integrated body (*wu*), mind (*mi*), and soul (*enu*) is necessary to achieve success. A few examples of how the game is played are given here; others will be found in succeeding chapters.

Stone valuables (*mokmok*, Arawe; *niglak* and *singa*, Kaulong—all three terms used interchangeably) are considered an ultimate measure of one's social power, but they are rarely displayed or used in any transaction today. They are kept hidden, usually in a limestone cave known only to the owner. Knowledge of their location is revealed only at impending death of the owner and then only to a single person, usually the eldest son or daughter. It is the ultimate (and rare) insult to say to another, "You have no stone valuables," with the implication that one has overstepped one's boundary of influence and importance with some inappropriate behavior. This challenge leads to the setting of a specific time and place for a public display and matching of stone valuables. The matching is one to one until one of the two players concedes, and this is expected to occur well before the loser's supply of owned and borrowed stone valuables has been entirely revealed. No one knows how many stones any other person owns, nor will anyone reveal this information to another. To do so would be to lose the intrinsic value and power these stones represent. It is thus quite possible for someone to claim to have stones, when, in fact, they do not, or to disclaim any knowledge of the whereabouts of such stones if one does not wish to invite a challenge to one's ability to display power.

I was told of a man close to death who revealed the hiding place of his *mokmok* stones to his young son, K, and told him to tell no one except his father's brother where the stones were hidden. After the man's death, although relatives pressured the young boy to reveal what his father had told him when they were alone together, the young man said nothing. Eventually, his father's brother arrived and K told him the location of the stones. When K grew up he inherited the stones, but when he himself lay dying he was unable to tell his own son, M, the location of the stones because M was in jail. M was to be released to go to his father's deathbed, but he arrived too late. I asked M about his father's stone valuables and he said, "I don't know where they are hidden." "What will you do about this?" I asked. "Oh, if I don't find them eventually I will hire someone to find them," he said, referring to the ability of some to send their own *enu* out on a search-and-find mission. Although I had no proof that M. did or did not know where his father's stones were, I grew increasingly suspicious that he was choosing to remain publicly "innocent" of this knowledge. This stance freed him of challenges in the community, where another man was also maneuvering for power. M seemed to me to be too calm about the "loss" of this important knowledge and the valuables that when "found" could be used to demonstrate his power. Had I not heard the earlier story (told by a close relative to the young man), perhaps I would not have been suspicious.

Similarly, magic formulae are kept secret and passed on only to single heirs and then only when death is close. Since no one else ever hears the empowering words of the spell, the display is merely in the performance and in the observed tangible results. Someone who has many spells, relating to similar objectives, has options concerning the use of particular ones. It is uncommon to use the same spell to affect the growth of taro, if the previous result was highly successful. With the next planting of the taro stalk, a less powerful and less effective spell will be used to make it unlikely that some jealous person will work counter magic on the garden. To an outside observer it sometimes appears that Kaulong continually invent new spells, although they claim that someone taught them. There is no way to check on the uniqueness of any particular spell, nor to determine how many spells anyone has. Whether one has learned any sorcery spells is of great concern to everyone. Many may claim to have such knowledge, but if they have not as yet displayed it, validation is based on probability and reputation alone. Those who have had their sorcery knowledge validated beyond doubt are either respected for their control or feared and derided for their lack of control. Sorcery knowledge affecting another's health is twofold: there are spells to cause the specific illness and spells to cure it—and a sorcerer should know both. In this special case, it is important to determine the definitive cause.

Knowledge revealed in songs (chapter 8) is very broad and of multiple origins and uses. For this reason song displays are perhaps the most important of all activities in which the individual self is publicly displayed. It was quite some time before I realized the considerable extent to which an individual uses song to express political and social knowledge. Depending upon where the song was being performed, in my house or in the variable situations of hamlet singsings, the singer could choose to reveal knowledge of foreign words or places, or to stress knowledge of the homeland (for example, to reveal the complete extent of his or her knowledge of bird classification, or the twists and turns of the road between two or more nearby or distant communities), or to give the names of famous men and women who have been known personally. The significant variables are, of course, the occasion and the audience, for all songs and the knowledge they reveal can be openly challenged.

To reveal enough to win the challenge in any competitive display is the aim, but to force an opponent to lose control is to end the game, perhaps permanently, a result not to be desired among the most adept and professional players, the big men (*pomidan*) or big women (*polamit*). If loss of control does occur, the challenger is often required to pay his embarrassed, and often weeping, opponent for having pushed too far in forcing him to reveal too much. Equals weep, pay, and shake hands and continue to have a relationship, while unequals get angry and violent and either fight or flee, thus terminating the relationship.

I found this out rather early in my Umbi residence when a young man with whom I had formed a close relationship of friendship chose to berate me in front of the entire community for not paying him enough for carrying in mail and supplies from Kandrian, a difficult trip of five days. Kaliam shouted and raved at me as the audience and I sat silently, but hardly tranquilly. At that time my own Kaulong was not up to arguing my side with any fluency, nor was it adequate to a more diplomatic response. As I sat, growing more frustrated at the seeming injustice of his raving, and furious at the others for taking neither his nor my side but simply letting the tirade continue, I found myself weeping silently. Immediately someone said, "she's crying." Kaliam stopped mid-tirade and within a very few moments came and held out a number of shillings. I was completely puzzled, but was told to "take them." When I hesitated, the instruction was repeated with great force, "You must take them, Jane," and I did. We were told to shake hands, and after this Kaliam and the audience acted as if nothing at all had happened. It was harder for me to forget, but it was obvious that I was supposed to—and eventually I did. Later observing similar instances of truly big men weeping in the context of important transactions, receiving pay and then shaking their tormentor's hand, I came to understand the power of this form of conflict-resolution among those who would be friends.

FINDING CAUSE: CALLING IN THE HANDS

It is unusual in Kaulong politics and life to attempt to find a definitive cause for any happening, particularly should this involve another's knowledge and activity as a single cause. In the course of daily social activity, multiple strategies to effect a desired end are far more often employed than a single means, thus leaving ambiguity in the minds of all (including the practitioner) as to which strategy worked, even as to whether the end was achieved through personal or nonpersonal activity.

As I discuss in chapter 3, any garden planting will frequently utilize multiple spells performed by one or more persons, and often in sequence before, during, or after a planting. When the taro grows well it is not important to determine whose spell was the effective one. And when someone is ill there are often multiple cures performed in close sequence, with the hope that one of them will be effective (which one is considered unimportant). And multiple explanations were given for the return to Angelek of the *enu*s of a mother and her son, while their bodies were still in Kandrian (see page 38). Finding a definitive cause was considered unnecessary. In any such discussion it is expressly stated that no one can really know which spell or treatment, or whether all of them together, brought about the observed result. It is usually considered to everyone's advantage not to resolve the ambiguity, for to do so may force the termination of a relationship, as well as provide an exact accounting of one's knowledge and self value. The exception being that it is to the sorcerer's advantage that people know of his power to cause and then cure.

In the Kaulong game, all players wish to leave the impression that they have more hidden knowledge which they could use if forced far enough (or too far). The delicate balance between revealing enough to win but not enough to lose is a game where bluffs, lies, gossip, challenges, and counterchallenges are acceptable strategies. I think I came to the first realization of this fundamental set of game rules when I had to repeat again and again what I was planning to do in the near future: go to the gardens, visit Ann Chowning in Dulago, go to talk to so and so, etc. No one seemed to believe me or accept my cultural premise that "my word is my bond."

The second affront to my cultural values came when I found myself increasingly infuriated at the tattletales: "someone is eating your melons" (and, "no, I didn't say anything to him"), "a friend of yours is at a distant village and has your cargo there and wants you to send carriers" (it turned out that a big man at that village wanted help in building a bridge over the river); and, "I saw X [a recently married girl] having an affair with Y" (a rumor that nearly led to a feud). In all these (and other) cases where the falsehood of the message was learned, no one blamed the messenger, even when it could be determined who sent the false message and why. Using such strategies to get someone to do what one wishes is expected of everyone—including, it seemed, the anthropologist, who in contrary fashion expected truth to be told, her word to be taken literally, and telling tales against another to be expected of children but not adults.

Because the Kaulong seek to play their political game with bluff and ambiguity, their society appears to be operating close to complete anarchy. However there are some special means and conditions by which the truth may be revealed. Significantly, in all these methods the sanctioning body is nonhuman, and the knowledge of how to force revelation of truth is known to all.

Some birds are considered to be oracles and may be addressed in an attempt to determine the possible reaction to a particular course of action. Chief among these is *kauk*, who is most commonly addressed when heard singing. If *kauk* continues to sing when asked a question— for example, "Will we find some pork to eat?" or "Will so-and-so be there when we arrive?"—the prediction is positive; if the bird becomes silent, the answer is no. No one seems to give much thought to whether the prediction proves true or false. *Kauk* is not consulted in serious matters, but serves to give some assurance to an otherwise very unpredictable life.

Since verification of knowledge comes only through demonstrated proof that it was acquired by direct contact, observation, or tutoring, all hearsay information is immediately suspected of being untrue, gossip, lies, or bluff. Apparently no one is blamed or judged for having either acted or not acted in regard to a piece of verbal information passed along through the bush. In an attempt to make such hearsay information believed, carriers of messages are often given a knotted croton leaf or a written note to bridge the gap between the originator and the recipient. Such a symbol is rarely considered an adequate replacement for direct contact and may be safely ignored if desired.

The only type of information that may be transmitted by word of mouth and believed by the hearer is news of a death of a relative. The truthfulness of such information must be without question, and such news is transmitted together with a shell valuable usually belonging to the deceased or to a close relative who was a witness to the death. As the news goes from messenger to messenger, so does the shell. The shell may be exchanged along the way for one of equal value. Today, word of a death is often sent to a kinsperson through the mails, but is always accompanied by a monetary note to validate the news.

If news of a death is later proved false, the sender is liable to death at the hands of the falsely bereaved kin. Of course, as with any precept, exceptions occur: I remember being completely puzzled by the quite vicious attack on a newly arrived visitor to Umbi by three successive waves of knife- and stick-bearing women of all ages. In the middle of the attack, the man extricated himself long enough to ask me for some money, which he then used to pay off the women and the attacks ceased. He was attacked, receiving a few cuts and many welts, I was told, because word of his death on a plantation had been falsely sent home and these kin had mourned him. Perhaps this is like the corporal punishment a Western parent might give a child who narrowly escapes being struck by a car after running blindly across the road. The Kaulong women were expressing their relief at his being alive by appearing to kill him.

Oaths of innocence are absolutely necessary when and if one is pushed to the extreme of showing one's whole hand of knowledge in any challenge of personal worth. There are two degrees of oath taking—one commonly used, the other more rarely. Commonly, one can swear on the name and power of fire (*yia*) that one is telling the truth: *yiaringin, yiasolei* ("it is the truth"). Fire cooks one's food (specifically taro) and makes it edible (raw taro is toxic). Should fire cease to work for you, you will die. One does not play with fire (including ashes and charcoal), or insult or anger it, nor does one call its name, *yia*, in vain. A big man or woman wishing to establish peace between two followers or between groups at a competitive hamlet singsing will walk between them with a stick of fire. To prevent a conflict, a stick of firewood may be planted on the entrance paths to a hamlet.

The ultimate strategy for determining truth (or innocence) is to call for a personal declaration of innocence from those judged to have the knowledge necessary to have accomplished the delict in question. There is a special deposit of water called *sasokngin*, found in only one locality (near Dulago) and widely traded from that source throughout the southwest New Britain communities. The water itself is believed to have the power to cause severe illness or death to those who do not tell the truth when in physical contact with it. Some people afflicted with this illness (which I tentatively identify as leprosy) were pointed out to me as having fallen ill after swearing falsely on the water. Trials held close to the water source (as in Umbi) involve washing one's hands or drinking while swearing innocence; trials far distant from the source (as in Angelek, where the price of the water is many hundred times inflated) involve holding a small vial of the water in one's hands while declaiming innocence. The belief in the power of this water is absolute and its effectiveness remarkable. Guilty persons usually choose to flee the region rather than face the awful consequences of lying "on the water." Their flight thus proves their guilt and the case is deferred until they should reappear.

Throughout my stay in Umbi, many trials were held to determine the sorcerer ultimately responsible for four deaths. In Angelek a sorcery trial was scheduled, resulting in the suspected person's flight out to Rabaul on the first available plane. When no one flees, or no one becomes ill, the final cause is left ambiguous, attributed to an unknown culprit, nonhuman spirit, lost soul, ghost, or (in areas contacted by the Christian missions) to God—or to all of these together. As it matters little which one, no action need be taken and the case is closed.

Once when three cans of salmon were found missing from my storage, some Angelek parents insisted on holding a water trial, against my pleas that this was not important enough for this kind of trial. The entire community turned out. Very young children were considered too young to understand the significance of oath-taking on water, while those from about six to fifteen years old were individually lectured by their fathers or mothers' brothers about what was at stake. They were told something to the effect that "Jane says she would not punish anyone for taking the cans, and that they would not be punished by any parent or other person if they said they took the salmon; that if they took the cans they should say so, for to lie 'on the water' would bring great illness and death. Did they understand?" All the children heard these words, and then were asked if they took the cans. None had. Then the adults who had been in the village at the time of the theft occurred took the oath. None of them had taken the cans. Satisfied that the theft was by person or persons unknown, the case was closed and the usual goodwill between the community and anthropologist was restored. Most significantly, I believe, this particular theft was taken to be an important occasion to transmit to children knowledge of the awful power of oaths taken on this water.

It was particularly interesting to observe that some individuals in Angelek had decided that water trials should be abandoned, and that monetary fines should be instituted to compensate for such things as injury and theft. Some court cases were subsequently heard (without the presence of *sasokngin* water), and fines were imposed on the guilty (but rarely paid). Those who supported reform claimed that the water was too dangerous to be used for any but the most serious crimes. It was, however, just because there was still a strong belief in the danger of the water that its use was so effective in eliciting final truth, and that monetary fines were so ineffective.

Two important aspects of the concept and management of knowledge among the Kaulong have been discussed in this chapter. One is that knowledge appears to be conceived and handled in many respects like other valuables in exchange transactions important to social life. One must use, display, and control knowledge in much the same way one uses and displays other tangible symbols of reciprocal relationships; self-worth is a balance of credit and debit and of degrees of power. Knowledge appears unlimited and infinite, available to all through personal effort, activity of body and soul, and acuteness of mind. Knowledge is both the equalizer and the source of inequality among people. Since all knowledge is useful to the building of the self, Western knowledge (including schooling, which is available to some living close to the coast) has value if appropriately used. However, there are very few opportunities locally to display knowledge obtained in Western schools, and, at least in the early 1970s, few had availed themselves of the opportunity to acquire this kind of knowledge.

The second important aspect discussed is that knowledge is considered an attribute of the individual self, acquired and controlled by the individual's mind. The result of this concept is a highly individualistic society where it is expected that no one will necessarily help another to achieve anything. Ancestors are not only dead, they are "only bones buried in the hamlet ground" or ghosts stashed away on a remote mountain; and since they are only bones, they cannot help the living. This was the emphatic explanation I received upon questioning Umbi Kaulong about why they rejected the "cargo" message of Koriam to which, apparently, the Sengseng of Dulago were listening. The cargo message involved ancestors bringing cargo to descendants—an act that was seen to be nonsense to the Kaulong. This individualistic concept was also behind the Angelek rejection of participation in the Local Government Council (as of 1974) on the grounds that promises to return the tax monies in the form of aid were false, because "everyone knows no one helps another person get ahead." Since the inland areas of southwestern New Britain had up to that time been largely ignored by all outsiders for as long as anyone could remember, there was justification as well as merit to their own explanation of the source of knowledge and power.

3/ In Forest and Garden

Knowledge concerning both practical and magical means of production is essential to establishing one's self-worth as *potunus*, human, in the eyes of others. In this chapter I discuss practical techniques and magic used in gardening, pig raising, and hunting and foraging. The rounds of garden work, raising and killing pigs, and hunting are governed to a large extent by the cycle of the southwestern monsoon, which brings rain to the southern slopes of the Whiteman Mountains, and by the northwest winds, which dump their moisture mainly on the northern slopes of the mountains while producing drying winds on the south slopes. It will rain at any time of the year in Kaulong territory, but the intensity of the rainfall varies.

The year can be divided into thirds, identified by the Kaulong as the time of rains, the hungry time, and the time of good weather and plenty of food. The first period, running from June through September, is known as *taim bilong ren* ("the rainy time")—118 inches of rain fell in 1963. Because it is a time of danger from flash floods and drownings and from falling trees, it is a time only for quick trips to the garden for food. Travel between hamlets is restricted, but the rainy season is a prime time for hunting wild pigs that are keeping dry in their holes. This period is, above all, a time for sleeping by the warm fires. I think that hibernation best describes Kaulong life during *taim bilong ren*.

Period two, from October through January, is known as *taim bilong hongri* ("the time of hunger"). (Rainfall recorded in 1963/64 was 38.22 inches.) This is the time for clearing new gardens, for trading and traveling, and for preparing for upcoming rituals. Because little garden food is available, people depend on hunting, gathering wild vegetables, and collecting insects, snails, and other small game found while clearing a garden to provide the major food source during this period. A toxic nut

Month	Rainfall (1963–64)	Season	Social	Activity Garden	Forest
June	16.49″	rainy	"sleeping"	small harvest	pig hunt
July	40.22″				
Aug	22.83″			clearing,	
Sept	38.63″			harvesting and planting	
Oct	17.59″	transition			
Nov	5.70″		"hungry time"		major hunting
Dec	3.88″	dry			and gathering
Jan	11.15″		"good time"	new gardens	
Feb	13.26″		trade, travel		hunt pig,
Mar	19.82″		feasting,		cassowary,
Apr	12.77″		singsings		fish, fruits
Apr	12.77″	transition		major harvest	
May	16.27″		with pig sacrifice		

FIG. 1. Seasonal activities

called *selemon* is prepared by cooking it, then soaking it in water for several days. The roasted trunk of a species of wild palm (called *limbum*) is eaten during this time, although in other months it would be considered pig food. Parents frequently send their young children to visit kin who live in locales where there are more garden resources.

The Sengseng consider the Kaulong lazy gardeners, because, according to Chowning (pers. comm.), the Sengseng do not experience a hungry period. I found periodic hunger characteristic of both Umbi and Angelek, and my informants said, and patrol reports confirm, that it has always been this way. I believe the lack of taro to eat at this time of year may be related to the low level of harvesting and stalk replanting during the rainy period, resulting—six to eight months later—in few mature taro plants to harvest. It is at the end of this hungry period when gardens begin to mature that people in Umbi might harvest a complete garden and call for others to help clear a new piece of the forest for planting stalks. The workers are fed harvested corms cooked

by the owner and host. Fancy parties include coconut cream and perhaps even rice carried from Kandrian by the host.

The third period, from February through May, is known as *gutpela
taim* ("time of good weather"). (Rainfall in 1964 was 62.12 inches.) This
is a time for weeding mature gardens and clearing new ones. It is also
a time for increased trade and travel to pig-killing ceremonies elsewhere, and for holding such events at one's home hamlet. As the
streams get low, it becomes possible to dam them or to use fish poison
to collect fish, eels, and shrimp. Hunting pigs and trapping cassowaries are common activities of men. Abundant wild fruits and nuts are
collected and enjoyed by all ages. Toward the end of this period just
prior to the onset of heavy rains in June, Kaulong conduct major garden harvests and replantings and sponsor many ceremonies in which
one or more pigs are sacrificed before people must trim their food
needs to a minimum for the onset of heavy rains.

HUNTING AND GATHERING

Subsistence for the Kaulong involves significant exploitation of the bush
and streams. In this regard, as elsewhere, success is a combination of
technical knowledge, skill, and special formulae learned through observation and direct instruction and with considerable practice. Without
taking precise count of subsistence intake (which I found impossible), I
estimate that in the rugged and remote inland Umbi region approximately 60 percent of the food is gathered from forest and stream; while
in the area around Angelek, 40 percent was hunted and gathered rather
than grown. Both Umbi and Angelek men said they preferred hunting
in the bush to laboring in the gardens: "My father told me to work in the
gardens in the morning, and then after my work was done, I could go
into the bush with my spear or blowgun."

In matters of prestige, a great gardener is more renowned than a
great hunter, although both tasks require acquisition and application
of specialized knowledge. Gardening is tedious much of the time, but
it directly affects one's reputation as a producer of two major symbols
of success: taro and pigs. A great hunter contributes considerable pro-
tein to the daily diet, which demonstrates his bravery, skill, strength,

and knowledge. Women also hunt, but less frequently than men; they spend more time in the gardens, cultivating edible greens and other introduced varieties of root crops, such as sweet manioc.

Men's hunting and fishing (in contrast to that of women) involve a more complex tool-kit and the use of dogs. The dogs are small and terrierlike, with pointed ears, bushy tails, and short coats of varied colors. Informants say they have always been in the bush. There are a great many wild dogs in the mountains. One of the strongest memories I have of Umbi is the wolflike howling of the village dogs taken up by their wild cousins, the sound echoing back and forth, and then the sudden silence. Because Kaulong castrate male dogs (like male pigs), bitches must be impregnated by wild dogs. Wild dogs are hunted for food, and their puppies are tamed and raised for use in hunting wild pigs. Kaulong feed their dogs no meat, but instead taro, tapiok, and other root crops. If hunting dogs are fed meat, it is felt that they will not help people to hunt game. Dogs are expected to hunt for their own meat and should call out to their owners when they corner some game. People expect dogs to work for them, not the other way around. The two puppies I raised in Umbi were just under a year old when they were taken with a pack of dogs on their first pig hunt. The male dog was lazy and returned by himself, but the female showed "great potential" as a pig hunter because she seemed to enjoy the whole process. Dogs find and corner the wild pig and call out to the hunter who spears the pig. Hunting with dogs requires magic spells, but I could get no details about this decidedly male business.

Pig hunting can be very dangerous. Wild boars have been known to injure severely and even kill a hunter and his dogs. Young boys in Umbi practiced pig-spearing by throwing sharpened sticks at a rolling disk of banana stalk, which represented the pig. They even encouraged my puppies to chase the rolling disk to get into the excitement of the chase. There is a special cry, similar to the battle cry, that a man makes as he carries in a wild pig. Children and women of the place dance and celebrate his prowess as a hunter. From December to June, we in Umbi ate wild pig an average of once a week.

When domestic dogs die their canines are removed and strung on long belts. These belts are part of the apparel of important men, who wind them many times around their hips. Sometimes these belts will contain human teeth interspersed between those of dogs, and a few belts I saw had large, old style (German, I was told), ceramic beads among the teeth.

Most unusual for Melanesia, the Kaulong use very long blowguns for hunting birds, fruit bats, and other arboreal animals, such as tree kangaroos and possums. Hunters carefully select the bamboo segments for size and bind them together (with small vine-rope and tree-sap) to form a tube fifteen to twenty feet long. The extreme length requires the hunter to use great skill in stalking his prey and in positioning himself, with his blowgun supported at both ends (to straighten the bore), as close to the prey as possible—often within a few feet. The dart, of hard palm wood with feathers tightly bound to one end to form a plug, is often three feet in length and does not contain poison. After inserting the dart the hunter grasps the proximal end of the tube between the fingers of both hands and with his mouth covered by his palms, he blows explosively. Often the dart finds its mark while still not entirely free of the tube. A bird or arboreal animal finds its way impeded by the length of the dart impaled in its body and eventually falls to the ground. Propelling the dart requires an enormous amount of breath, and people told me that they encourage young men to play panpipes (see chapter 8) in order to develop their lung capacity.

Cave bats abound in this limestone country. Using torches, the hunters enter the enormous caves and kill the escaping bats with sticks. They must be careful not to mention what they are doing, calling the bats by hidden names, else the cave will collapse and trap the hunters. Bats that escape are hunted with the blowgun.

Men trap cassowaries and bush fowl with snare traps laid across paths in the forest. In good weather they go to the river to spear large freshwater eels and fish. They use a small snare on the end of a stick and a lure of rotten meat to catch shrimp. Their method is relatively unproductive compared to that of the women, who catch large numbers of shrimp with their bare hands while crawling upstream during the hot dry season (a delightfully refreshing enterprise).

Wolio, Anut, and Homung—the major taro spirits—control the large eels, which are said to be the spirit's pigs. Men use spells to induce these spirits to show them where their pigs or eels are to be found. In return, the men reportedly give some pork to these spirits (although when pressed I could uncover no specific occasion when this had been done). Pigs and eels are considered to be the same kind of food: when consuming pork is tabu, for example, after the death of a close relative, eel is also forbidden. I can attest to the similarity of taste between these two prized foods.

Often while clearing a new garden area both men and women catch a great variety of animal and insect food with the aid of machete and axe: possums, bandicoots, snakes, frogs, ants, grubs, beetles, and caterpillars, which are eaten most commonly. Men and women gather wild yams, mushrooms, a great variety of fruits, nuts, and wild edible greens (ferns and the like).

In addition to providing daily food, the forest also contains resources valuable as trade items, medicines, and raw materials for manufacturing trade goods. Raw materials include fibers for skirts, bark for cloth, lizard skins and feathers, bamboo for musical instruments and blowguns, and honey. Vine-rope is used in lashing together house and garden posts and logs and for making fine net bags.

But the bush also harbors dangers both from cassowaries and wild boars and from the numerous spirits inhabiting sink holes, underground rivers, deep pools in the streams, particular trees, and, indeed, almost any significant feature of the landscape. I visited one such dangerous place, which was also a source of drinking water, at a refuge site in time of war. We descended the mountain and then, in the darkness of dense forest, we followed the path as it wove its way between weirdly eroded and twisted limestone walls to an enormously deep hole in the bottom of which was swiftly flowing water. I was told not to go too close, for the spirit within would grab me and pull me into the hole. However, when the people of the place had been under siege, then a strong man would go to this hole in the middle of the night's darkness and pull up water for the people to drink. I was taken to the place of one spirit who lived in a sink hole under a rock and who sighed and sometimes roared in a frightening way—it was I believe a blowhole for a underground stream.

Then there are the spirits that may be delocalized, in particular the *inaling (esusu)*, or female spirits, who lure men to follow them and forget their wives and children. The spirits that inhabit the bush surrounding the clearings are invoked to threaten wandering small children. Some of these localized spirits are said to be able to make a woman pregnant or cause one to fall from a tree.

The forest is a place where one usually goes alone to be with the coolness, quiet, and beauty. Kaulong seek out solitude and say that one can have peace only by living alone. But this peace does not come easily in a dangerous forest of bottomless pits, falling trees, wild pigs, cassowaries, sorcerers, and spirits. And living alone in the forest does nothing to enhance a person's reputation and prestige.

GARDEN PRODUCTION

The Kaulong are taro gardeners. Taro (*Colocasia esculenta*), called *nga* in Kaulong, is considered to be *the* essential food for human beings, enabling them to maintain health and promoting bodily growth. While it is common for people to exist for a number of days without taro (during the hungry period for example), people always say they are hungry when a day does not include taro. No form of meat should be eaten without taro, and it is quite impolite to present meat to anyone without an accompanying portion of baked taro. Finally, a man is not a complete human being (*potunus*) without at least two to four taro gardens in production at one time.

An old man named Punuli, living near Angelek, told me that when he met Americans on patrol during World War II, he was asked, "What do you eat?" "Taro," he replied, and added that it was "strong for them" and "if they had no taro they would die." One American asked to try taro, and Punuli's wife roasted and scraped some and put a piece of the inside "meat" on the American's tongue. Then Punuli gave some to every American. They said it was good. After the third group of Americans came, Punuli said he couldn't give them any more taro because all their food was gone. The American went to look at the gardens and saw the taro was small and told Punuli to bring his people to the coast, that he would give them food. They got so much rice from the American that even when the gardens were good again, they still had rice. Punuli told me this tale to illustrate that taro to them was symbolically the same as rice or bread was to Americans.

Among the Kaulong, Sengseng, and others of this region, garden sites are not specifically owned by any individual or group. I was told that no one need ask permission of anyone before clearing a site. Named garden sites are usually found near a hamlet clearing and are where descendants of prior gardeners should plant their taro. "One should plant where one's father planted before," but the only reason seemed to be that "father knew best." Should someone else start to clear such a garden site, however, no offense was taken. I heard of no cases of conflict over garden sites. Whereas second-growth gardens are easier to clear than primary-growth sites, I saw almost an equal number of primary- and secondary-growth gardens cleared and planted.

Garden sites are judged ready to be replanted when the timber that has grown up inside is of sufficient size to make a strong fence. The fallow period varies according to the growing qualities of the site, and it can last from ten to twenty years.

A good gardener typically has taro gardens in three or four stages of growth at any given time: a newly cleared garden in which to plant the stalks harvested from a mature garden, and a third and possibly fourth garden in which the taro is maturing, or perhaps a fourth just being cleared and fenced. In the more remote areas around Umbi these gardens were usually jointly managed, and one's taro plants were dispersed throughout three or more gardens. This reduces the risk that the taro will fail to mature because of adverse soil conditions, the steepness of the garden, taro disease, marauding wild pigs, theft, or a host of other problems believed to affect the health of the taro.

In the Angelek region, the gardens were most often cleared and planted by one person or perhaps two brothers, rarely more. The gardens were apt to be contiguous rather than scattered around the landscape, as they are in Umbi. In Angelek, protection from adverse taro magic was usually given as the reason for private rather than jointly managed gardens.

There was some division of labor by sex in the physical preparation and care of taro gardens. Women preceded the timber cutters and slashed through the underbrush with machetes, releasing the clinging and hindering vines. Men then cut the timber. In many areas of this region the prime rather than secondary forest requires considerable skill in timber cutting. The ultimate exhibition of skill seemed to occur in what I called garden parties. As the women freed an area of vines and brush, the men organized their timber cutting so that when all was ready, a single "king pin" of a tree was sent crashing onto other partially cut trees so that all the trees fell in succession like dominoes, to great cheers from men, women, and children. It was obvious to this observer that there was, in such a display of skill, a large element of aesthetic satisfaction that went far beyond the mere utility of clearing a garden site.

The fallen timber is used first to build strong fences. The trunks are laid between two parallel rows of upright posts and are lashed with lawyer vine (*kanda*) into a strong, four-to-six-foot-high barricade against wild and domestic pigs. Other timber is used to construct a garden hut, often an open lean-to but sometimes closed with four walls constructed in the same way as the fence with a roof of lawyer vine leaves covering all. The interiors of these garden huts have two or more sets of five to eight poles laid loosely on two horizontal logs placed on the ground along two long sides. These sets of poles are used as beds or benches, the width of the set expanding and contracting as needed for the shifting number of occupants. It is in these garden huts that married couples spend most of their time, sleeping close to the garden in order to protect it and to ensure their own privacy. Husband and wife share the garden hut unless there is a teenaged daughter, who will share with her mother while the father builds a second hut for himself.

Planting taro may be done by men or women. I usually observed men planting, which involved wielding the heavy seven- to eight-foot sharpened poles. They lifted them high and then forced them a distance into the ground, pushing them forward, back, and around to enlarge the hole. Then the man tossed a taro stalk into the hole. He completed the job by pushing and breaking in the side of the hole with his foot.

If it is dry enough, some of the leafy brush is heaped and fired and the ashes are spread out over a small area. Taro is the main crop, which is said to grow better in ashes. Other plants are subsequently added to the garden. A*ibika*, *bubak*, greens, sugar cane, pitpit, cucumbers, sweet potatoes, yams, sweet manioc bananas, and tobacco are the most common secondary plants. Some gardeners may add sweet corn, beans, tomatoes, pumpkins, gourds, and other introduced plants. Typically, it is said that with the exception of bananas and tobacco, these secondary crops are women's crops, planted and cared for by them.

Of all garden crops, only taro requires the addition of magic to grow and mature. The first step in a sequence of magical activities is the performance of spells that (in Angelek) can call back and/or steal a garden's fertility. In a region where ownership of garden land is absent, this type of "fertility" spell gives the possessor certain claim of priority to the site. At the least, he should be consulted by another gardener wishing to clear and plant there. If the spell is not performed, I was told by one spell owner, the garden will be a poor one at best. He

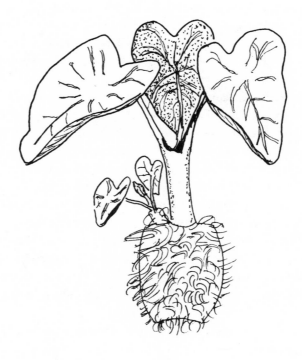

FIG. 2. Taro

illustrated his point by telling of a man who cleared and planted a particular garden site while he, the spell owner, was away working on Manus (and therefore could not perform the spell). The taro grew very poorly; in fact, nothing came up at all.

When taro is harvested, the edible corm is cut away from the stalk, leaving a concave piece of the corm attached to the stalk, which regenerates into a new edible corm. Kaulong told me that the cut is best done using a clam shell, since a knife is said to make too clean a cut and jeopardizes the regeneration. People eat taro leaves as a "green." But it is the stalk that is inherently valuable.

Taro stalks are inherited, traded, imported, and exported. The elaborate local taxonomy reflects the variable histories of specific plants. In some instances, a variety parallels a genealogical descent group; in others, a local group origin; and in still other cases, its own personal history as to who planted or imported it.[1] When someone said, "This is my grandfather's taro," it was clear that it was not only the same variety as the grandfather had planted, but was considered to be the identical plant (stalk) that the grandfather had planted. The taro stalk has an immortality that is taken as a human model, as we shall see in chapter 9.

Stalks must be replanted within three days of being cut from the corm, or they rot and die. When people plan a residential move, they must plan for their taro's move well in advance. A long-distance move will usually take a year or more as the person is said to be "walking his taro" (i.e., planting) ever closer to the eventual destination. When someone goes away he must ask another to care for his taro stalks. The caretaker assumes both the responsibility of planting, weeding, harvesting, and replanting and the right to eat the taro corms.

While adequate practical knowledge of taro care and classification is essential for successful gardening, all taro corms are ultimately controlled by major spirit beings. The particular spirit is not the same for all Kaulong regions, nor does it appear to bear any relation to linguistic

---

1. I did not systematically investigate taro classification, and my knowledge of the complexities comes from observation and informal questions and discussions held with a variety of gardeners in both Umbi and Angelek.

boundaries. For example, the Kaulong of Umbi and the Sengseng of Dulago recognize the same taro spirit named Wolio, whereas the Kaulong of Angelek recognized two major spirits, Anut and Homung, to whom all taro magic was addressed. There are many spells dedicated to these major spirits, no taro corms will come to the garden unless magic is performed. In Angelek I was told that these spirits operate with help from a snake named Amat. If Amat sees a garden full of taro, he will tell Anut and Homung not to send any more. Caterpillars and snakes are special garden inhabitants and should not be disturbed or, if eaten, their bones should be returned to the garden where they can look after the taro. These major spirits—Anut, Homung, and Wolio—all live in a hole near the headwaters of the Ason and Alimbit rivers.

In Angelek I was told that there is a mountain between Lauring and the road, on top of which there is a small bottomless hole, so crooked that you cannot see inside. In the early days, there was a "rope" (a vine) rising out of this hole and going up on top of a large *malais* tree, then on down to the coast and the islands. This rope was the "road" on which all taro walked about. But then the rope broke, and all the number-one taro fell down on the islands and is called *auring* (or in *tok pisin, namba wan*) taro. All other varieties of taro, called *anhaung* (or in *tok pisin, namba tu*), fell back into this hole where taro can now be found. While number-one taro is big, number-two varieties are sweet. Number-two taro is considered to be *potunus*, or human. Once a child of number-two taro got lost and cried and its mother came and nursed it. For this reason, if a pig breaks into a garden of number-two taro and eats just a few taro, people will kill the pig because it is as if it ate a human being.

When one makes a spell for taro in Angelek, the taro comes from this hole. I was told that during hungry time (September to March), the area around the hole is just bush, but during the time of plenty, the area around the hole is completely bare, just like the village clearing. This is because the taro has trod the place bare on its way to the gardens.

Like many other major Melanesian gardeners, Kaulong believe taro can walk about at will. The gardener's first task after the garden has been prepared is to coerce a controlling spirit—such as Wolio—to send the corms to the garden. Inducement involves bespelling the taro stalk and often the ground in which it is planted. And while it is most common for the spell to be silently spoken over wild ginger root (*hengel*), which is then chewed and spat over the stalks bespelling them, not all garden magic involves ginger. Water, the croton called *eun*, and another plant called *epi* are also frequently used. One man left a very tall tree in the center of the garden so the taro would see it and know where to go. Taro also walks about at night and people say that someone sleeping close to the garden can hear it. One man told me that after he had seen Europeans planting gardens without magic, he tried to do the same at home in Angelek. "Nothing at all came up," he said—proof that here, at least, magic was an absolute necessity for growing taro.

During the growing period other spells may be performed—spells to protect the garden from specific harms. Most common spells involve decorative and bespelled crotons that are placed in various parts of the garden to ward off any magical attempt to steal the corms as they walk about during the night, to persuade the spirits to send more taro, and to enhance the growth of the corm. And there are spells to cause illness to any poacher. These may be put in place as the gardens near maturity.

There are spells to protect against diseases or too much rain or sun or other climatic extremes. At the time of my stay in Umbi, taro blight was beginning to cause considerable concern. Good-weather magic is very rare; it involves the use of crystals and is considered to be very powerful magic as it can cause the water essential to taro's growth to dry up. Rain magic is commonly known and when successful causes unusually heavy amounts of rain to fall. I was told that everyone knows some rain magic, but as a result of a former *kiap*'s threat to jail anyone who made rain, no one would admit to it. However, Umul came visiting one day after an unusual dry spell and we sat commiserating over the drying of our gardens. When I asked if he knew how to make rain, he immediately said, "No," but without pausing to take a breath told of making rain magic in his garden that morning. Why wasn't it raining now? "Because I was foolish and kept working in the garden," he answered. "I should have gone home to sleep. Rain won't come if you keep working." I learned that belief in the efficacy of the spell is essential to its effectiveness. Magic only works for the believer.

The number and kinds of garden and taro-related formulae appear to be practically infinite, but all are individually owned and are an important consideration in the evaluation of a person's knowledge. As I mentioned in chapter 2, management of this knowledge is extremely important in the game of politics. One successful gardener told me that he was deliberately not using a certain formula in the replanting of a particular set of taro stalks at this time because, having used it just previously when the taro had grown to noteworthy proportions, he did not wish to display such success two plantings in a row—"because people would begin to talk" or be jealous and then might perform harmful magic on his garden. A man who has many formulae relating to any particular activity has alternatives and choices to make in the display and validation of knowledge. Not everyone has appropriate spells, but the gardener may hire one or several people to perform the desired spells for a price. Most gardens are under multiple spells throughout the growing period, thus which spells are most effective is ambiguous, allowing each performer to believe his was the one that worked best.

Although most garden spells are in the hands of males, some Kaulong women have spells to ensure growth and health of the crop. I saw them performed only twice, in Umbi. The owner of a garden hired a group of women to clean the maturing taro, using coconut shells fastened to sticks to scrape weeds away from the stalk and to heap soil around the base of the taro stalk. I happened to sit near a group of three taro stalks that apparently had been overlooked in this clearing and scraping. Much to my surprise, at the end of the ritual, the women all rushed to this "forgotten" clump and broke the stalks and coconut-shell scrapers. They then planted the scrapers upright in the clump with the taro. This will ensure the growth of the taro, I was told. The owner then served the women rice that he had bought in Kandrian, carried (all fifty-two pounds of it) on his back to Umbi, and spent the day cooking for them.

The magic formulae of the gardens are passed on from father to son, from mother to daughter, and less commonly from a mother's brother to

Bridge over the Alimbit River

The village of Umbi, cleaned and prepared for the *Kiap*'s visit

The front room of my house in Angelek

A sister from the Sacred Heart Mission checking the children of Angelek

Election information provided in Angelek

A typical hamlet with main house (*mang*) and fruiting trees

Three girls of courting age

Kaliam catches a parrot that has eaten too much taro
from Kaliam's garden to be able to fly away.

Nakling weighs a murmut that he plans to cook for my dinner
in order to determine what he will charge me.

Debli sings taro magic spells into water, while garden owner Ningbi waits for the water to be poured over his taro stalks.

A "big man" pours "poison water" over the hands of a suspected sorcerer to determine guilt or innocence.

A young hunter uses a twenty-foot blowgun.

In the dry season, pools in small streams can be dammed
and the water bailed out to gather shrimp and, perhaps, fish.

Expert timbermen balance on crude platforms
while cutting virgin forest for a new garden.

As gardens are cleared, the logs are made into strong fences
to keep both wild and domestic pigs out.

Harvesting taro

Three young men—(*R to L*) Kinegit, Gaspat, and Mikail—
at the start of their prestige seeking.

A woman clears and burns brush in a new garden.

Girls begin garden work at a young age.

Children play in a mature taro garden.

Elderly women are the prime caretakers of very young children and pigs.

Young girls pose for the camera.

The effects of head-binding in infancy can be seen in this girl's
elongated skull; here, she drinks water from a coconut shell.

First menses ritual for Pangel at Angelek. The young woman's head is shaved in longitudinal stripes, and she wears a new *songon* (skirt). The women swing a men's ceremonial belt against her back as they sing.

Women dance at conclusion of first menses ritual, clowning in men's ornaments and trousers.

A young man from the interior, dressed to attract females

Shells placed on the pig's body by the groom's kin
are evaluated by the bride's kin.

A mother holds her infant, whose head is bound, while her older daughter plays with a new puppy.

sister's son. Each recipient, selected on the basis of relative age and potential, receives a different spell. A first son or daughter may receive the most potent spells, but if judged not as worthy as a younger son or daughter, he or she may receive spells with less proven power. Ground-fertility magic, I was told by a first-born son, is always given to the eldest son. I did not record a single case where magic was passed on to some-one other than son, daughter, or sister's son.

Although many will reportedly hire another to perform special magic formulae on their gardens, I was unable to obtain any examples of garden magic (or for that matter any other kinds of magic formulae). I was told that these individual formulae are not for giving, "they must stop in the mouth."

Significant differences in the management of gardens between the two Kaulong areas in which I worked probably result in large part from the differences in terrain. The rugged steep slopes of the limestone ridges in the remote interior of Umbi apparently limit the size of any individual garden. Here, a single gardener would typically plant taro in a number of different and shared gardens at the same time, which I interpret as a way of reducing the natural and human risk factors such as marauding pigs, landslides, and (magical) theft. In Umbi, sharing gardens typically means sharing labor and ritual as well. In contrast, while the more gently undulating terrain near Angelek permits much larger gardens, I noticed hardly any shared gardens and a heightened fear of magical theft of ground fertility and/or taro corms.

Gardening is not easy. It requires constant clearing of the forest and then maintaining the clearing for the next nine to fifteen months while the garden is planted, protected, and eventually harvested. As the months wear on, the fence begins to rot and must be maintained or pigs are sure to invade. Pigs are devastating to a taro garden—they eat the corms down to the beginning of the stalk and thus prevent the plant's regeneration.

Wild pigs may be speared on the spot (the source of much of the pork consumed), but word should be sent to the owners of domestic pigs to come and collect the pig. Only after an owner has ignored a number of such messages may a domestic pig be killed. Exchanges of valuables in payment for taro destroyed and pig killed will eventually restore harmony between the gardener and pig owner. Everyone said that the loss of taro was greater than the loss of a pig. The former can never be replaced, the latter can.

PIG RAISING

Raising pigs is an important adult activity for both men and women. Transactions in pork are central to the most frequent and significant intergroup political activities. While the total number of pigs raised by the average adult rarely exceeds one per year or two per married couple, pork is an important symbol of political and social power. Pig raising is difficult in such an ecologically marginal area. There must be a surplus of cultivated taro and other root crops to feed the pig. The owner's personal relationship with the pig must go beyond feeding to include grooming and training. While piglets may be put on a leash for a short time, once they become bonded to a human caretaker they are left to roam the extensive bush during the heat of the day and are expected to return at dusk for grooming and supplementary food. The most common problem in raising pigs is taming the pig adequately to keep it from invading gardens or going feral and to help it lose its fear of humans. There are magic formulae and special techniques to aid this endeavor. Keeping a pig healthy, safe, and out of the gardens is considered a learned (not inherited) skill.

Keeping a pig healthy involves an extensive knowledge of what a domestic pig may or may not be permitted to eat. Varieties of pigs may require different diets. Debli acquired a "dakso" pig in Umbi. This pig was descended from a pig called "dakso," an imported European pig originally acquired at a plantation on the north coast of New Britain. Debli gave his dakso to K, an old woman who had survived her husband's death, who agreed to care for it. Because K had too many grandchildren living with her, none of whom paid attention to the special treatment the dakso required (e.g., being given only fresh water from round holes and only human—not pig—food, and being allowed to eat and sleep in quiet), Debli built K a special house for herself and the pig. He planted a taro garden to feed the dakso and was responsible for all of the pig's food. K, the caretaker, would be paid when the dakso was eventually sacrificed. Pigs generally eat small or substandard taro and yellow, not white, sweet manioc, although I heard the reverse in Angelek. Manioc (*tapiok*) was introduced by Australian agricultural officers to guard against the dangers of depending on one major root crop, and while white manioc is considered human food it is secondary to taro in importance. A type of *limbum* (palm) and a nut called *selemon* are known as pig food (but people will also eat these during the hungry time). Absolutely forbidden to the dakso were any food leavings such as the bones of wild bush rats, lizards, wallaby, insects, or fish and shrimp. Ordinary pigs will effectively clean up these discards.

In Umbi, it was rejected as "untrue" that small piglets would be nursed at the breast—"the pigs teeth would bite the woman's breast," but in Angelek when I fed my piglet milk, I was commended for doing so. My Angelek informant said that he had seen his grandmother nursing a tiny piglet. This, he said, was the proper way to care for an unweaned piglet. The child who was nursed alongside the piglet considered the piglet to be its sibling, having had the same mother.

In infancy, bespelled powdered lime is blown into the piglet's nostrils to make it forget its natural mother and bond to a human caretaker. Male pigs are castrated when quite young. Initially a female pig is no more valuable than a male pig. A female that is allowed to bear a number of litters (rather than being sacrificed in the first or second year) is more valuable than one sacrificed with few offspring.

The most valuable pig is a "tusker." Some male pigs have their upper canines removed, permitting the lower canines to grow unimpeded and perhaps in a full circle to reenter the lower jaw, a process that takes ten or twelve years. Specialists are paid handsomely for removing the upper canines. After this procedure, the owner of a tusker will employ many spells and all-night hamlet ceremonies to enhance the tusker's growth and ability to withstand accusations of taro destruction or will pay the compensation necessary to keep a gardener from spearing the tusker.

The ceremony in which a tusker is sacrificed is a great event, often years in preparation. After the ritual butchering, the lower jaw with its pair of encircling tusks is given to a visiting trade partner who in the old days was said to have to legitimate his ownership and eventual wearing of the tusks by killing someone. The two spiral tusks are then made into an ornament that is worn hanging down the owner's back or is clenched in his teeth so that the encircling tusks appear to come out of the wearer's own mouth. Displaying a pig's tusks in one's own mouth usually occurs in an intergroup situation where tensions are high. As I shall argue in chapter 10, the wearer is saying to others, "Watch out, I can be like a pig. I am powerful and dangerous."

To make a pig grow rapidly and to great size means keeping it alive for a period of time and performing special magic formulae. Both men and women own and raise pigs, although I know of no tusker raised and owned by a woman alone. It is more usual that such a pig is the joint responsibility of one or more men together with one or more women.

Almost without exception pigs are raised with the expectation that they will be ceremonially butchered and distributed as pork to people outside the immediate hamlet. I knew of approximately thirty-eight pigs sacrificed at hamlet rituals, while at least an equal number of others were killed as they were caught marauding in another's garden, after going feral due to neglect, or with some other reason given and accepted.

There is an annual cycle of ceremonial pig killing. Most of the killing occurs during the "good time," when there is less rainfall and greater ease of travel to distant hamlets to participate in such rituals. I believe this is a conscious effort to prepare for the coming rainy season when there can be little garden clearing or planting and thus less food for all, including pigs. One man who killed all his pigs just prior to the rainy season said that he was following the dictate of a dream he had had recently. Most families will negotiate to reduce the number of live pigs to one or two, enough to carry over through the rainy season and through a period of hunger occurring just prior to the good season beginning in early January.

Sacrificial pigs are killed in the morning following an all-night song ceremony (*lut a yu*). Some of these ceremonies are held as rites of passage. In a tooth ceremony, for example, the blood of a sacrificed pig is rubbed on the child's head to celebrate the complete eruption of the child's first teeth. *Lut a yu* (singsings with pigs) are also held for male initiation (and sometimes for female puberty rites) and for mortuary rituals. Pigs are also killed during marriage exchanges, at peace-making, and at burials, none of which involves all-night singing beforehand.

Sacrificial pigs are butchered into two principal pieces: the *banis* (the ribs) and the *het* (the head). The "rib" portion is skinless and without fore- or hind legs but includes the hams or hips and upper rear thighs. The "head" includes not only the head, but also the entire body skin with its underlying layer of fat and the forelegs, all left articulated to the skull. The two hind legs, minus "hams" that are part of the *banis*, are minor portions.

No owner or caretaker will ever eat his or her own pig. When the big tusker at Dulago was killed, its former owner and ceremonial host made magic causing a great rain that flooded the Ason in which I nearly drowned on my way home. I was told that the owner had made the rain to erase his sacrificed pig's tracks so he would not see them and feel sad. When my pig Gudeo died (mysteriously—but I was too sad to push the cause to any conclusion), people fully understood my tearful instructions to butcher, cook, and distribute the meat throughout Angelek, as well as my request not to let me see any of it. Joining me for my dinner of rice and fancy canned meat and a small bottle of scotch were all the young people who had helped me take care of Gudeo, who had slept with her in my cookhouse after she outgrew my upstairs house, and who said they, too, were too sorry to eat any of their pig.

In the Kaulong world, the forest and the garden are two contrasting spaces in which to live and work and become human. The forest is quite clearly the preferred place of the two, but it is equally clear that it is a place where humans are just another creature, occupying the same space as animals, insects, birds, and spirits. But while both men and women spoke of the forest with an emotional attachment quite unlike the way they spoke of a garden, it was in the gardens that they worked to become differentiated and human.

The gardens, however, have no permanence. The clearing made is later abandoned to the forest and may never be cleared by the same person twice. For a year or two a person may fill the garden space with taro and pigs, but the taro and pigs move with the owner to a new place and the garden eventually reverts to the animals, birds, and spirits. The position of pigs vis-à-vis humans is parallel. Both should sleep in the garden hut. During the day the pig and human may roam separately in the forest gathering food. Humans, like pigs, should have sexual relations only in the forest. It is to distinguish human from pig that humans should learn to work in the garden clearing where no pig should be.

Children of both sexes gain most of their subsistence knowledge from observation and practice, and usually only the formulae are formally transmitted and then usually only to fully adult offspring. Children, however, are frequently asked to participate in the performance of a magical technique by fetching and holding the water to be bespelled or the ginger root, but they are unable to hear the silently recited spells. As the children grow and of their own volition begin to demonstrate what they have learned, elders evaluate their progress in acquiring knowledge. Girls are said to acquire garden knowledge faster than boys because "they are greedier than boys" by nature. Women also have a special corner on pig-raising knowledge, although this is not exclusively theirs. While both men and women hunt and gather wild food in forest and stream, men have additional knowledge of specialized techniques using the blowgun, the spear, and dogs. In some subsistence activities men and women have different skills and techniques as well as formulae, and in others there is no differential knowledge according to gender.

It was especially apparent that there was no necessity for a man to be married to have extensive gardens; in fact, men said, "It is better to have mothers and sisters to help in the gardening than a wife; the former are more reliable."

Hunting, gardening, and raising pigs are not just subsistence activities but are also for the purpose of trade. All items produced through one's labor, including pigs, are traded. Special products of the forest, but not food, are also traded (for example, skins, feathers). In chapter 4, I discuss the use of gold-lip pearl shells (*Pinctada maxima*) to negotiate exchange relationships.

4/ Saying It with Shells

In 1922 Bronislaw Malinowski published his now-famous study of the Kula regional exchange system from the perspective of the people of Kiriwina in the Trobriand Islands. Since that time additional studies of the Massim exchange system have greatly increased our knowledge of the complexity of this Papua New Guinean trade (see, for example, Weiner 1976; Leach and Leach 1983), and there have been a number of other comparable studies that have dealt with Highland areas (Strathern 1971, Healey 1990, for example).

The trading system of the Vitiaz Strait (Harding 1967, Pomponio 1991) is one of the few systems in Island Melanesia outside of the Massim that have received serious study. Traders from Siassi, acting as middlemen, moved commodities between New Britain and the Huon Peninsula region of Papua New Guinea. The traders also traveled eastward along the south coastal region of New Britain where they linked up with Arawe Island traders, who then carried the trade farther eastward at least as far as Kandrian (see map, p. 4).

The Arawe Islanders directly traded with coastal people who are economically, politically, and linguistically linked with each other and distinct from the inland peoples. I do not believe the inland Whiteman language group of people was ever significantly linked in direct trade with the coast, however a number of rituals and songs whose origin is said to be the "coast" have been introduced into the interior, and in the early 1970s I knew of a few marriages between Arawe-speaking people of the near Kandrian coast and Kaulong in the Angelek region. People in Umbi and Angelek remember the first steel axe traded inland, and occasionally other items (such as wooden bowls) made their way into the interior. It is quite possible that going out of the Whiteman language region were dogs' teeth, bark cloth, manganese oxide, and spears, but there is no evidence that this trade was a significant part of the interior people's life. We need a great deal more information before we can document the interlocking of these routes.

It was of interest to find that while the Sengseng of Dulago traded to the coast (south/north), no Kaulong did. The Kaulong of Umbi traded with the Miu to the west and Sengseng in the east, while those of Angelek did not trade with the Miu but with the Gimi to the west and with Sengseng and Karore to the east.

While each subregional system is quite distinct there are underlying similarities. This is an exchange system that uses gold-lip pearl shells as valuables and as markers of value of both goods and services. I am defining a valuable as an item whose intrinsic worth is uniquely recalculated at every event in which it changes hands. Gold-lip pearl shells supplanted an earlier use of *mokmok* stone valuables but did not devalue the stones. There is considerable complexity in the use of shells which serves to differentiate participants in ability, motivation, and knowledge. Exchange is the language of politics and it is characteristically Melanesian that a large part of the oratory is in nonverbal exchange.

As I have shown in chapter 3, there is little gender distinction in daily household or subsistence activities. Similarly, as we shall see in chapter 5, the public arena in which exchange takes place is open to both men and women, although the quantity of exchanges is greater for men than for women.

What is reflected in the exchange system is the independence and autonomy of the individual over anything resembling a social order. The self-developing individual Kaulong typically expresses little concern with any larger aggregate of people beyond a personal egocentric network of exchange relationships. Within such a network, each individual establishes his or her own place. Negotiation for social position is typically concealed in nonverbal acts whose primary aim is to avoid any ultimate evaluation of one's personal social worth. At times it seemed to me that the Kaulong, who always deliberately chose to make ambiguous what might easily be made explicit, represented an archetypical society close to total anarchy. I show in this chapter how the Kaulong manage to express nonverbally what they seek to conceal, e.g., that as humans they do depend on others. It is through exchange that they achieve a level of *shared* understanding about, and order in, their social world.

THE LANGUAGE OF SHELLS

In this region of southwest New Britain, before there was any contact with German patrols or recruiters for labor plantations, according to my informants the polished and pierced stone objects of various sizes, shapes and hues—generally called *mokmok* in Arawe and in Kaulong *niglak* and *singa*—were held by men of power and influence, *pomidan* (hereafter big men). These objects were used in two major contexts: the exchange of pork and the granting of permanent sexual rights in women.

The origin of these *mokmok* stones is not known by my informants or to me. The former say "they belong to the ground like the bones of the dead." In Angelek I heard a story that a great big "mother" of all *mokmoks* came out of the ground near Sankiap on the other side of the river south of Umbi. This "mother" stone gave birth to all the little *mokmoks*. When I asked if one could see this mother of all *mokmoks*, I was told that after she had given birth she disappeared. In Umbi, I was told that the *mokmoks* bubbled up from an underground river somewhere in the region to the southwest of Angelek. The source is obviously considered to be within the region but distant from any one group. Currently *mokmok* stones are kept buried in the ground, often under decorative bushes or fruit-bearing trees, or kept in limestone caves hidden from all but the current owner. The stones are considered extremely significant in the validation of personal power when that is challenged but are rarely used in any context in which ownership is transferred. However, I heard that *mokmok* stones were demanded by a sorcerer when he was hired to kill another and by powerful men when a daughter or niece (ZD) was to be married. Although my data are not definitive, it does appear that some women own *mokmok* stones.

Gold-lip pearl shells, perhaps traded in from Arawe, were in circulation before German recruiters arrived on the local scene. Older Kaulong agree that they were limited in number, large, and unshaped, although their exterior surface was polished. Only big men were said to have held and transacted with these shells, in the same contexts as *mokmok* stones and sometimes together with them. My informants say that the first laborer from the Kaulong region to return from a German plantation brought with him a number of gold-lip pearl shells as well as steel knives and axe heads. Thereafter, the local people insisted that recruiters give shells and knives to parents before any of them would allow their sons to be recruited. More shells entered the exchange system and the resulting increase allowed the system to expand. Significant inflation came with the ending of World War II when the naval base on Manus opened for laborers recruited from southwest New Britain. Manus is now considered the ultimate source of gold-lip pearl shells.

I was repeatedly told that the primary reason for going to work on Manus was and is to exchange wages for shells with which to enter into the local exchange network upon returning. People say that even the laziest one among them would return with ten to twenty shells, while many could obtain the maximum, said to be about fifty. Currently the exchange system involves women and children, as well as young men, their elders, and the acknowledged big men, as active participants. Certainly inflation has made it possible for so many to participate; however, I do not consider that universal participation is the only result of inflation. What may be more significantly attributed to the inflation in shells is an increase in the number and contextual range of individual transactions. With pacification, travel became safer and more people were able to enter into the system at an earlier age. Individual exchange networks were also enlarged to include more people in more contexts and in more distant areas.

The rules or grammar of exchange do not seem to have changed, and this has resulted in a system that can become more complex for each participant as his or her network enlarges. This complexity is also self-limiting. Only a few people have the quantity and quality of knowledge to build and maintain the most extensive networks. Most individuals are only able to maintain a moderate-sized network and some are able to handle only a very modest network. None of my informants was willing to estimate the size of any other person's network or divulge the size of their own. This is but another example of the desire to leave important measures or causes ambiguous, but it also means that I was left to make my own estimation.

It is important to emphasize that all who exchange are considered *potunus*, and that there may be a rare few who manage to rise over the top or fall below a minimal level of humanness. Superhumans and subhumans, as I will show in the next chapter, are recognized and talked about.

Foreign currency has also filtered into the region: first, a small amount of German coins, followed by the wider spread of Australian money, and, following independence, the national currency. These monies were rarely used in any local transaction during the period of study except when there was an overriding reason for not demanding a shell in return for an obligation. "I asked for money because I know [he/she] doesn't have any [i.e., good] shells" was a common explanation for asking for money, or "I changed my shell for money in order to buy something at the trade store," or to buy a plane ticket to Rabaul, or to Hoskins—in other words, in order to trade in the money world of the outside. In Angelek, I was told that old German coins with a hole were becoming very "valuable." For example, some people took one or two of these coins to Rabaul and when they were ready to come home, found that one such coin could be exchanged for the Australian money needed to buy a ticket back to Kandrian. I was also told that these coins were being hoarded and hidden, much like the *mokmok* stones.

My astute informants were well aware of the implications underlying the intrinsic differences between coin and shell as mediums of exchange. They understood that coins were anonymous in that one man's coin always equalled another man's coin of same denomination. And further that two (shilling) coins could equal one (two-shilling) coin. Shells are not anonymous, each shell is distinct from every other shell so that X's shell can not equal Y's shell and no two shells could ever equal one. As one frustrated transactor exclaimed to his trade friend: "I can't buy pork from you, you always return my shells. How can I buy it? I only have shells. I am not like White men who have plenty of something to buy things with—I only have shells. Money has been given to us by White men to help us, but you won't take money and you don't like *my* shells." Clearly any transaction involving shells is a context in which more than the exchange value of the transaction is being communicated by the symbol. As I shall discuss later, the very ambiguity of the message coded makes the shell the overriding symbol of choice for nearly all transactions.

Evaluation of the Pearl Shell: The Euk

The gold-lip pearl shell has a value measured in foreign currency just as it comes from the ocean, but it is not considered a symbol for transaction without some modification. The skin must be removed by polishing the outside with pumice, a stone, or a steel file. The less rounded edge is then filed to approximate the curvature of the more rounded edge, but also leaving a projection, called the "ear" (*kinan*) of the *euk*. Finally, a hole is drilled in the apex of the hinge area from which to fasten a holding rope. The gold-lip pearl shell is thus transformed into a symbol of transaction, into an *euk*.

Any further modification does not increase the value of the shell. Further modifications are extremely frequent, however, and in many

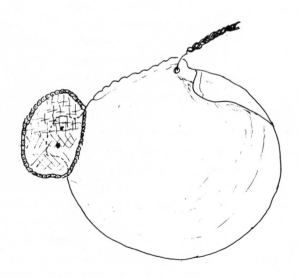

FIG. 3. Gold-lip pearl shell (*euk*)

cases very elaborate. Woven covers are made from plant fibers to cover the "ears," and these may be further decorated with nassa shells (*tambu*), colorful seeds, feathers, plastic, or other materials. The holding rope itself may be elaborately decorated with additional substances. One of my informants asked for and received lengths of my unusual (to them) long, straight hair to use as decoration for his shells. All informants agreed that such packaging has no effect on the true value of the shell but that the aim is to make the shell "attractive." Considerable time, effort, and sometimes expense are dedicated to packaging individual shells in one's possession, particularly in anticipation of an important transaction. (Interestingly, shell magic is not applied to the shell but rather to the person, with the aim of increasing one's chances of making a good negotiation.) Such attention to individual shells by each successive owner certainly serves to increase the temporary owner's knowledge of the special characteristics of that particular shell. This intimate knowledge is absolutely necessary for the successful trading of shells.

Shells are evaluated according to the following structural characteristics: size, weight, thickness, right or left configuration, balance of configuration, and miscellaneous qualities. I consider each in turn.

1. *Size*. Although there is a continuum of sizes, two groups are recognized. The two groups are stored separately from each other, but are often used together in important transactions. Large shells (*emtartngen*) are often given personal names and are used in pork transactions and in certain aspects concerning granting of sexual rights over women. Informants are less inclined to assign money equivalents to these large shells than they are to the smaller ones. The large shells are sometimes exchanged, however, for from five to ten 1974 U.S. dollars. Smaller shells are usually not named and are used in a great variety of exchanges involving goods and services and in a number of other contexts as well. Only shells near the extreme ends of the size continuum are acknowledged to belong to one or other grade. Most middle-range shells are open to debate in any context.

2. *Weight*. As shells age they lose weight in proportion to their size. The heavier (newer) shells are more valued. Negotiators measure weight by clicking the shell with their finger tip and evaluating the "ring" of the shell in the context of their total experience and memory.

3. *Thickness*. If the shell is translucent when held against the sun, it is downgraded.

4. *Right or left configuration*. As the pearl oyster is a bivalve, the shells come in two configurations called *ngolong*, left-eared, and *wzshu*, right-eared, depending on the position of the "ear" when the inside surface is toward the viewer. A right-eared shell is more valued than a left-eared one. Both are required in pork transactions and should at least be offered in equal numbers, or with more right- than left-eared shells.

5. *Balance of configuration*. On the back surface of the shell the arch of the apex should be steep, well formed, and smooth. The hinge area on the inside should be small. These configurations are judged to be positive if consistent with the size of the shell.

6. *Miscellaneous qualities*. Various marks and blemishes on the inner and outer surfaces are also used in judging quality. My knowledge of these criteria is limited by my experience. Experience in handling many shells over a lifetime is the only way one can gain a sense of the comparative value of any of the circulating shells. The value of each shell is renegotiated at every transaction.

The Rules (Grammar) of Transaction

The rules governing any shell transaction are few and simple to learn, yet quite difficult to apply without the expertise that comes with long experience. The subtle implications of each of the rules involve concepts critical to effective negotiation and "speaking" well with shells.

The first rule is that shells must circulate through a minimum of three new owners before being offered to a previous owner. In actual practice it is rare that someone will accept any shell he or she has previously owned, and whoever offers such a shell is considered singularly inept. One of the implications underlying this rule is that once one has negotiated with the shell and established a value for that context, one does not wish to renegotiate the value of the same shell in another context. It appears that people always seek to upgrade their shells and always seek higher value shells than they had before.

The second rule concerns who has the right to control the timing of debt payment. All transactions involving payment for goods or services are credit negotiations with a customary and necessary delay between the initiation of the debt and its payment. With the exception of pork transactions (a special class), the creditor has the right to seek out the debtor when he decides the debt should be collected. There is an implication here, often verbally stated, that the longer the debtor is made to wait before being asked to pay, the better shells he or she may be able to "find" and offer to get rid of the obligation. Here time equals interest on the debt. In pork transactions, however, the debtor must initiate the payment, offering whatever price (quality and quantity) of shells he or she thinks is appropriate to end the obligation. These shells may or may not be acceptable and thus interest and value are directly and overtly negotiated at every successive step of the pork settlement.

A third rule is that satisfaction with a shell received in transaction has no time limit. Shells accepted in any transaction may be returned to the previous owner at any time as being unacceptable payment for the debt. Once a received shell has been used in any further transaction, however, the first transaction is considered completed. It is also understood that any uncompleted transaction at the time of death of one of the exchangers is inherited by sons and daughters of the deceased, who must complete it.

Most adult Kaulong may have from ten to thirty shells in their possession at any given time, each one individually governed by these rules. A very influential man brought with him to a marriage transaction (described in chapter 5) more than a hundred shells. It is clear that keeping in mind the limits and possibilities of the messages encoded in one's current stock of shells is not easily learned, nor is everyone equally endowed with the mental capabilities required for expanding one's participation in the system of shell communication. Thus it is that individuals may be differentiated from each other. Everyone has the opportunity to engage in shell transactions, but only a few will have the ability and motivation to achieve fame and power.

As young men and women are learning shell transacting, their shells are kept for them by an older sibling. Young men stated a preference for their older sisters to have the care of their shells. At the least, this means that any negotiation is under the eyes and tutelage of the older sibling. When a shell is obtained and taken to the sibling, that sibling may say, "This is a poor shell. Go back and ask for a good one." And so the learning begins.

I, too, learned to speak the language of shells as young and middle-aged men gathered in my house to work on their shells. Hours were spent in changing the decorative "packaging," cleaning and polishing them, and, most importantly, talking about the relative merits of each shell. As I began to acquire shells, I was constantly asked to show my shells and I received lectures on each one many times over. That said, I never felt fluent enough in this language to initiate transactions on my own.[1]

The Contexts of Shell Transaction

The messages and metamessages that shell use communicates are embedded in the contexts of transactions. To understand what people say with shells requires an exhaustive survey of these contexts and settings.

Contexts in which shells are used may be usefully divided into two kinds: those in which one shell is directly exchanged for another, called *potupan*, and those in which a shell is exchanged (*tok pisin, dinau;* Kaulong, *naum*) for some good or service.

To *potupan* is to offer a shell to another with the implicit message that the receiver must hold the shell and begin to look for a matching shell to offer in exchange. One gives a shell in *potupan* to establish a new trading relationship or reaffirm an old one. In the special trade relationship known as a "pork road," the *potupan* shell is a promise to attend a singsing and be a potential receiver of pork. Shell-for-shell exchange is also found in the context of marriage exchanges when sexual rights to a woman are exclusively allocated to her husband. (They do not relate directly to those rights, however.) In all these cases the meaning of *potupan* is the same: the shell will be followed by a reciprocal visit, when a particular kind of exchange is expected. Examples of these follow.

1. My own collection ranges from one moderately good one with a name to one tiny shell, so devalued by its size and condition (scratched, blemished, etc.) that it had been given to a five-year-old child, who offered it to me in exchange for some rice.

Just prior to a visiting kinsman's departure homeward an individual may offer her or him a shell for *potupan*. The visitor in accepting the shell agrees to a continuing exchange relationship with the donor. This type of exchange is often the first any young person enters into with someone outside the natal village. The receiver must hold the shell until the donor, "following his shell," arrives at his kinsman's place. "Following a shell" is a legitimate reason to travel outside of home range. I knew of only one man in Angelek who had a partner among the Kaulong in the region of Umbi. When one of my Umbi friends visited me in Angelek, he did so only under the protection of Kandrian. Some government employees dropped him off at my house while they inspected a bridge and picked him up on the way back a few hours later. No amount of assurance on my part regarding his safety could allay his anxiety at spending the night somewhere where he or his family had no trading partners.[2]

The return visit is usually made several months to a year after the initial gift. The delay is considered necessary to allow the receiver to "find" a matching shell. When the exchange visit is made, the two transactors *kimkimwhal*—"match" the shells. The shells must equal each other on as many of the evaluative criteria as possible (right/left-eared, size, weight, and markings). The matching is not easy; it is rare that the first shell offered for matching is accepted, or for the best match to be offered first. Eventually a match will be agreed upon and the *kenwhal* (exchange) made. Each shell may now be used by its recipient in further transactions and in other contexts.

A *potupan* with a visitor (usually a kinsperson) sets up an exchange road between the two exchangers. Over this road the partners will make repeated visits to each other carrying goods to exchange or collecting debts (*naumngin*) and maintaining an established quality of transactional relationship between themselves. The quality of this road may be renegotiated at any time at a different level with a new *potupan* or matching of shells.

2. When strangers were immediately suspected of evil doing and ambushed and killed, such legitimacy was extremely important. Even today, visitors traveling "without stated purpose" outside their own range are in danger. They may be sorcerers.

Some exchange roads are also pork roads along which the partners agree to accept portions of pigs raised and sacrificed by their partner at special ceremonial occasions. A person intending to sacrifice a large pig (a tusker or a sow who has given birth to many litters) or lesser pigs that he has raised attempts to exact promises from both old and new pork partners that they will attend the ceremonial affair and be a potential recipient of one of the major portions (ribs or head) into which all pigs are butchered. The invitation accepted, the potential guest gives a shell to the visiting host, which the guest subsequently "follows" to the affair (called *lut a yu*, literally, "a sing with pigs") held at the host's place. The particular shell given is for *potupan*, and the host must keep it and be prepared to match and exchange it with his guest before any further transactions involving the piece of pork take place.

In addition, in some of the negotiations involving the actual pork, the receiving partner may insist on also receiving a *potupan* shell from his host, as a promise that the host agrees to be a pork-receiving guest at an affair to be given by his partner at a scheduled time in the future. In these cases, the *potupan* transactions are quite separate from those in which shells representing the value of pork received are negotiated and transacted.

I turn now to those *potupan* exchanges of matched shells that occur in the context of marriage transactions, but are not themselves part of a marriage payment. The matching of shells takes place between the participating kin of the bride's and groom's sides at the conclusion of a long series of other presentations of shells, which include the bride and groom but involve shells that are *not* matched.

The matching exchanges exclude the bride and groom. One of the two groups collectively presents six to ten shells at a time, throwing the shells on the ground in front of the other group. Individuals in the receiving group decide which of the shells they can or wish to match personally, and they make an immediate exchange. Any shell unmatched is returned. The groups continue the presentation, matching acceptance and rejection until no further exchange is desired by either side. Knowing that such an exchange will take place, kinsmen of both bride and groom assess their competition and arrive at the event prepared to match any shell presented to them at the level they wish to establish. Of five such transactions at which I was present, two were deliberately competitive affairs in which the brides' kin were effectively humiliated by being offered shells of a quality known to be higher than they could reciprocate. While in both cases the marriage transactions as a whole were completed, there was little doubt in anyone's mind as to the level of so-called "equality" of the two groups linked now by a marriage.

In these shell-for-shell exchanges, it is clear that the aim is to establish either a new social relationship or to renegotiate an old one at a new level of relative equality. Each individual is responsible for establishing his or her own network or exchange partners and for deciding what level of equality that particular relationship represents. People only establish trade partnerships with kin, so it follows that all trade partners are considered kin. If my father traded with Y's father, then Y and I are brothers. The cultural ideal of equality between such partners is so pervasive that if any cause for unbalance between the two occurs, shells may be offered outright to readjust the relationship.

In establishing these dyadic relationships, negotiation may be easy or difficult depending on a number of variables. Estimating one's partner is essential, and how accurate this estimation is will be reflected in the skill with which the exchange is made. One's partner is not just a single personality, but a link in other networks of relationships. Thus when thinking of specific shells, one must calculate a trade partner's potential access to shells as well as his possession of certain shells at any given time. Another important consideration is the achievement drive of the partners. The most highly competitive exchanges were observed to occur when very strong, powerful men were involved. An ambitious person seeking to increase his or her overall ranking welcomes invitations (challenges) from powerful people, for one reward of success is a relationship of high quality.

The *potupan* exchanges resemble those found in other Melanesian societies, in which a symbolic marker or "valuable" is used to express a type of exchange often referred to as "ceremonial." Ceremonial exchanges in these societies are quite often distinguished from utilitarian exchanges, where goods and/or services change hands with or without

special markers of the transaction. Markers of utilitarian exchange frequently differ from each other and from those symbolic of the ceremonial exchanges. Among the Kaulong, however, the same symbolic
marker is used in the ceremonial *potupan* exchanges and in the commercial transactions involving payment for goods or services. Indeed, individual shells themselves are interchangeable between the types of exchanges.

Every adult Kaulong is a link in a network through which tangible
and intangible items of any and all classes enter, circulate, and leave
this particular regional exchange system. For example, many Kaulong
in Umbi had important exchange relationships with the Miu to the
northwest and with the Sengseng to the east. The Sengseng of the
interior had direct trade relations with Sengseng who had moved close
to the coast, and to the east with the Karore. The Kaulong of Angelek
traded mainly in an east-west direction, personal networks extended
westward across the Alimbit to Gimi and eastward across the Ason
(Apaon) to the coastal Sengseng and Karore.

What is important to note here is that every Kaulong is engaged in
commodity exchange with *potupan* partners, and this at a minimum
will include members of his or her close kin group and hamlet affiliates
and, at a maximum, partners in several different language groups.
Any commodity produced by one's own labor or obtained from another is exchangeable for shells, with two exceptions. One important
exception is that which is considered "food." "Food" is given as a
service and compensated for as such. I shall return to this shortly. The
second exception is that one's children are not transactable commodities and one could argue (as I will later) that children are not thought of
as products of one's labor.

Common items produced for exchange are surplus crops—banana,
coconut, betel (areca) nuts, tobacco, taro plants, imported edible and
decorative plants of all kinds, and live piglets; manufactured items—
such as barkcloth and skirt fibers, spears and carved shields, drums,
lizard-skin drumheads, fine net bags, lime, and salt; and special natural resources—red ochres, *egit* (manganese oxide), and water both for
drinking (in times of drought) and for trials, and, lastly, imported
items—axes, machetes and knives, clam shells (for separating taro

corm from stalk), calico, clothes, peroxide and hair dye, sweet smelling perfumes, oils, lockable boxes/cases, and money. While some of these items are produced by males or by females (the barkcloth and skirt fibers, respectively), most are produced and exchanged by either sex and often by both as a team. It is through these productive activities that one can build up one's trade and exchange network and increase the number of shells one controls. It is interesting that, unlike in the Massim and Siassi regions, there is little specialization between communities in manufacturing goods for exchange. Where there is regional variability in raw materials (e.g., minerals, woods, and fibers), these items are significant in the trading, but the general trade seems generated by the exchange of similar items and to be less dependent than some other regional trading systems on culturally constructed differences in the production of trade goods.

In commodity exchange, the number of shells expected in return will usually be agreed upon at the time the object is given, although like all such transactions this is on credit. The skilled commercial transactor usually has an operational plan in his mind concerning his total debts and assets at any given time and thus specifies which debt will be paid from which asset.

To be successful in the commercial market, one must be both a consistent and successful producer of goods and a skilled social manipulator. Underlying these qualities is the acquisition of special knowledge of both an esoteric and a practical nature that enables one to increase the chances of success and to judge one's debtor accurately as to the chances of getting a specially desired shell or at least a better one if one holds out long enough. The style with which a person carries out commercial transactions communicates much useful information about that person and the quality of his or her knowledge, both to the other transactor and to any witnesses to an exchange.

Whereas *potupan*, or the matching of shells, establishes an agreed upon level of social equality between the transactors, commercial exchange is directly reflective of an established inequality between the transactors. One sells something to extract shells with the explicit aim of getting greater value than one has given out, thus obtaining a personal advantage over less skilled and knowledgeable individuals. Consistently successful people gain prestige, fame, and what Kaulong call "a name."

Exchanges in which shells are used in compensation for receiving nourishment are quite distinctive, and it is to these that I now turn. To the Kaulong, nourishing food is quite specifically mother's milk, cooked taro, and cooked pork.

For infants and children up to three or four years of age milk is considered the sole nourishing substance. While they may receive other ingestibles, they are thought to "starve" and not grow well unless they have access to milk. Deprivation of mother's milk was far more common in the past, when it was customary for mothers to be strangled when their husbands died. I often heard how unfortunate it was that some person was stunted, physically and mentally, because he was deprived of his mother's milk. Individuals frequently talked about the "milk" compensation they would demand of their mother's brothers, who had strangled their mother while they were still nursing.

For older children and adults, "starvation" and stunted growth are considered likely if access to cooked taro and pork is denied them. For those who provide these essential foods, labor and other assistance and food are expected in return. However, should this reciprocal feeding or the supply of labor be interrupted in any way, then a reckoning of the account must be made and shells are given to anyone who has contributed any of these particular items at any time in the past. Typically this reckoning will occur when an individual marries, and such payment occupies a large amount of time at the marriage negotiations and settlement. Significantly, in contrast to parents and other close kin who receive payment for contributing nourishment to a bride's growth, male siblings of the bride, who may also have contributed food to their sister's growth, receive no compensation for this, nor do they eat any of the pork given to the bride's family by the groom. Brothers do not close out their account with their sister. Between married sisters and their brothers there is continued exchange of food for labor throughout their lives. This is not the case with other kin of the married sister, as I show later.

Upon a person's death, all those who have fed the deceased in the past are compensated by those who are nonresident members of the same hamlet. As the nonresidents come to the hamlet to see the grave, they give a shell to those who provided the care.

Feeding is but one kind of personal service that requires compensation in shells; curing, midwifery, ritual sponsorship of menstrual and/ or tooth-blackening ceremonies, preparation of grave and body, as well as performance of all special magic formulae all are paid for with one or more shells. Some are paid for in the context of marriage negotiations or death and burial rituals and others at the time the service is performed or when solicited.

In addition, taking care of another's personal or jointly owned property—caring for taro while the owner is away, tending another's pig, caring for the plant resources of a hamlet including the trees and common house—is compensated with shells. These services are paid for when the owner returns to his taro, or when a nonresident visits his natal or affiliated hamlet place. There is almost no service given that is not compensated with shells, should compensation be requested.

Tabu Removal Shells are used in transactions to symbolize the removal of personal tabus. A woman is isolated from her husband and the community in a special hut during her menstrual periods. Her isolation is complete: she may not touch or eat anything with which a male may subsequently come into contact, for it will cause him serious illness. When the menstrual flow ceases, someone (husband or father usually) must give her a cooked taro with a shell, signaling that she is no longer dangerous and may return to her normal place and activities. When a close kinsperson has died, some individuals of their own volition assume either a taro or a pork restriction (never both or they would starve, I was told). Until another member of the hamlet gives them cooked taro or cooked pork with a shell, their self-imposed restriction will continue. In neither menstrual nor mourning prohibitions may the restricted individual request release from the tabu; others must signal their willingness to readmit the person as full a member at the previous status quo.

The strictest behavioral tabus are imposed when an individual marries and becomes sexually active (for the Kaulong these are the same by definition). Each married Kaulong is immediately isolated from his or her spouse's cognatic kin (alive and dead). For the rest of their lives, they may not eat or drink in front of an affine considered tabu nor may they speak the affine's name or use any word from which the name was derived, nor may they fight any affine. Other restrictions are also imposed but may be removed one by one, affine by affine, by the newly married's offering of a shell and its acceptance by the affine. Until permitted by the affine, no newly married Kaulong may speak to, walk behind, or raise any part of their own body above the affine. They may not eat any food carried on the affine's head or passed over the affine's body (including the affine's grave). Only when an affine accepts an offered shell specifically for one or the other of these tabus is that restriction removed (discussed further in chapter 7).

We have seen that in the lifting of the menstrual and mourning tabus, others indicate when the individual's relationship with them is to be normalized on the same basis as it was before the restriction. This is not the same with the affinal tabu lifting. Because the individual considered tabu is now engaging in sexual activity with a member of their kin group, any prior relationship with this person, based on behavior appropriate to an unmarried person, is wiped out. Each relationship between the newly married person and his or her spouse's kin must be reestablished on an entirely new basis: that of a married, sexually active person.

The distinction in all these cases as to who may set the time and occasion when the shell may be successfully offered is indicative of the locus of power in the different contexts. The nonequality between givers and receivers in these contexts is symbolized by the single nonreciprocated shell given in the transaction. Unlike the *potupan* exchanges in which shells are matched before exchange, or the exchanges involving goods or services (including release from tabus) where there is only a single shell movement, the final exchanges I discuss below appear to have qualities of both forms.

Where a relationship previously established has broken down because of the inappropriate behavior of either or both of the individuals concerned, restoration of the status quo may be achieved by the exchange of shells, without matching, but with sometimes long intervals between the two parts of the transaction.

Causing injury to another person, whether physical, mental, or emotional (shame, *mangin*), may be compensated with the payment of shells or the exchange of shells. Theft of another's property may also be redressed with a shell payment, either with a single shell or with an exchange of shells. In both cases the result is the reestablishment of the previous relationship without change. Where there is an exchange of shells, mutual blame is acknowledged, or more commonly a mutual desire to overlook the trouble that has caused the relationship to break. Where there is a single-sided payment, there is an acknowledged blame and thus an inequality which the payment abolishes. Escalated to a scale involving many people, wars and feuds may be ended with either kind of payment in shells.

While it may seem to be stretching the category to include among these conflict cases those payments made by brothers to their sister's deceased husband's kin (when today they do not strangle their sister), in the Kaulong mind this payment is absolutely necessary in order to reestablish a relationship between the two groups of affines to a state existing prior to the marriage of the sister and her deceased husband. This payment for sparing the woman's life is to balance those shells that were given by the groom's kin to the bride's kin as payment for her death. These shells given to the bride's kin at the time of the marriage negotiations were not reciprocated. Since she did not die when her husband died, the payment is returned and the marriage "annulled."

Finally, between those who *potupan*, the ideal of equality is so strong that any imagined cause for inequality is usually quickly addressed with the payment of shells. For example: A presented pork to B. B's lot of offered shells to pay for pork received from A, an established pork partner, were rejected four separate times over a period of many months. B, in complete frustration and as a challenge, declared the transaction (and debt) finished, and implicitly the partnership as well. A then carried a small pig to B's hamlet and presented it with a shell, whereupon B walked away. A then presented the pig a second time with two shells, and again with three shells, and finally a fourth time with four shells. B told me that he considered the four shells were to pay for the four previous rejections of his shells by A. B thereupon kept the four shells, ate the pig, and his next lot of shells in payment for the pork (the first pig) were accepted by A without question and equality was restored. And another example: both Ann Chowning and I were considered to be unusual assets for our local communities. *Potupan* partners of the headmen of Umbi and Dulago came visiting, traveling from distant places. Each visitor separately complimented our headmen on what a wonderful thing it was to have us (wealthy individuals) in their community. Our headmen told us that they were in this manner pressed into giving their visitors a shell outright, to balance the inequality. This was because these trading partners lived so far away they could not benefit from our presence even through "trickle down" principles. Actually, our local headmen first asked us to pay their trade partners, a request we declined even as we attempted to gain explanation.

The Meaning of Shell Exchange

It should be apparent that there is almost no relationship or context involving two or more individuals that is not marked by the giving and receiving, or matching, of gold-lip pearl shells. Evans-Pritchard remarked, in connection with the Nuer's concern with their cattle, that the "more simple is a material culture the more numerous are the relationships expressed through it" (1940:89). Certainly the Kaulong have a very simple material culture and the contexts in which gold-lip shells are used to express social relationships are multiple. It must be emphasized again that the system is open to all members of the exchanging society without restrictions by gender or age or any other distinctive marker. Therefore what is being communicated must be relevant and important to everyone at all times. It must also be noted, however, that not every person engages in this form of communication to the same extent, therefore while they all share a common concern, they do not share equally in that concern.

I believe the shared individual concern is one's relative ranking in the society at large vis-à-vis other participating individuals. We have seen that in the visitors' affinal and pork *potupan* one establishes or resets differential levels of social equality with designated others. The equality that is marked by the matched shells is directly pertinent and reflects the particular dyadic relationship and only indirectly the ranking of each of the exchangers in the society as a whole. Any individual will be assessed by others on a social-worth continuum, by both the numbers and quality of the individually established exchange relationships that he has managed to create and maintain. In chapter 5, I discuss in greater detail the differential levels that may be attained in Kaulong society.

Not only is every exchange relationship set up individually and at a negotiated level of equality, it is also considered renegotiable at any mutually agreed upon time. The gold-lip shells, which when matched symbolize these equal relationships, are symbols of the level of equality that has been expressed in that part of the exchange action. The shells themselves allow a nonverbal statement to be made but do not stand for that statement by themselves. The fact that no individual transactor will use the same shell to express the equality of another relationship (or in any other context) allows the necessary freedom from exact accounting or interpretation that a verbal statement would establish. Ranking within the egalitarian framework of the *potupan* exchange relationship is a dynamic condition (or person) requiring constant feeding to continue and which only death can stop, much the same as maintaining the growth of a plant or child.

One's social network can only expand in quantity and quality with the continual input or feeding of new shells with which to symbolize each new link or restate old ones. All productive activity considered human in nature is convertible to shell symbols. That which man and woman can make through their own efficacy, they can control and exchange for shells. Thus differential ranking is a measure of differential efficacy in human productive activities as well as in the subsequent shell transactions that make production explicit and by which one is known. It is significant that for the Kaulong and their exchange system neighbors, little gender distinction is to be found in either production or exchange. What is significant is that children, human offspring, are not symbolized within the many contexts where shells are found.

The use of a single symbol for the wide range of contexts becomes understandable if one interprets the ultimate message I am giving my trade partners with every shell exchange as follows: that I am saying something (always somewhat ambiguously) about my personal efficacy in producing things and in relationships by which my social ranking is established. But the shell itself cannot be used as a standard of that rank alone, for just as any person's rank is relative and dynamic, so is the value of each shell used to symbolize the rank. What has never been set by using a standard symbol (such as words) can always be renegotiated. For the Kaulong, verbal communication is always evasive and ambiguous, for once an explicit statement is made it is rarely forgotten. No personal evaluation is absolute unless one is nothing, without any worth, a social nonperson, a rubbish man, without efficacy or the ability to make or produce anything. Such individuals do exist in theory and fact, and they form a bottom line from which to measure one's own self-development. There is no upper limit, although there is some evidence that behavior that goes beyond a certain degree of acceptability, to what we might term despotic, the Kaulong consider to be nonhuman, or "like a *masalai*" (bush spirit, *tok pisin*). To be human is to be judged only in relation to other humans and by activities understood to be human. To be competent, perhaps exceptional, in shell exchange is tantamount to being human, *potunus*.

5/ *Pomidan* and *Polamit*: The Kaulong Elite

In the preceding chapter I mentioned the fiction of equality that prevails between trading partners. This equality is symbolized periodically by the successful *potupan* exchange of pearl shells. I argue that equality among traders must be symbolized because it never really exists. No two people are ever seen to be the same, to have the same knowledge, talent, or personality.

Children are considered to be the exact *replacements* (*senis* in *tok pisin*) of their parent(s). But children do not automatically inherit the social position of the parent; they must reestablish, by their own acts, the various facets of their parents' identity, and, ideally, they will go further and make their own "name." Nor do children inherit much of the tangible wealth produced or the knowledge gained by the parent. These, too, must be regained by the child.

In this chapter I discuss how gaining social position may be accomplished from childhood to full adulthood. I show that equality of opportunity is theoretically open to both genders, but because men and women are not the same, inequality also exists between sexes. The reasons for this will be discussed more completely in following chapters, but it is important to stress here that Kaulong, unlike many Highland Papua New Guineans do not have a marked division between the sexes in labor, ritual, or in economic goals. Much of the flow of daily life for both Kaulong men and women is interlocked in similar activities with similar personal aims; what varies is the intensity with which exchange activities may come to consume one's daily life, and this intensity is potentially greater for men than for women. Women complained that they must periodically interrupt their personal working for renown to give birth, and also when menstruating.

One class of songs (sung during rituals) is grouped under the category of *pomidan* (important or "big" man) and *polamit* (important or "big" woman). These are songs in which the singer lists all the important men or women known personally to him or her. Each song has a chorus in the form of a phrase denoting an activity which is repeated after each name and which marks the subclass of the song. Songs that list men all end with the name *pomidan* and those listing women with *polamit*—described to me as referring to the "boss" or the "big name" of the class. The form and performance of songs will be discussed further in chapter 8, but here, as an introduction to activities involving big men and big women, I list the chorus-activity lines for *pomidan* and *polamit*.

Men (*pomidan*)	Women (*polamit*)
1. He collects debts	1. She wails
2. He goes traveling	2. She blames me falsely
3. He makes holes with digging stick	3. She kills (strikes) me
4. He sleeps with *egit* (mineral)	4. She makes net bags
5. He breaks *kina* shells	5. She hides
6. He gives talk/spreads message	6. She ties up firewood
7. He digs wild yams	7. She dances in ceremonies
8. He hears a message	8. She whistles in dances
9. He kills (strikes) me	9. She collects vine-ropes
10. He jokes/lies	10. She gossips
11. He steals axe	11. She calls out/summons
12. He collects house beams	12. She cares for descendants
13. He bathes	13. She is pierced with spear
14. He recruits for a feud	14. She remains alone
15. He stands with a shield	15. She comes to me
16. He travels with a shield	
17. He rests under a selemon tree	
18. He calls pigs	
19. He calls for taro-spoon (he's toothless)	
20. He is a craftsman	
21. He has cassowary feathers on his head	

In all I collected thirty-one songs in which important men are listed and fourteen in which important women are listed. With such a small sample, I have made no correlation between the number of times an activity is duplicated in my collection and the relative importance of that activity. It is possible to see in this collection of songs a catalogue of most of the activities that characterize all adult men and women. In this chapter I discuss the way in which an elaboration or intensification of these and other activities differentiates men among men and women among women.

The names of men and women in the songs are individually selected by the singer—with the caveat that the singer should know the individual listed by sight and from personal contact. In the ideal form the names of individuals are given in order from the least to greatest, smallest to biggest, reputation. But with the exception of these songs, I could obtain no independent ranking of individuals. Truly big men, such as Maklun, and rubbish men, such as K, were almost universally at the top and bottom, respectively, of everyone's song list. For the women, Lipok, a truly big woman, was equated with Maklun. I also found it instructive to compare the song listings of "important women I know" sung by the same singer in his early teens (in 1968) and as he sang it six years later. As a teen, he listed his younger sisters, then other young women living in the same community as he, and finally his mother. His 1974 listing included other more distant and more senior female relatives he had come to know in the interval.

Songs sung by individuals of moderate and high reputation usually included only other individuals of roughly the same ranked status. These songs are usually sung in a competitive public forum and thus are a fairly good indicator of a singer's reputation or social ranking, at least so far as he or she wishes to make public.

The system by which individuals are ranked vis-à-vis others is dynamic and constantly and purposely kept in flux. One individual can over many years gain renown, only to lose it with great rapidity. The system is relative. One only has rank above others if one exceeds the expected and shows his or her *greater* knowledge and ability to make things happen. However, by demonstrating knowledge one also puts it up for challenge. Mili sang a song listing places along a distant road.

A visitor remarked to me after Mili had left that "he doesn't really know this road, he's never been there." This turned out to be untrue, but that is the nature of political challenge and rebuttal.

Not everyone wishes to achieve the greatest possible power among his or her fellows. Many are content to make a modest reputation as a productive human being. Others desire to do a bit more and become the leader of a hamlet; and once in a great while (speaking historically), there appear men, and perhaps women, whose superior intellect and ability is matched by their great ambition to achieve fame of international dimensions extending beyond the local language group. These people also achieve fame that lasts long after their death. In Kaulong all these individuals are termed *pomidan* (*midan* is singular; *pomidan* plural) or *polamit* (I recorded only the plural form for big woman, having never heard *lamit* used). Only if one falls below the modest level expected of an adult person, does one fall below the level of *midan*. I know of only one man and no woman who achieved this low level of personhood. In fact, as I write this I wonder if it is possible for a woman to become what in *tok pisin* is known as *rabisman*, rubbish person. I shall return to this in future chapters.

THE IMPORTANCE OF *BI*

As is found commonly in Melanesia, kinship linkages are not traced through many generations. Among the Kaulong, I found that after five or six generations the apical ancestral person was merged with the male or cross-sibling pair who, according to the origin myth of a particular place, gave rise to the group of cognates associated with that place. The geographical place is referred to either by using a proper name (e.g., Angelek) or *bi da nu*, our place. Origin myths vary somewhat, but typically relate how an ancestor emerged from a hole in the ground or from a branch or trunk of a tree. Depending on the particular group and their associated myth, a single male or a pair of cross-sex siblings emerged to begin what are referred to in *tok pisin* as the *lain* (line) of descendants associated with the place.

The first action of the ancestral male, in the myth, is always to select and clear a piece of ground and thereby create a *bi*, a place. The preferred choice for a *bi* clearing is on the top or on a shoulder of a ridge, with a steep approach on three sides. Preparing the clearing, which rarely measures more than a hectare or two, also involves using the felled logs to build a main hamlet house (the *mang*). A ficus tree is planted in the center of the clearing if one is not already growing. When it grows tall, the ficus will serve as a defensive position in time of attack: women and children climb high into the tangle of aerial roots; while men, also in the tree branches, hurl spears down onto their enemies from their superior position.

The founder and later affiliates of the hamlet plant permanent and fruiting trees, such as breadfruit, areca (betel) palm, coconut palm, Malay apple, *galip*, banana, pawpaw (papaya), although the latter two may also be planted in gardens. These trees are placed to surround the clearing.

The mythic ancestor, so the stories go, is eventually seduced by a traveling woman and begins to produce a line of descendants or, as the Kaulong frequently said, "he 'fathers' a line." In some stories where a brother and sister emerged together, the account includes her seducing a traveling male, then following him to his place where she gives birth to or "mothers" a line of cognates associated with her natal place and complementary to her brother's line. In those cases where a single male emerged, his daughter is said to "mother" one line, while he and his sons "father" the complementary line or lines. The term *kuk* ("gives birth to") is used in both cases. These complementary lines of descent together encompass the group of cognates who consider themselves as *poididuan* or closely related kin ("brothers"), sharing a similarity of biogenetic substance not only with each other but also with a place and its resources.

One such group of cognates, for example, traced its relationship of substance and placement to a hill upon which grew a magnificent mango tree. Out of that tree the apical sibling pair was said to have emerged some four or five generations ago. The hilltop place is known appropriately as Asa (literally, "The Tree"). The brother cleared the ground and then went to a pig distribution, leaving his sister at home. The sister seduced a visiting man from the Gimi linguistic group and followed her husband to his home many miles distant where she gave birth to a line of descendants. Today her third- and fourth-generation descendants periodically travel to Asa and, upon arriving there, place a number of gold-lip pearl shell valuables on the roots of the mango tree (which is still standing) to be collected by the living descendants of the apical brother. These shells are considered payment to the caretakers of the shared ancestral home who have kept the place clear, maintained the fruit-bearing trees, and looked after the bones of those buried there. By this act of payment for services rendered and by their visitation, the descendants of the sister reaffirm their claim to Asa and to their share of the fruits of the trees planted in the clearing, and most importantly, they reassert their "brotherhood" or kinship with those who now live at or affiliate with their ancestral place.

All productive resources of a place are shared equally by those who maintain their affiliation through visitation and care of the place. Daughters and sons benefit equally from their parents' activities in relation to the establishment of these plants and persons representing the perpetual resources of the hamlet. The responsibility of maintaining the production of these resources is shared equally by resident and nonresident children of the place. As the fruiting trees die, young sprouts or offshoots are planted to replace them and to maintain the original plants' place in the clearing. Similarly, as people of the place die, they are buried in the main hamlet house (*mang*) by their descendants as replacements (*senis*) for them in the affiliated group of cognatic kin.

Replacement is seen as an exchange or substitution of similar entities. In order to maintain the world order, only a minimal one-to-one exchange or substitution is required. Surplus products (fruits or children) are items in which all members of the cognatic kingroup share and should distribute through exchange activities. Kinsmen who belong to a place-affiliated group call each other *poididuan* and characteristically initiate and maintain *potupan* exchanges concerned with the distribution of equal shares of the common heritage. Competitive exchange, which may also take place between these same cognates, involves such nonshared items as pigs and other personally created wealth.

Those ancestral places where the apical ancestor emerged from the ground or tree are points of reference for the most inclusive group of affiliated kinsmen (*poididuan*). But these places are far more than mere points of reference. They symbolize the core meaning of kinship and of being. Coming from the same place is the essence of sharing an identity not only with other people, but also with all the nonhuman resources of the place as well. There are strong emotional ties to the ancestral places, their associated trees, and the house-site mounds indicating the burial place of past affiliates. Even when a hamlet is abandoned and the fires are cold, the ficus, coconut, and other trees remain for a time as markers of one's identity. A Kaulong usually traces and maintains a relationship with affiliates of no more than three or four ancestral places. Rarely does a Kaulong maintain or even know of all the ancestral places he or she could claim through grandparents. A big man or woman, however, is such a rare or exceptional individual and will maintain, through active visitation, exchange, and trade, significantly more place ties and kin relationships than an ordinary man or woman.

Secondary and less inclusive lines of relationship to places and affiliated groups of kin are formed every generation following the ancestral one, for according to the Kaulong model, only one son need remain at his natal place to bury his father and replace him in the hamlet. Other sons most frequently move out and clear new ground and thereby establish new places. While such segmentation is the model, considerable variation in the actual history of every group shows that some sons affiliate with their mother's natal place, headed by their mother's father or brother; or several brothers may remain with their father and continue to cooperate closely and noncompetitively after his death, usually when one is clearly dominant politically over the others who are less ambitious. A married sister may remain with a politically dominant brother. Frequently, a sister's daughter returns to her mother's natal hamlet and finds a husband there among the children of her mother's brother, who are her "brothers." In so returning she is considered to be a *senis* for her mother, a replacement in the social universe of her mother's natal place.

Residential flexibility is more a reality of Kaulong life than is implied in the above principles. Throughout a lifetime, both male and female Kaulong, married and single, frequently shift their actual residential affiliation among three or more places to which they trace a relationship to the founding male or his sister and where they can claim a share of the productive resources. Some individuals shift their residential affiliation on an almost annual basis, others less regularly. Frequently, the underlying reason for the shift is conflict over shared resources and rights. The most common course of conflict resolution among kinsmen is, first, a separation to avoid physical combat, followed by a negotiated compromise. Such a conflict resolution is based on the fundamental principle that normally it is more important to maintain the unity and solidarity of the affiliated group than to establish political dominance or priority of rights leading to fission.

To summarize, the model is one of overlapping ancestral place-oriented cognatic kindreds, which are arranged conceptually in a hierarchical scheme according to their historic setting in time and space. Utilizing this native model, men and women establish personal networks by reaffirming relatedness through travel and trade and through permanent or shifting residential cooperation and affiliation. Links in personal networks are created and maintained or broken and dissolved through continued or discontinued personal action. This action is guided by balancing sibling obligation to share and cooperate with personal desire for individual renown. The basis of the model is derived from the cooperative cross-sex relationship of the original apical sibling pair, associated with the creation of the shared substance, place, and heritage—all of which contribute to a shared identity. In chapter 6, I return to the all-important cross-sex sibling pair.

Now the importance of the hamlet, or *bi da nu* ("our place"), in the making of big men and women must be considered. The number of affiliates of any one hamlet or *bi* is rarely more than fifteen men, women, and children who are usually, but not necessarily, closely related as members of an extended family of three generations or as joint fraternal family members. The main hamlet house, the *mang*, is where unmarried male affiliates sleep and where married males will sleep when visiting the hamlet. Married couples, as we have seen, usually sleep near their gardens often quite a distance away from the hamlet. The hamlet leader's wife frequently sleeps in a second, cruder house—a *mok*—located in the clearing where she can look after her young children and pigs. Visiting women will also sleep in the *mok*.

I have emphasized sleeping rather than occupying or living in these houses and huts because it is only in sleep that there is any necessary separation between married and unmarried and between male and female. The reason for these restrictions concerns the Kaulong definition of marriage: any two people of opposite sex who share the same house overnight are, with a few exceptions, considered married (see chapter 6). Women are usually permitted in the *mang* during daytime and occasionally overnight when there are more than two or three women and no available *mok*.

The *mang* is not just for the living to sleep in. Deceased affiliates of both sexes will be buried in the dirt floor of the *mang*. Each successive burial may impinge on a former one until there is no more room, at which point a new *mang* will be built and dedicated with a ritual. As I visited hamlets with a long history of occupation, I was shown where previous *mang*s had been built within the perimeter of the clearing. Not too far in the past, the skull and certain arm bones of ancestors were exhumed, ritually treated, and used as the focus of important ceremonies. These skulls were kept in the *mang* until the Australian government enforced their reburial (see chapter 9). All important exchanges and all singing ceremonies take place on the *bi* clearing. It is where all the activities that define *potunus* occur: it is *the* unambiguous human place.

CHILDREN OF THE PLACE

Ideologically, any child is seen as a replacement of either parent. A daughter can replace her father or her mother, and a son can be his mother's or his father's replacement. No allocation is made until the child is able to make the decision on his or her own, and there is no firm or ceremonial declaration.

Children of either sex are greatly desired, particularly by aging parents. Infanticide does exist, but usually because the new child follows too closely a previous child who still needs its mother's care and milk. Such a close birth is shameful for both parents as well. It is not unusual for children to "die at birth" or to be "thrown away into a hole." Sometimes an attending woman will rescue a child who has been "thrown away" and raise him or her as she would her own. The child, however, is always known as the child of his or her birth mother. It was significant that in the remote inland regions Chowning and I noticed an almost total lack of any deformity or disability that might be attributable to genetic or birthing disorders. I heard of only one case (when I asked): a person called Damaksi (meaning "one more") who was born with six fingers and toes. The mother chopped off the extra digits when the child was only a few days old.

Birth takes place outside of the *bi* and outside of any garden. One of those I saw took place in a rock shelter, giving the scene a rather Paleolithic atmosphere. The process is intensely polluting. Only one or a few women are allowed to approach the birthing site.

The mother and newborn return to the *bi* when all bleeding has ceased. She and the child are greeted by a number of women, and she is usually given some gifts (skirt materials, calico, tobacco are the main ones) for which at some future date she will pay. Together with the presentation of the gifts, some of the women clown (see chapter 6).

While the mother is the prime care- and food-giver to the child initially, after about six months this care is shared by the father, older siblings, and other hamlet residents. The care is constant. The infant is held or carried in the caregiver's arms (no sling or net bag is used), and sleeps across the thighs or cradled under a warm armpit as both child and caregiver sleep. For the first three years or so, a child is rarely out of physical contact with another person.

Children are weaned around four or possibly five years old. There was one three-year-old for whom her parents had tabued all liquid of any sort, save her mother's milk. This was so she would remain hungry for her mother's milk and thrive. During the "hungry period" a man asked me for food and when I said "we should save it for the children," he said, "Nonsense, they have their mothers (to feed them), it's us old people (he was in his thirties) who should be fed." Various foods are tabu for young children: *bubak* (a wild sugar), wallaby, eel, snake, and a large variety of frog. The first two will make the child sick, and the last three one may only eat as a full adult and after receiving a ritual treatment which negates the danger inherent in these foods.

A child's teeth must never be mentioned until such time as its full set of baby teeth have erupted else the child will never grow. Then the father will rub the baby's head with pig blood and may give it a name by which it will be known through adolescence and perhaps beyond. This ritual will often accompany another involving the sacrifice of pigs.

While mothers begin the feeding, it is the responsibility of all hamlet affiliates to contribute food to the growing child. Men should bring not only taro but also pork which they get by going to other places to *lut a yu* ("sing with pigs") and by entering into pork transactions. A few weeks after "the first ever" twins were born (chapter 6), I was told by the *tultul* of Umbi that only one of the infants was human. "Why?" I fearfully asked. "Because I gave both of them pork fat to eat and only one ate it and so is human." (As I discuss later, humans eat pork while pigs and other nonhuman monsters eat humans.) I was known to refuse pure pork fat, too, and I feared for the humanity of both the infant and myself.

Sharing food is perhaps one of the most important social lessons imparted very early to children. I once gave seven bananas to seven very young children, aged two to six. Under the direction of two mothers, the children broke their bananas in half, ate one half and gave one half to another child. Then each was told to break the half they had just received into two parts and give one away. Fascinated I watched and counted as each of the bananas was broken into thirty-two pieces! Children who do not wish to share turn their backs on another so that "no one will see" him or her eat without sharing, but if a mother or other socializer is close by, the hoarder may hear sharp words being said about "a stingy person." Typically, when members of a household eat together each person will repeatedly cut portions of his/her taro or pork and give a piece to another in exchange for a piece of theirs even when the original portions are identical in quality and quantity. In a society in which sorcery is rampant, I thought that this was an excellent way to ensure that those who ate with you were not poisoning you. Some confirmation for this interpretation came when I sought a cause for someone's illness. Sorcery was discarded as an explanation because, while the patient was visiting a known hot-bed of sorcerers, they had shared food with him.

The Kaulong meaning of sharing I found to be contrasted sharply with that of the Tiwi of North Australia, where I learned that you honor someone by asking for something and if you don't ask, it means you don't need or want it. In Kaulong one should never ask because it shames one's host. I was told, "people should see that you want something and offer it to you."

The pattern of Kaulong sharing is one in which those who have some item can choose those to whom they desire to give it and thus create or maintain a relationship. All children are taught how to share, for it is by sharing that one can gain respect. It is only through increased production that one can "share" that production with others by giving and thus enlarge one's own social network. When one is given a share by one with greater prestige, the receiver moves up in the hierarchy of respected people. The one who gives signals his belief that you are capable of being in his network. Sharing then has nothing to do with establishing equality among sharers and everything to do with establishing inequality.

The ones ultimately responsible for the continued growth of a child are its parents. However, some children are seen to be exceptional at a very early age, and these children appear to become children of the place, with every hamlet affiliate responsible for and taking an interest in the child's physical and intellectual growth. These are children who are already seen to have a self, or *enu*, of greater than usual size. These are the children who are bright-eyed, fat and active, with shiny skin, and bubbling over with good humor and joy at being themselves. They often begin singing before they speak. They are clowns, perceptive of everything around them and able to repeat, imitate, and mimic. Their language learning is accelerated and they quickly come to know the names of important things. At a tender age these children, female and male, are seen to have the potential to become great midans, perhaps one whose name will be remembered for a long time and who will bring fame to the place. Because they show such great potential their entire childhood education and growth are intensified and carried out by all close hamlet affiliates and close kin who are nonresident.

I knew one such charmer in Angelek. I was told that if anything ever happened to this four-year-old, his parents would hang themselves in shame to accompany their child to the mountain of ghosts. The shame, I was told, was because they did not look out for him well enough, and perhaps others in the hamlet who had shared in raising the child would accuse them of not looking out for this child of the hamlet. Kawang, the young child, once performed an original dance to the acclaim of nearly two hundred people participating in a very important ceremony in a neighboring hamlet. His father told me that the son had invented the step when he was visiting in another hamlet. He collected many stones from under the house verandah and carried them to the stream where he threw them into the water. Then he called to his mother and aunt to come and see what he had done. When they came they saw him dancing on the stream bank with his two arms churning in front of his body as his feet stamped the ground. This exceptional activity is typical of exceptional children, my informant added. Kawang frequently performed his dance on request.

EGIT, TOOTH-BLACKENING

Manganese oxide (in Kaulong, *egit*), a mineral found sporadically throughout the region, is traded widely to locations that do not have a local source. It is an essential part of the ritual celebration of young adulthood. Although it was (in the past) universally applied to young men with a few exceptions, I know of a few cases where young women received *egit*. I do not believe, however, it was ever a universal ritual for women.

The mineral is chewed together with powdered lime, and then placed along the inside of a six-inch piece of bark from a twig no more than an inch or so in diameter. The treated bark is then placed inside the young man's mouth so that the *egit* is held firmly against the outside enamel of his teeth. For a week the boy lies in the hamlet *mang*, is allowed to eat nothing, and can drink little. Water must be poured down his throat so as not to touch his teeth. Informants told me that the mineral burned their gums and the inside of their cheeks and mouth, and that they were so weak that when they went to relieve themselves outside, someone had to help them.

During the time the boy "sleeps with *egit*," as the Kaulong say, the sponsor of the youth arranges nightly rituals in which members of the host's hamlet and those in related hamlets sing *sasungin* songs appropriate to the occasion, as they circle around the central clearing. Following the final night of singing, a pig is sacrificed and the pork distributed to visiting pork partners, and the young lad is released from phase one of the ritual.

By hosting the event, the sponsor gains prestige. Most frequently a father hosts his son's *sasungin*, but it was a common alternative to have a mother's brother "pull" his sister's son to his (MB) and his sister's (MBZ) natal hamlet in order to gain prestige through hosting the ceremony. This may well be the first obvious effort to influence a youth to switch allegiance from his father to his mother's brother. As I shall discuss in following chapters, having children is a gravely dangerous activity because of ideas about pollution, but it is also necessary in order to have a *senis*, a replacement. If a man can "pull" his sister's son to become his *senis*, living in his hamlet, in order to bury him when he dies, the mother's brother accomplishes reproduction of a replacement without the danger of sexual intercourse (see chapter 7).

At the end of a week, a curved boar's tusk would be put in the boy's mouth and pulled strongly against the teeth. If the *egit* stayed on the teeth, he could then go on to the next phase. This second phase lasted from one to three months during which time the young man would live in the bush, accompanied by his own friends. They would hunt and the young man would give his food to his parents. He could eat no warm or hot food. When he drank, the water must go straight down his throat; and when he ate cold taro (provided by his mother), he must swallow that, too, as he could not chew food. During this time he should not look at any young women.

Panoff (1966) writing of the Maenge of southeastern New Britain where a similar practice occurs, says that the Maenge equate manganese oxide with menstrual blood, which they say has a similar odor. The Maenge believe the treatment of men's teeth with the mineral will protect them from the polluting evils of menstrual blood. The Kaulong did not make this connection, but it may be just that, not knowing of the Maenge at the time, I did not ask.

When the black mineral is firmly fastened to the tooth enamel, the young man may return to his hamlet and fully participate in events that take place there. And he gets a new name—one that has -*egit* for a suffix. His teeth are jet black and, importantly, invisible. White teeth are an important characteristic of spirits and monsters (including pigs) who inhabit the bush and prey on human beings. Adult human beings by definition eat pork and do not have white teeth.

I knew of two women in the Umbi region whose father had sponsored a *sasungin* for each of them. The only reason I could elicit was that he had no son at the time. The two women were fully adult when I knew them, and I was told that they were very strong women, that they did things a little bit differently from others and therefore should be treated differently as well. Women who do not have their teeth treated with the mineral acquire very dark teeth through chewing betel (areca) nut, pepper leaf, and crushed lime. I was told I should chew betel so that I could have "nice black teeth." I tried to comply, but was hopeless at spitting the blood-red juice any distance away from my body. My description of the tooth-cleaning ritual I underwent twice a year to get whiter teeth did nothing to alter their belief that I was a very different kind of person.

In the Angelek region, I witnessed first menses ceremonies for several girls as this ritual was slowly being introduced from the coast into the interior. I will save discussion of this until my discussion of gender in chapter 6.

YOUNG ADULTHOOD

In mid- to late adolescence young men and women have an enormous amount of freedom. Traveling with others of the same and opposite sex and often alone, young men and women visit relatives at near and distant hamlets, sometimes living at their mother's brothers' hamlet(s) for extended times. Much of this visiting is for the purpose of attending all-night ceremonies, "singsings," to help in making gardens, or to gain knowledge of "roads" through the bush that link hamlets.

Young girls are said to settle down faster than young men. Girls are greedy and think of food all the time and therefore like to work in the gardens. Young girls also begin taking care of piglets. Boys are less likely to work in the garden than to try their hand at hunting in the bush or using the spear and blowgun.

Young men in particular are watched to see if they begin serious gardening early and if they appear anxious to go on trading trips, learning new places and new faces. If a youth shows promise, she or he is supported, receiving more attention than usual, and from more people than just the parents or mother's brother.

There was one family in Angelek with four sons. The father, Posin, had been a government-appointed headman, now retired, whose wife had died with the birth of the youngest boy, now twelve. "Dapper" was the adjective that came to my mind every time I saw Posin. Even in the height of a rainstorm with mud the prevailing skin cover, when Posin came visiting, his skin was shiny, without a trace of mud and seemingly unaffected by the rain. Posin's two oldest sons were well-established gardeners and traders. The third son (in his late teens or early twenties) began his first garden while I was there. This garden was characterized by everyone as a good one, large, properly cleared, and well-tended. This young man was consistently included in local lists of "good" gardeners, even though he was the youngest by far. The three older sons did their best to send their youngest brother to school in a village six miles away (a twelve-mile daily walk). They plotted a route for him that led past their gardens so that he would be fed in the morning and have taro to eat while at school and a meal as he returned. This was notable in a culture where typically teenagers and all adults cook for themselves.

Both young men and young women begin participating in the many ceremonial singsings held in other hamlets and, of course, in their own hamlet. Singing is extremely important to individual prestige and acknowledgment as a human being for both sexes. Songs are learned through participation in the singsings but also through tutoring before the event by members of one's own hamlet. "Everyone sings," I was told, and I was given the names of only two people in the region who were known not to sing: one was a hearing but speechless man, and another was just said not to like singing. Clearly it was expected that everyone can and would sing, just as people can learn to speak. Actually, singing begins early in childhood, but it is the young adult for whom it becomes a focused goal. People sing as they walk through the forest on the way to gardens or to hunt in the morning and frequently as they return from the forest and garden in late afternoon.

KAULONG ELITE BEHAVIOR

Ideally, the road to success among the Kaulong is open to any ambitious person willing to work hard at raising taro and pigs and at the business of establishing and maintaining trade relationships with distant as well as near kinsmen. It is open to those with the talent and intellectual ability required to keep track of increasingly complex and numerous debts and the symbols of those debts, the gold-lip pearl shells that circulate throughout the region. The way is open to anyone with the physical stamina and courage to travel widely and frequently through dangerous and difficult countryside between widely scattered hamlets inhabited by friends and enemies of different dialect, language, and ethnic groups in order to participate in political ceremonies (at which fighting is a frequent expectation), to collect debts, and to make one's name known throughout the region.

While the road to success and fame is open to all, some members of the society have a head start from the beginning, especially those born into a hamlet where there is a *midan* of sufficient renown to provide the necessary intensification of a child's education and also a model of appropriate behavior. Behavior of the elite is considered to be different from that expected of ordinary members of the society. The elite are said to follow different rules and strategies, with exceptions to the norm often becoming the elite rule. When this system is played to the fullest risk, a person may overplay the role and enact unacceptable exceptions and become a feared despot liable to assassination (by spear or sorcery). At the other extreme, a person may underplay the expected role and lose followers to a more attractive and exciting opponent, or even lose elite status altogether.

The elite play roles in both the private and public arena. In the private sphere of the hamlet they manage all the resources of the hamlet: adults, children, fruiting trees, bones of the ancestors. No harvesting from the hamlet trees and no ceremonies may take place without permission of the *midan*. Troubles that arise between members of the same hamlet are settled by the *midan*. Hamlet managers may or may not be married. When organizing any event, they call upon all affiliates, men and women, to participate. An elite *midan* will have the ability to attract many permanent affiliates, frequently including less ambitious brothers. An elite *midan* will often attract an elite sister (and her husband and children) to his hamlet. But I found that most often an elite woman chose an elite man to marry, and that together they were a powerful combination of talent, intelligence, courage, and influence.

In the public sphere the elite travel often and widely. They attend more ceremonies and bring more pork home to the hamlet than the nonelite. They arrange pig sacrifices on the hamlet ground, spilling the blood on the bones of the ancestors, and give portions of pork to visiting trade partners. The sacrifices can involve one or more pigs. If the latter, the *midan* tries to get other hamlet residents to schedule their pig killings to coincide with his, thus making it an even greater event.

While a woman frequently travels with her husband, she just as frequently may set off on her own, particularly if the journey is not a long one and is to her natal hamlet. However, some women travel alone to visit distant trading partners and such behavior is noteworthy and typical of elite women.

When elite men and women travel, their movement is known. Their direction and destination is also known and word is spread in advance of their arrival. I was told that *midan* alone were permitted to blow panpipes (*lawi*) as they walked along the trails. Blowing *lawi*, it was said, makes the road shorter and less difficult and gives notice of peaceful passage through the forest. When an elite person arrives at the designated hamlet, all affiliates are expected to leave their gardens (often many miles distant) and be waiting at the main hamlet to show proper respect. Respect behavior is marked: children are hushed and kept out of the main hamlet house (*mang*) and hamlet women are not usually found sitting in the *mang*, where they would normally be found during the day. Special food is prepared—for example, taro with meat and perhaps greens and coconut—and is served first to the elite visitor. If the visitor notices anything unusual in the hamlet, a compliment to the host will usually bring a compensating gift of some kind. (This is what happened when the headmen of Umbi and Dulago were complimented on having wealthy anthropologists in their hamlets.) There was never any doubt about the elite or nonelite status of a visitor. Elite females traveling alone or in the company of men were always accorded special respect from men and women alike.

To conclude this discussion, I look briefly at four examples of elite behavior, three of them male and one female.

I first met Lipok when she was brought to my house in Angelek to be introduced to me. I addressed her in Kaulong whereupon she grabbed my arm and pulled me out of the house and proceeded to dance with me around the clearing all the while singing in delight, "She speaks our language, she speaks our language." Lipok was at least eighty years old by my calculation. She had first been married to a man who died. This was before the Australians arrived, but she had somehow avoided being strangled as was customary. Instead, she married a *midan*. I believe that Lipok herself chose to marry this man rather than be strangled to be with her first husband. I was told that if a man was "big" enough he could pay for her shame of being sexually active with two men. In time the second husband died, and this time she chose to remain single. Her own status and power combined with the power of pacification permitted her exceptional behavior. When I knew her she managed her deceased second husband's hamlet, living there alone but with many willing younger kinsmen nearby should she require help. Her daughter was married to the Angelek *midan*, Kamil, and Lipok came frequently to Angelek to help her son-in-law and daughter, although she did so with a style calculated to maintain the complete and unquestioned respect and undying loyalty of all those privileged to be called her kinsmen.

Lipok came to me one day and requested my immediate presence at "her place"—her daughter's cookhouse close behind my own house. As I was busy with some duty at the time, I said I would come in a little while. This reply was inappropriate. I was to come now! Those in my house emphasized that her's was a command I could not ignore. Lipok handed me a warm piece of cooked pork when I stepped into the cookhouse. I said how wonderful it was, I would save it for dinner as I had just eaten. "No! You must sit here and eat it now," she told me, and continued, "I've been watching you and you always give food to those young men who work for you. That's not right. This is for you and you alone." I am not sure why she did not want to help feed the two young men of my household, but I am sure that she was putting me clearly in her debt, and that I was honored by that debt relationship, and, finally, that whatever Lipok wanted from me or commanded of me she would get. Most importantly she would be respected by me as a *polamit*, an elite woman of very high status.

Whenever Lipok came into Angelek, I noticed the usual activity became more subdued. If she spoke, one had to listen very well because she spoke quietly. Lipok was said to have outlived her "time." Her skin was very loose and wrinkled, but her eyes sparkled and her voice was firm as was her step. She was said to have acquired a great deal of knowledge, to have made good gardens and raised fat children and pigs, and to have traveled to many singsings. She was compared to Maklun, the great man to whom I now turn.

Maklun was a man in his seventies whose fragile body belied the strength of spirit within it. He wore his hair in long dreadlocks covered in red ochre (*emi*) in the style of all truly great men. Red ochre when rubbed on a skull is said to "cool" it, and it is possible that it has the same effect on a living head. Maklun spoke excellent *tok pisin* and was the appointed *luluai* of Lapalam, a large administrative village in which his younger brother also lived. The two brothers maintained separate *bi*, one north of the village and one to the south. They were at times competitors and each was known as a *midan* of some notoriety. Of the two, Maklun had the widest network of trade partners and the widest reputation, extending over many hamlets. He commanded distant kinsmen to help build him a new *mang* and to contribute pigs to his singsings. He called for labor from nonresident kin to clear a new garden. Maklun even defied the Australian law of the time by asking his kinsmen to exhume the skull of one of his distant brothers, who had been a big man of a hamlet over ten miles distant from his own.

When they carried out the important ceremonies involving the skull, he also participated (see chapter 9).

Few would dare challenge Maklun, for if they did he could totally embarrass any challenger by presenting him with some highly valuable item which he knew could not be reciprocated. He was said to have more *mokmok* stones than any other person known to my informants, and to have significantly more shells. He brought more than three hundred shells to a marriage exchange. I watched in great admiration as he and his equally able and elite wife selected shells for *potupan* with a swiftness that could only come from a precise knowledge of each and every one of their three hundred shells, as well as those shells that were presented to them. It was an extraordinary performance.

Maklun was a man quick to lose his temper and raise his voice, and he frequently reduced an opponent to tears in the course of a transaction, necessitating his paying a shell to his victim to maintain their relationship. He was known as the hardest shell bargainer of the entire region, the hardest to get to accept one's shells as being of sufficient value to erase one's debt to him. He was known to have taught many in his hamlet (both male and female), and kinsmen in neighboring hamlets, the fine principles of shell evaluation and negotiation and to have given them appropriate magic spells ensuring success in financial transactions. He commonly demanded and got double value for any exchange. Although those who entered into transactions with him complained loudly outside of his hearing, they considered themselves both fortunate that he considered them worthy of a relationship and courageous in daring to transact business with him or one of his group.

Maklun hosted his nephews' tooth-blackening ritual. I was invited (primarily because the mother of one of my household assistants came from Maklun's hamlet) to attend one of the ceremonial night-long singsings. I was then asked to remain for the final night after which a pig would be killed. This I did, and was about to leave to return home when I was told that Maklun wished to give the pig to me. I consulted my companions who said, yes, I should buy it, but it would cost twice what anyone else would charge for a pig, and that Maklun would want shells as well as money. They offered to help me by taking care of the shells. Maklun then said that he wished me to have the pig because I had spent two nights there and I had fallen on the path. When I returned to Angelek with the pork, and it had been cooked and distributed, people came to me saying, "I hear Maklun gave you this pig." And I began to build a reputation.

Maklun was an excellent example of a *midan* who had reached a critical level of renown. He was widely known to be over-hard in his dealings and in certain ways had defied customary behavior—for example, by giving the pork to me instead of to a pork partner who had expected to receive it. At the same ritual, Maklun invited a member of the native police (who appeared with a message for me) to stay for the ritual and to sleep in the *mang*. Again, exceptional behavior. By defying Australian law and managing the skull removal and ritual under the very nose of the Kandrian administration, he also placed his reputation on the line. Commonly, a *midan* could do as he pleased, but if he went too far there were checks. Most often these checks were expressed as "a woman would talk," i.e., would say to her husband, "why don't you do as X does and bring back pork for me to eat?" and the husband would get jealous and kill X, either with a spear or with sorcery.

But Maklun seemed to be a master at walking the political tightrope, a position I believe he relished for the excitement it provided. Not only was he able to juggle all the personal relationships with friends and enemies he had cultivated in his personal network, but he had also very successfully widened his network to include Europeans, all of whom added considerable variety and spice to his life and an additional measure of prestige.

Kamil was the leader of the hamlet in which I lived which was itself a portion of the administrative village of Angelek. Kamil was neither the *luluai* nor *tultul* of this village, nor had he ever held one of these positions. He was, however, considered to be the only big man resident in Angelek. The village men's house was considered Kamil's *mang*, and his control over the hamlet portion of the village land area and over those of the village residents who considered themselves members of Kamil's hamlet was absolute.

A slightly balding man in his sixties, Kamil spoke no *tok pisin* except for a few guidebook phrases that he would address to me in a friendly, jesting manner, although most of our conversations were held in Kaulong. His face was etched with kindness and good humor and his intelligence shone through his clear eyes. My first impression of Kamil was of an elderly, mild, and inconspicuous man.

During the ten months I lived in his hamlet while he was alive, I observed Kamil in a variety of leadership situations. He bought his eldest son a wife in two separate rituals of transaction in which he effectively belittled his son's in-laws with an embarrassment of valuable shells that they could not match. He conducted singsings for a variety of occasions on the hamlet ground near the graves of his father and other deceased kinsmen, although none of these involved pigs. He traveled to about six pork-receiving singsings at other hamlets and fed his hamlet membership with cooked pork. He controlled the harvesting of the coconuts and breadfruits growing in the hamlet, and he brought up for hamlet or village discussion a variety of disputes involving members of his hamlet and he participated in their settlement.

Kamil would tolerate no dissent among or concerning his hamlet residents and was outstanding in his immediate reaction to such disputes, dropping all other activities and pressing for immediate settlement. He would frequently supply both parties to the dispute with the necessary shells to exchange to establish peace. For example, I was called to his garden hut one day to treat both his son and son's wife who had hurt each other in an argument. Mikail, Kamil's son, was accused by his wife Wiame of spending too much time in the *mang* with the men and going to ceremonies without her. She struck him on the knee with her machete, causing him to fall to the ground with a nasty cut, but not before he had struck her on the mouth with his fist, causing her to bite through her lower lip. All of this took place in her husband's parents' garden house and thus she had seriously breached the tabu against all violence in front of in-laws. I patched them both up, and then Kamil told me that he was coming to Angelek and there would be an all-night ceremony of singing called a *dikaiyikngin*, an affair where the local group sings while walking in a circle around the hamlet clearing. Kamil arranged for word to be sent to all of Mikail's kin living within traveling distance, and to all of Wiame's kin, telling them to come and sing at Angelek.

At dusk the local group began the singing, with both men and women leading the singing and all participating, including the young men and women. Men beat *kundus*, hourglass-shaped drums. Children hung around and watched or, as the time went on, slept. An hour or so before midnight, some of Mikail's relatives joined the local group in the circular singing. When dawn broke, Kamil gave shells to his daughter-in-law, which she gave to each of Mikail's visiting relatives, holding her head bowed and not looking them in the eye. When this was done, Kamil discussed with others the probable reason for the absence of any of Wiame's relatives. Deciding that it was not possible to know why they did not come, Kamil decided to hold a *dikaiyikngin* for a second night, just in case the word came to them too late for them to make the first affair. The second night's singing proceeded as before, but none of Wiame's relatives came. "Probably because they felt Wiame to be in the wrong, particularly since the fight took place in her in-law's presence."

Kamil demanded and received complete respect for his person and his position and would tolerate no show of disrespect, however slight, demanding payment with a quiet voice should anyone violate his sense of what was required. I learned this in no uncertain terms fairly early in my stay in Angelek. My household had feasted on a delicious bandicoot cooked with coconut cream and Chinese cabbage. There was soup left over, and as Kamil passed by my front door I asked him if he would like to have some soup. He said not a word and went to his own house. Shortly, someone from his house came to me and demanded I give two shillings to Kamil. "Why?" I asked. I did not get an immediate answer but paid the shillings, and shortly after this Kamil came and climbed into my house with a gentle smile and kind greetings to all of us. After Kamil left, I asked my two young helpers again to explain why I had to pay two shillings. I was told that it was because I had offered Kamil soup. I still did not understand. They explained that I had insulted him by not offering meat, but only soup which was a leftover. Since everyone else in the community accepted any leftovers I offered them, clearly Kamil was not like everyone else.

Kamil, unlike Maklun, never raised his voice in anger, although I never saw him lose a verbal challenge. He had a delightful sense of the ridiculous and because he was absolutely sure of his position of respect, he often acted the clown for the amusement of all. I saw no other man do this. Kamil was not one of the truly renowned *midan* in this region, but he was not too far behind. Moreover, he was content with his level of fame, having satisfied his ambition.

Kamil was the best example I knew of a "talking man," a category of person distinguished from a "fighting man." Talking men were said to have a higher status than fighting men, because they were always in control of their *enu*, their self. My assistant Gaspat was also known as having great potential as a "talking man." I had noticed that mothers frequently asked Gaspat to discipline a wayward child. After Gaspat inflicted a few slaps and blows to the child, the mother would call the child to her, holding out a stick with which he could fight back, and she would then cuddle her child and protect him within her encircling arms as Gaspat got in a few more licks. Gaspat told me that everyone knew that he was a talking man and would not become angry and lose control and, therefore, he was preferred as a discipliner of children.

My final example of elite behavior is of Pomegit, who must have died about 1900. His brother's grandson related the story to me in Umbi. I had asked the grandson to tell me who had the most *mokmok* stones, and he said that Pomegit had had more than anyone else in the past or today. Pomegit was a *midan* who had demanded absolute silence of everyone when he was in a hamlet. Children, dogs, and even birds must be controlled and remain silent. When anyone had showed him disrespect by crying, talking, or chirping in his presence he had insisted on immediate payment of a *mokmok* stone. No other payment would satisfy him. He had murdered many individuals, but no one had ever attempted to kill him in retaliation. "They were too afraid," my informant said. But Pomegit did eventually die. His ghost, however, did not go to the mountain where all human ghosts go, but into the river, underneath the water where he still exists as a *masalai* (a localized spirit).

Like other Melanesian big men, the Kaulong *midan* are self-made men and women, who through recognition of their personal attributes gather followers to reside in their hamlet or, if not, to cooperate frequently in joint ventures. Followers do so for what they themselves may profit in terms of prestige, which may trickle down from those they help. Kaulong *midan* achieve their renown without the aid of any nonhuman spirits or ancestors. Ancestors are quite removed from the living. While hamlet ceremonies involving sacrificial killing of pigs expressly allow the pig's blood to cover the bones of the dead ancestors, there is no concept that these dead bones have any ability to aid the living (see chapters 9 and 10).

Taro spirits are the major spirits who help those who know the appropriate magic spells needed to induce the spirit to bring corms to the garden. Some spells are more powerful than others, but none of these spirits is in control of or benefits any one individual.

The Kaulong at the time of my study appeared to be very conservative in adopting new ways of achieving success. In Umbi, few had any use for money, for they desired little in the way of tangibles outside of those produced locally. My presence introduced to the area both money and the desire for things money could buy. But money cannot buy prestige.

Alternative paths had been chosen by fewer than fifty individuals from the entire inland region (from all four language groups) as of 1974. About a dozen individuals had received more than five years of schooling, and I knew of only one Kaulong who had completed secondary schooling. While many had gone to work in other areas, most of this work was unskilled or semiskilled (such as driving a taxi or being a member of the Pacific Island Regiment.

I know of only two local men who chose to take nontraditional roads to success. One ran a trade store five miles inland from Kandrian that was in its first shaky year of existence in 1968. Another man had decided to plant coconuts and had a small plantation of fewer than five hundred trees. A number of other individuals planted more coconuts than they needed for consumption with the aim of selling the surplus, and one or two had planted small coffee groves. In 1968, none of these entrepreneurs had any great expectations for the success of their ventures.

A "new way" was proposed by Koriam, elected member of the House of Assembly representing the region, 1964–78. While some of the Sengseng decided to try this new way—involving giving up old habits and calling on the ancestors to bring wealth and prestige—none of the Kaulong found the message attractive. The Kaulong actually laughed at the idea that their ancestors would help them. "Everyone," they said, "knew that their ancestors were nothing but bones." In 1974, the government was attempting to draw the Kaulong into the local government, saying that if they paid taxes to the local government council, the council would help them. This my Kaulong informants also laughed off. "Why should anyone want to help us? No one ever helps another without asking for a high price. Everyone knows that if we want to get ahead, we must do it ourselves."

6/ We Are All Brothers and Sisters

Distinctions of gender, categories of maleness and femaleness, are topics that have received considerable attention in Melanesian ethnography during the past three decades, beginning with Read's work among the Gahuku Gama in the Eastern Highlands (1965). In 1964 Meggitt characterized distinctions made between the Eastern Highlands and the Mae Enga of the Western Highlands as that between "lechers and prudes," respectively. Following this, literature on the Highland societies has shown the diversity and complexity of gender definition and relationships to be far too great to reduce to quick labels (see, for example, M. Strathern 1972, 1988; and A. Strathern 1972; Herdt 1980; Gillison 1980; Berndt 1962; and others).

It was not long into my initial visit before it became clear that Kaulong attitudes and practices relating to sexuality were quite distinct from those previously described. During the first week in Umbi in 1962 and while my ability to communicate verbally was extremely limited, my house was suddenly invaded by my two young male assistants, closely followed by two young women, each brandishing long supple sticks with which they attempted to strike the young men as they struggled to hide behind me and the mosquito net draped over my bed. The women were more successful than the men, but after a while the battle ceased, leaving me completely puzzled as to the initial cause or final solution. The boys showed me the welts they had received, some of them bleeding. I asked them, "Why didn't you fight back?" "Oh, that we cannot do," they replied. "Why did they cease fighting?" I asked. "Because we promised them some money," they replied. The final question, "Why did they begin to fight you?" was answered, "That is the fashion of girls."

Shortly after this I learned that while some men appeared to enjoy the violent courtship of young women, they were literally scared to death of marriage and told me that many men postpone marriage until very late in life when, they said, they were ready to die. Some men managed to avoid marriage altogether.

If this were not intriguing enough, I observed genealogically close siblings of opposite sex engaged in the intimate behavior of grooming each other: seeking and removing and biting to death lice from each other's head. Eventually I heard of and observed many instances of extended close contact between mature but unmarried men and women. For example, while the hamlet house was generally a place where unmarried men slept, women were free to enter the house during the daylight and on certain occasions to sleep there.

All of the above behaviors illustrate distinctive attitudes toward behavior between men and women, brothers and sisters, husbands and wives, contrasting with what had been described in the literature on Highland New Guinea societies. In some instances, it appears that in regard to marriage Kaulong are the greatest "prudes" of all Melanesian groups, yet concerning attitudes toward polluting aspects of womanhood—which in the Highlands lead to extremes of avoidance among adult men and women (including husbands and wives, brothers and sisters)—the Kaulong appear remarkably unconcerned. And lastly, it appears that Kaulong men marry women they call "sister," and women marry men who are their "brothers."

I begin my discussion of gender in this chapter with an examination of consanguineal and asexual parallel (same-sex) siblings and follow this with an examination of the consanguineal and asexual opposite-sex siblings relationship. I argue that the asexual parallel- and cross-sibling models reflect, respectively, the Kaulong ideals of gender similarity and differentiation. I conclude this chapter with a discussion of the essential and categorical distinction between men and women: the woman's ability to kill men through the pollution of their maturity, and in periods of menstruation and childbirth. The sexual cross-sibling relationship of husbands and wives is discussed in chapter 7.

The basic contrast between parallel- and cross-sibling relationships (both asexual and sexual) is that in the parallel relationship there is competition and conflict, while in the cross relationship, conflict is explicitly curtailed and cooperation is an obligation. I conclude chapter 7 with a discussion of the sibling model of reproduction of society, in which I argue that Kaulong avoid the shame of sexuality by striving for a situation where asexual cross-siblings replace themselves as a *sibling set*, implicitly denying sexual reproduction.

CATEGORIES OF SIBLINGS

The Kaulong term *poididuan* was usually glossed by my informants in *tok pisin* as *ol barata*, "all brothers," and in this sense included all members of a cognatic kingroup without regard to sex, generation, collaterality, or known genealogical linkages. This term, then, denotes an inclusive category of kin from a global social universe.

There is no other term by which one may refer to another as a sibling in Kaulong without distinguishing both the speaker's and referent's gender, thus implicitly indicating the parallel or cross-sex nature of the relationship:

Sibling (unmarried) Terminology

	parallel-sibling	cross-sibling
male speakers	*worok*	*elut-ngo*
female speakers	*edok*	*wili-ngo*

These terms are extended fully without qualification to all categories of siblings throughout the most inclusive ancestral group of cognates who can trace a relationship through either males or females to an ancestral founder of a named *bi*. When exact relationships are not known, correct terminology is applied according to any one of the following principles: (a) if two individuals refer to each other as "sibling" so do their children refer to each other as "sibling"; (b) a child of someone you refer to by a parental term (*inu*, mother; *iok*, father) is called by you "sibling"; (c) a parent's parallel (same-sex) sibling is referred to as a parent: a father's brother is *iok*; a mother's sister, *inu*. While parents' cross-siblings (mother's brother, *wiheng*; father's sister, *daso*) are distinguished from mothers and fathers, their children are *not* distinguished from children of mothers and fathers. Thus, all of ego's cousins, parallel and cross, are considered and referred to as siblings.

Siblings who share one or both parents (sometimes extended to a common grandparent) are considered to be "one-blood" siblings. Unfortunately, I was unable to elicit a Kaulong term for this distinction. The *tok pisin* phrase *won blut* was mostly used to explain to me why a particular brother-sister pair could not marry, and also to explain the sibling relationship that above all others contained the greatest *caring* obligation among cross-siblings.

Parallel-Sibling Behavior

The following discussion considers the model for siblings of the same sex. The model is a male model and is cogently outlined in a story concerning the origin of three types of fighting spears, personified in the narrative as three brothers.

> There are three brothers who go to a pork distribution and ceremony (singsing). The two younger brothers fall asleep during the singing. The older brother sings and is given pork during the distribution. He goes to find his younger brothers and sees them asleep, locked in the hamlet house. He returns home alone.
>
> Middle brother hears his older brother calling him and he tries to get out of the house. Finding the door locked he begins to dig under the walls, tossing dirt on top of his sleeping younger brother. Younger brother awakes and accuses middle brother of waking him suddenly while his soul is still about and thus trying to kill him. Younger brother fights middle brother until both of their shields and spears are broken and they fall asleep again.
>
> Then the youngest brother hears his oldest brother calling and he tries to get out of the house. Finding the door locked he digs under the wall, tossing dirt on top of middle brother and

waking him, and they resume fighting. They fight until all pieces of the shields and spears are but splinters. They fight with their fists, then fall exhausted upon their beds and sleep.

Oldest brother finds them and, angry at their continual fighting, he sends them away, giving each a portion of raw pork. Middle brother throws his piece away when it begins to stink. Youngest brother makes a fire and cooks his pork with wild yam and eats it.

Youngest brother then clears a *bi* and builds a house. He clears a garden and watches various plants which of themselves come up and grow in his garden. He then watches a wild pig eat some sugar cane and he tries some himself. The pig then eats bananas, then *tapiok* [manioc], then taro; and by following the pig and through trial youngest brother discovers how to prepare each for eating by man (e.g., some such as taro must be cooked while others may be eaten safely in a raw state).

One day the youngest brother sees a woman smoking a leaf and she gives him some and he discovers how sweet tobacco is to smoke. She also gives him betel nut. The woman stays, and the two "sit down" together.

Youngest brother then thinks of middle brother and decides to visit him and bring him tobacco, betel, and taro. The two brothers talk and promise to visit each other regularly to exchange pork. Youngest brother returns home and finds the woman gone. He calls to Sakul [a bird] and tells Sakul to find a woman for him. The bird does so, leading a woman to youngest brother by singing sweetly. Upon seeing the man who sent Sakul, the girl decides to stay. She becomes pregnant and youngest brother tells her to send word to her mothers and fathers to come and be paid, so that she may stay with him.

After youngest brother pays his wife's parents, he thinks again of middle brother and, taking pork, he sets out to visit him. He meets middle brother, who is on the road on his way to visit youngest brother. The two brothers decide to sing and to exchange pork.

As they sing, oldest brother hears them and comes to the singsing. The two younger brothers are afraid of the foreigners (who come with older brother) and want to fight. Oldest brother stops the fight and says, "We are all of us from a long-way place," thus identifying everyone as strangers to each other. Middle brother replies that he comes from Aingon. Youngest brother says that he comes from Miu. Then oldest brother says he is from Kaulong [in this instance a specific locality]. Once their place and identity is secured, the fight [and the story] ends.

Within this story all aspects of brotherly (and male) behavior are noted and marked. The placement of women in this male world is also made explicit. These points are first listed and then discussed below.

1. Oldest brother has dominance and control over younger brothers. Birth order is principally important only for the firstborn.

2. Through hard work, keen observation and, clever thinking anyone can achieve success regardless of birth order or specific instruction. One can acquire important knowledge through experience alone.

3. Males are completely independent in subsistence production and in preparation of food for consumption. Men can live alone and succeed.

4. Brothers fight. Men fight. If you wish not to fight you live alone.

5. Visiting and exchange of pork and other garden products should take place between brothers. They should share and exchange (and not fight).

6. Social interaction with men from other places occurs at planned events where exchange of pork is preceded by singing as an alternative to fighting, but where fighting is to be expected.

The above is the male Kaulong world, one that does not necessarily include a man's female cross-siblings (sisters) or women in any way. It is noteworthy that the three brothers have no sister and the wife, no brother, only a mother and father. Wife's brothers do not receive any of their sister's marriage payment. Their absence here is explained by this aspect of cross-sibling behavior. In the story women are seen as seducers of men through gifts of tobacco and betel (in reality usually bespelled) and, most importantly, as producers of children. The wife in the story chooses whether to stay or not, but once her husband pays her parents (after her productive abilities are shown) she, like all women, is married for life.

When giving oral narratives of descent (pedigrees), an informant's own direct ancestor usually is listed first in any sibling group regardless of whether that ancestor is male or female. Following this preference, male siblings usually are listed before female siblings. Both males and females are given in birth order, but separated by gender. The salience of the firstborn male in these pedigrees reflects the preference given to the eldest son, although all siblings ideally share equally in the parental estate.

Magic spells and stone and shell valuables are important items individually possessed. Men pass on spells to their sons or, rarely and exceptionally, to daughters when they are judged to be more qualified. Women pass on spells and their own valuables to daughters. All informants agree that it is natural for a man to give his firstborn son the best spells. The eldest son also is given the father's store of stone valuables, some of which he should hold in trust for his younger brothers. Ideally, the oldest brother should care for the welfare of the younger, using his greater inherited knowledge and wealth on their behalf. Oldest brothers advise younger and help them in their financial transactions. The stated ideal is that all should live together with the eldest as hamlet leader and with the younger ones helping in the older brother's production of garden produce and pork. However, set against this ideal is the acknowledged reality that competition and jealousy among brothers naturally leads to fighting and to the eventual establishment of independent hamlets by ambitious and talented younger brothers. While separation of equally ambitious brothers is expected, it is also common to find two brothers, single or married, cooperating in particular garden or pig-raising enterprises at any given time. These cooperative ventures are found among other kin dyads as well, but it is characteristic for such ventures to be extremely flexible and variable in personnel from year to year and from enterprise to enterprise.

Males consider marriage necessary only for the production of a child to replace them in the social universe. Marriages of brothers should follow in sequence of birth order, the eldest marrying first and then giving his sanction to younger brothers' later marriages. I was told that, ideally, the youngest brother should never marry. Rather, he should remain free of female contamination in order to be available to care for his older brother's children after their father has died (of women's contamination) and their mother had been strangled and buried with her husband.

The acknowledged fragile ties between male parallel-siblings are expressive of the entire male world of the Kaulong. Mutual aid is expected among brothers although it is not seen as a binding obligation. Rather, it is expressed as something to be desired: "If I so desire, I will give food to my brother and he will give food to me, or I will help him in an exchange and he will help me, or I will give food to my brother's children and they will work for me." Individuals are encouraged from childhood to be completely self-sufficient. It is not considered aberrant to live alone, preferring to cooperate with no one in the production of food and wealth resources. Single as well as married men may achieve great renown by attracting other men and their wives to cooperate in joint enterprises that produce great amounts of wealth for all to exchange in wide personal trade networks. A man does not necessarily need a wife for success. According to informants and genealogies, it was not uncommon that a few big men in the past were never married. Some men attributed their success to the help they received from their mothers and subsequently from their sisters, and expressed the belief that these kin were more reliable help than were wives.

In contrast to the unisexual man's world, a woman's world is bisexual, although much of the same emphasis on independence and self-sufficiency in economic production and transactional relationships is also a part of a woman's socialization. As we have seen, there is little in the daily economic life that a woman cannot or does not do. Only heavy timber-clearing and the laying of logs for fence or house walls are considered exclusively men's work. All other work can and is done by either sex: indeed, when it comes to garden work, women are said to learn at an earlier age for they are considered to be naturally greedy for garden products.

Just as brothers are expected to fight each other, so are sisters. To illustrate this point, a father told me of a fight between his two grown daughters. It seemed one had declared a preference for the moon, and the other for the sun! Exchange of words soon led to a physical battle which went on for some time before the father felt he had to step in because his daughters appeared close to killing each other. When women fight, men usually do not interfere. Women fight with their fists, while men fight with spears.

Competition between sisters is frequently concerned with getting a husband. As discussed in chapter 7, women are the aggressors in courtship, and this aggression is physical. While some men choose to flee from all women (and marriage) for their entire lives, a few manage to marry more than one wife at a time. However, any man wishing to take an additional wife can do so only with the permission of his first wife. Without this permission the courtship by the potential second wife is seen as adultery and resulting conflict between the two women is so intense that suicide of one or the other is expected and sometimes accomplished. One of my friends continually complained to me about the inability of his two wives to get along. He eventually settled one of them in his garden hut and the other in his Umbi house. Even this didn't solve his problems. "Are they sisters?" I asked him one day. "No way!" he exclaimed, "No man would marry sisters. Everyone knows sisters always fight."

Ideally, brothers should cooperate and so should sisters. In both cases the cooperation is not expected but is earned. "If I want to help a parallel-sibling I will, but I can't count on a parallel-sibling to help me."

As I discussed earlier, trade relationships are primarily built upon the parallel-sibling relationship for brothers as well as for sisters. Each trades with his or her same-sex trade partners whom they refer to using sibling terms, and this trade is essentially competitive. It is only through an initial *potupan* exchange of shells (a totally voluntary act by both parties) that a peaceful but competitive parallel-sibling exchange relationship is launched.

Barkcloth and Fiber Skirt: Cross-Sibling Relations

Kaulong make a significant distinction among those siblings who are descended from a same ancestral cross-sibling pair. Those who are descended from the brother are in the category of *da mulu* (of or from barkcloth), while those descended from the sister are in the category of *da songon* (of or from the fiber skirt).

It was well into my third visit to Kaulong before I was made aware of this most subtle yet culturally significant distinction among those who are otherwise considered as siblings. I had been able in Angelek to import enough rice to sell some to those in the community who were finding it hard to feed their families during the "hungry time." I sold after dark, in part to discourage over-reliance and to limit the sale to those in the immediate neighborhood. One night I was told by a friend not to sell to a man who lived but a short distance away, "because your supply is getting short." Shortly thereafter the same friend said it was all right for me to sell to another man who lived in the next community at a greater distance. Puzzled, I later inquired why he had made the distinction. "Because the first man is *da songon*, and the second man is *da mulu*." It was the first time I had heard those words used in such a way.

Mulu is the very long strip of barkcloth that men used to wrap around their loins (before calico); it is painted in a design depicting a vine with thorns, called pig's teeth (*yu ngin*). *Songon* is the fiber/leaf skirt worn (in 1972) nearly universally by women.

The categories "of the barkcloth," and "of the skirt" refer to descendants of an original founder of a *bi*: A man, or cross-sibling pair, emerged and cleared a place. The man/brother acquired a wife and proceeded to "father" a line of descendants; while his/their sister seduced a passing male, followed him home, and proceeded to "mother" a line of descendants for her natal place. Both groups of children call each other sibling, but the brother's children are *da mulu* to the sister's children, who are reciprocally *da songon* to their mother's brother's children.

"So," I asked my rice advisor, "what difference does it make that one man was *da songon*, while the other was *da mulu*?" "*Da mulu* are more important," he replied.

I was told that each group of cross-siblings divide their children into these categories. Thus, the parental model is generational and does not extend through time. From the children's point of view it is also generational. My true siblings and I and my father's brothers' children are "of the barkcloth" to our father's sister's children, while my true siblings and I and my mother's sisters' children are "of the skirt" to our mother's brothers' children.

While the model is expressed and explained by the Kaulong as a generational one, without time depth, it is significant that the distinction was most often verbally evoked when two individuals wished to reestablish a distant relationship on the grounds that they belonged to complementary lines descended from an apical brother and sister pair three or more generations removed. If the situation called for solidarity leading to fusion of interests, then the barkcloth/skirt distinction was discussed in terms of its equality and complementarity, implying the social solidarity of the people of one place. A common situation was trying to persuade a trade partner to accept a gift of pork with its obligation for return with interest.

If the situation called for a distinction to be made between individuals, however, then the barkcloth/skirt distinction was made on the basis of giving those born of the brother prior rights or consideration over those born of the sister. Commonly this arose when there was *conflicting* interest in a shared resource, such as my supply of rice.

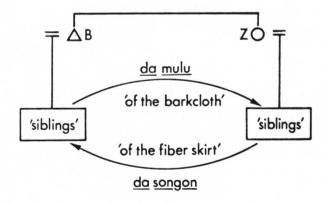

FIG. 4. Barkcloth and fiber skirt distinction

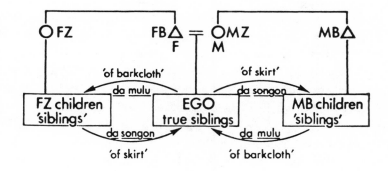

FIG. 5. Siblings borne of cross-siblings

It is important to understand that while the principle of distinction is made on the basis of gender of the cross-sibling parent—born of man, born of woman—the categories of descendants are made without regard to their gender.

Consanguineal Cross-Siblings

The *mulu/songon* distinction among groups of siblings is a model for relations between cross-siblings of the closest kind, "one blood." Caring for each other is the key quality of the brother-sister relationship. Caring is shown in many ways: by supplying food (taro and pork) without compensation throughout the life-span; by helping to raise children, pigs, and taro; by giving support (shells, songs) in times of competition with others and even in battle.

A man told me the following story. When he was young, he and his brother were fighting and his brother bit him on his leg. The leg became infected and eventually got so bad that the smell of the gangrene drove all his relatives from the hamlet house in which he lay. They left him alone to die, he said. Then a sister heard of his plight and she came and took care of him. She slept in the house with him and spent months constantly applying native medicines to his leg, cooking him nourishing food, bathing him, and giving him water to drink. My informant concluded his story with the comment that it was not until his younger brother had undergone the tooth-blackening rituals and was prohibited from chewing anything that his leg began to heal. I asked my friend whether he had paid his sister for her labor. "No," he replied, "one doesn't pay a sister for this kind of help, but I might take her a shell someday [many years after the event] to say thank you."

Kaliam, one of my household assistants, had been cared for by an older sister when he was a baby. "She carried me all the time, and gave me things to eat." This sister had married a man from a Miu-speaking community quite a distance from Umbi. The brother acquired a number of items known to be in demand in the remote Miu region: a wooden lock box, calico, mirrors, axe heads, and coconuts, and went to visit his sister. He had intended, he told me, to trade these items for shells, but his sister *shamed* him by telling him he was remiss in not coming to visit her for so many years. So he gave all the trade items to her and came home without shells. But in listening to Kaliam's tale, I noted his facial expressions and tone of voice, which conveyed to me his sense of honest pleasure at his sister's show of affection and caring.

Older sisters are preferred over brothers, and, indeed, all other kin, for keeping a man's shells for him. Sisters will not use the shells for their own purposes, and they will keep them safe. A young brother counts on his sister to give him good advice in shell transactions, advice that comes automatically when he goes to collect or deposit shells. A man can always count on a sister to come to help prepare and or harvest a garden, build a house, or care for his pigs. I was told a sister is more trustworthy than a wife in these endeavors.

Shame (*mangin*) is a very strong emotion among the Kaulong, and it is principally felt when sexuality is involved. If a man was shamed by inadvertently exposing his genitals to a woman (by slipping on the path or being interrupted while defecating), his usual recourse was to commit murder—not necessarily of that person to whom he was exposed. Significantly, if the woman was a close sister a man was not shamed.

Consanguineal cross-siblings should not fight, but brothers have a measure of authority, reflective of the *mulu/songon* distinction, over sisters. Brothers exercise this authority, sometimes with physical force, quite specifically in relation to their sisters' sexuality.

KAULONG SEXUALITY

> In the beginning women carried spears and shields and
> went to the "singsings" and fought, while men slept in the
> bush with their sickness. Then the women asked the men to
> carry their shields and spears and in return the men gave the
> women their sickness. Now men go to the "singsings" and
> fight while women sleep in the bush with their sickness.

Gender in Kaulong is given for all occupants of a place (humans,
domestic pigs, and dogs), who are linguistically differentiated *at birth*
into discrete male and female categories (*wala*, female; *masang*, male).
Animals of the forest do not appear to be initially so differentiated.
While in humans, gender distinction is also made in all reference and
address terminology relating to kin categories, there is little distinction
in socialization, or in gender of the socializer, throughout the early
developmental period of life. Fathers and mothers, as well as other
close affiliates of the *bi* of all ages and either gender, share in the
raising of children of the *bi*. This joint responsibility is particularly
noticeable when a child is exceptionally robust and vital, a child seen
to have great potential for self-development.

There is regional variation in the age of appropriate assumption of
gender specific genital coverings (barkcloth, *mulu* [now cloth], for
men; plant-fiber-skirts, *songon*, for females). Generally, by the age of
ten, individuals have regularly assumed such distinctive clothing.

Activities of children are as undifferentiated by gender as are those
of their elders. In patterns of approved aggression, however, there is a
noticeable gender distinction, and socialization for aggression begins
very early in life. Young, toddling males are encouraged to play
roughly with other boys (usually but not necessarily their brothers),
and are given sticks to return the attack and are urged to persist and
defend themselves and not to run away. Boys are also taught to avoid
such behavior with girls (usually but not necessarily their sisters).
Young, toddling girls, on the other hand, are encouraged to act aggres-
sively toward young boys, usually striking blows with sticks given to
them by their adult (and usually female) caretakers. Since boys may

not return a girl's attack, they can only run to escape, and the girls are encouraged to keep up the attack by pursuing the escaping victim. Hand-fighting is considered appropriate between girls. The differential training in cross-sex aggression is directly related to the all-important pattern for courtship leading to marriage, as we shall see in chapter 7. But before discussing this, it is necessary to examine more closely beliefs concerning the major distinction to be found between men and women, the menstrual/childbirth "sickness" and its power to contaminate and cause illness in males.

From sometime before puberty to after menopause, females are considered capable of polluting men. The ability, or power, is a continuous one with periods of increased intensity during the menstrual blood flow and during childbirth. While in these two intensely polluting conditions, a woman must remove herself from the *bi*, stay clear of all gardens and dwelling places located there, and avoid all drinking water supplies and sources. She may not touch anything with which a man may come in contact. During these times, the polluting effect spreads laterally in all directions from the woman. Periodic total isolation of the woman from men is the most efficient means of control.

In contrast with the concept of periodic lateral contamination, mature women are also considered at all other times to be capable of polluting anything they pass over or rest upon; the pollution is thought to spread vertically and directly downward, permanently affecting anything below.

Female pollution is dangerous only to males. They become contaminated and are made ill by ingesting anything so polluted, or by consuming anything that itself has been in contact with a polluted object, or by placing their own body directly underneath a contaminated object or polluting woman. There is some indication that males only gradually become susceptible to such contamination. If it so happens that a mother resumes menstruation while still nursing a young male child, the child will normally accompany his mother into isolation and is not polluted. Even if weaned, young sons are frequent visitors to their mother in her menstrual isolation. Young lads are frequently sent into contaminated areas by older males, to retrieve objects of value before the objects become seriously affected.

The illness that results from female pollution is respiratory and prolonged, and accumulative pollution will result in an early death. European medicine will not cure such respiratory disease, I was told; only
women have the appropriate knowledge, and even they cannot forestall the expected death due to women's powers.

The concept of vertical pollution results in men's adoption of certain
habits while traveling in the forest and in certain architectural features
for garden huts and major dwellings. While on the trail, men must
take care not to pass under any fallen tree or natural or constructed
bridge, for men always assume that a woman has walked on the tree or
crossed over the bridge. Women need not exercise such care as they
are not subject to pollution. All drinking water comes from springs,
because it is assumed that women have crossed over or through all
flowing streams or rivers.

In the *bi* and in the garden all houses were traditionally built on
the ground. Raised houses, which the Australian administration ad-
vocated as being healthier, were unpopular because of the health
problems they caused for males. Not only were they much colder in
the rainy season and made inside (sleeping) fires unsafe, but once a
contaminating woman had been inside such a raised house, no male
could sit underneath or retrieve or use any object that fell through
the floor boards. No male could eat food which was cooked underneath the house and the raised floor made inside cooking difficult
and dangerous. Wood stored under the house could not be used for
cooking.

Ann Chowning (with the Sengseng) and I (in both Umbi and Angelek) lived in raised houses. Our hosts' accommodation both to
ourselves and to our living arrangements differed. In Dulago the
Sengseng classified Ann with the grandmothers—presumably postmenopausal and therefore nonpolluting. Her male assistants both sat
and cooked food under her house. Women, however, were not permitted to enter her house nor sit on the firewood underneath. In
Umbi, my hosts classed me with the mothers—but, interestingly,
they considered me personally to be nonpolluting, and men felt safe
sitting underneath my house and eating food cooked there by my
assistants even as I was above them inside the house. Women were

permitted in my house but not while any men were sitting underneath. In Angelek, my raised house was too close to the ground to permit anyone to sit underneath, much less cook there, but my split-palm floor allowed many valuables to escape into this danger area where only women and quite young boys were allowed to venture and retrieve.

In the traditional houses (*mang* and *mok*) there are usually two or more bed/benches made of loose poles supported on parallel logs with fires built between the beds. Cooking is restricted to one particular fire or to one particular region of the larger *mang*. Food is stored above or away from the bed/benches where women sit, and firewood for cooking is kept in between roof beams and water containers hung from the side walls. In the *mang*, single men commonly cook their own food and some married men prefer to cook for themselves there as well, considering the possibility that food cooked by women has been prepared carelessly and/or on the wrong fire. While some men expressed fear that a particular woman might deliberately feed them contaminated food, most informants merely considered women to be careless and unconcerned generally about this contaminating matter. I rarely observed women showing any concern for their polluting effect on men, with the exception of mothers, who regularly protested when their young sons were sent to retrieve objects dropped by older men through the floor of my raised house.

Daily female pollution is conceptually well-defined. Avoidance of such vertical contamination is fairly easy and does not necessitate lateral separation of the sexes. As we have seen in previous chapters women as well as men freely enter the main structure of the *bi* and involve themselves in discussions and activities occurring there during the day. At night the structure is usually restricted to males for sleeping, a restriction relating to incest and marriage tabs more than to pollution, as we shall see below. Close bodily contact is permitted between primary kin of opposite sex from infancy throughout adulthood. As we have seen, one-blood cross-siblings maintain the closest of all primary kin ties well into adulthood, with the possible exception of mother and son.

MENSTRUATION AND CHILDBIRTH

Periods of intensified pollution during menstruation and childbirth, when the pollution spreads laterally from the woman, are the only times that necessitate the separation of a woman from the physical domain of all men, including the house, garden, and mutually used possessions.

Menstrual huts are built at the periphery of the central clearing, or outside the garden fence just beyond the cleared areas. Husbands and brothers are anxious that the huts be far enough away to protect them from the contamination but close enough so that they can protect their wife/sister. The isolated menstruating woman is able to collect her own food from the forest and bathe in the streams, but drinking water (always coming from a "pure" source such as a natural spring) and garden produce must be provided for her, left nearby for her to collect if the supplier is male. She wears special disposable green-leaf skirts and uses disposable green-leaf water and lime containers. The smoke from her fire is considered to be dangerous to men should they be able to detect it. When her period ceases, the woman must await the offering of a shell by a man of the hamlet before she can rejoin men in common activities.

My data show that traditionally in Kaulong there was no ritual marking the onset of menstruation. From locations near to the coast, however, there is a menstrual ritual being introduced into the interior region by inmarrying women from the coastal Arawe-speakers. This ritual involves shaving the young girl's head in a distinctive pattern, which is then painted in red ochre. She is ritually presented with special skirt fibers and materials and given symbols of production (for example, taro stalk, sprouting coconut, yam, etc.) as well as firewood, which transforms raw taro into food. She is told the special names of the objects, skirt fibers, and menstrual blood. She is also instructed on pollution and restrictions. Parents, married males and females and unmarried females, observe the ritual. Observers were said to be important in order that the girl's condition become known so that the public (men) would observe caution and not become affected through her expected lack of concern and probable carelessness.

The ritual was being performed on selected young women by women who themselves had undergone the ritual. The songs were in an Arawe language and translations were only vaguely known, as were any "explanations" of the meaning of the various plants and objects. While I saw three such rituals, I was not successful in finding anyone who could give a coherent explanation of the events.

The ritual itself includes older women, who "clown" and are paid for their work by the girl's father. Clowning behavior typically involves cross-dressing by women who don pig-tusk ornaments and dog-teeth belts and barkcloth, calico, or even trousers. They direct verbal, sexually loaded gibes indiscriminately at all men, flipping their breasts at them, squirting milk in their faces. Clowns often directed their attention in my direction as I was trying to record the activity simultaneously on tape, notebook, and film. They usually managed to disrupt my work, which was their intention; and once, laughing in frustration, I put aside my tools and joined them in their antics. This was well received and I received my pay from the father the next day, along with some notoriety and fame. Ritual clowning also occurs during the return of a new mother and child to the community and during marriage transactions and in some pork distributions such as occur at tooth-blackening.

While I found it easy to collect data on menstruation from both women and men, and on childbirth from women, I found it impossible to collect data from either men or women on beliefs about conception because of the extreme shame of sexuality.

Childbirth may take place in a rockshelter or hut placed within the "forest" and outside any clearing. The woman has usually arranged for several other women to take care of her throughout the birth and for the subsequent period of isolation. Although attendants are usually mature women, some teenage daughters were known to have been sole attendants of their mother. There was one much talked about case where a husband took care of his wife in childbirth. He was said to have been so jealous of his wife he would allow her no company other than himself. The child died and his wife nearly followed, and he was taken to court by his wife's relatives for his inappropriate behavior.

All those who attend a woman in childbirth and those who later visit must remove their normal clothing and don disposable leaf skirts, and they must leave behind all possessions. The birthing place is extremely contaminating and should these women return to their own place without washing and destroying or leaving behind all they have used while in the birth-place, males will be affected. Males usually do not visit the birth-place under any circumstances.

The fact that infanticide took place in the isolated birthing place was talked about quite freely among women, but I can recall no case where a man was present at such a discussion. I was told of women who gave birth to "snakes" (without arms or legs) or to a *masalai* (ogre), who were immediately strangled or smothered as they were obviously not human beings. Children who were born too soon following a previous child were frequently strangled or "thrown away." In the latter case they might be rescued by one of the attendants and raised by her.

I frequently asked Kaulong in both Umbi and Angelek if there had ever been twins born. I showed them pictures in magazines of twins and indeed of quadruplets and quintuplets. Amazement was the response, and then comments that animals have multiple births but never Kaulong. Therefore, when Debli rushed into my house one day, saying I must go stop Molme from killing one of her sons, I did a double take. "You mean she has given birth to two boys?" "Yes," he said. Molme was the mother of three older children and I felt it was not my place to interfere here. I took the coward's way out and delayed my visit to her for a day, when I was considerably relieved to find her nursing two healthy infant sons. The infants were sleeping, each stretched out along a forearm with his head in the palm of her hand and with his legs hanging down like tassels from her elbows. She had already bound the boys' heads with soft barkcloth, fastened with a thin vine wound firmly but not tightly around the frontal and occipital bones. For weeks she carried both of them in this fashion, and I remember seeing her walk up the slippery path to the village carrying the boys and at the same time balancing on her head a full net bag of taro corms, above which was a load of firewood topped with her axe. Then came the time when the twins were about eight weeks old and she allowed her husband to carry one. Eventually her eldest son (fifteen years old) and daughter (twelve years) helped her care for the boys.

In spite of my passive noninterference, I believe that my presence in Umbi itself caused Molme to reconsider the effect that birthing twins would have on the community and on the community's relation with the government. I found the community reaction fascinating. Men, by and large, were amazed that *their* women could give birth to two at one time—"it had never happened to us." Women were not so adamant that it had never happened before, and I am quite sure that they had regularly killed any second infant and never told the men.

Men came to me to ask what they should do about the twins: should Molme and her sons go to Kandrian to the clinic? As Molme seemed to be feeding both infants quite well, I said I didn't think it necessary. Molio, the *tultul*, worried about the event, gave both infants some pork fat to chew. He told me he was now convinced that only one was human and the other was a *masalai*, because one liked the pork (as humans do) and the other did not (*masalai* prefer to eat human flesh). I feared for the one who rejected the pork fat. I, too, couldn't eat pure fat, I reminded Molio, sacrificing my humanity for the sake of the infant. However, when I left, the twins were still flourishing.

The logistical problems the twins caused for Molme were clearly illustrated to me by this case, and I could well understand mothers' desire to space children at three- to up to six-year intervals. Kaulong explicitly say that the reason for this spacing is so that each child is given all the food and care it needs to ensure its survival.

A new mother and her child return to the *bi* when her bleeding ceases and after she is offered a shell by her husband. Mature women in the community may clown and present the new mother with skirt materials which, today, may include calico. The first time I saw this I did not understand what was going on under my house. Investigating, I sat among the women and watched them behave in all ways similar to a drunken orgy—although I knew no alcohol or other intoxicant was available. Men doubled over with laughter stood at a discreet distance, but close enough to hear the words these wild women were uttering. One lady came and sat in my lap. Unfortunately, our combined weight caused the bench of slender poles to collapse, sending me head over heels with my legs in the air. The women were horrified (it was very early in my stay) and they took their merriment to another locale, much to my distress.

A woman dying in childbirth was not unknown, as became clear in genealogies and in stories from informants. If the mother hemorrhaged, there was nothing that the attendants could do. Sometimes when a woman died in childbirth her husband hung himself in grief. While there was an expectation that widowers might marry again, many did not, particularly if they had children, which the father then proceeded to raise alone. Any surviving infant would be given to another caretaker to nurse and raise.

In spite of the rather restricted nature of female pollution, Kaulong males showed an extraordinary amount of fear and anxiety concerning it. Given the equation of sexual intercourse with marriage and contamination, male fear and avoidance of all three was an impressive and distinctive feature of Kaulong life, as is discussed in chapter 7.

7/ The Reproduction of Siblings

Having described the consanguineal, asexual sibling relations (both parallel and cross) and shown them to be models for male and female gender, here I will focus on the sexual relationship formed by the marriage of individuals who consider themselves cross-siblings (sister and brother). I believe that Kaulong consider marriage for any purpose other than reproduction to be cognitively inappropriate. People marry only to have children, who will be their personal "replacements" (*senis* in *tok pisin*) in the social world. Therefore, I argue that a set of cross-siblings seeks to replace itself in the natal hamlet clearing and thus maintain its continuity of human social life in the forest.

In Kaulong, it is not possible to speak of premarital sexual relationships, for there is but one word, *nangin*, to refer to both sexual intercourse and marriage. Men are afraid to engage in the most polluting of all relationships with women, that of sexual intercourse/marriage. I argue that the men's model of social reproduction is one based on the seemingly asexual reproduction of tropical plant-life where new generations are cloned from the old without sexual contact. In the brother's view, he strives for replacement of generation in the hamlet by controlling his sister's sexuality and its products.

COURTSHIP

Expected and legal premarital heterosexual relationships exclude *nangin*/marriage in any form, but do not exclude a variety of courtship activity on the part of unmarried males and females. Although men are scared to death of *nangin*, many young men are very interested in courtship, which does not necessarily lead to *nangin*. However, it is appropriate only for females to initiate any act of courtship. If a man

158

initiates such action it is considered to be a crime of rape, punishable by death.

Courting women may offer cooked food, betel nuts, or tobacco to a man or they may initiate a verbal encounter with mildly suggestive joking (*tok pilai* in *tok pisin*). Frequently women will physically attack a man, singly or in groups, using any weapon at hand, but most typically supple long switches. The courtship with physical attack is called *ulal* and is part of pig-killing ceremonies or singsings, but is by no means restricted to those contexts. Men may reciprocate only in the verbal joking. They may not strike back in the physical attack, but are expected to pay shells, money, goods, and/or food to the women who attack them. *Ulal* and *tok pilai* should take place only between unmarried, sexually mature, but eligible individuals, with the exception that very young children practice with any available individual of the appropriate gender regardless of eligibility of the relationship.

Given that it is a woman's right to initiate courtship, it falls upon the male to try to influence the choice of the female in some appropriate fashion. This they can do in a variety of ways. They travel and attend singsings and other gatherings in places where they know there will be eligible females whom they will try to induce to fight them. And, if they so desire—and many do not—they do everything they can to make themselves attractive to the females. In Angelek, where many had access to European-style clothing, the young men used to gather in my house prior to a singsing to iron their best shirts and shorts. I did not provide the iron—a cast-iron, coconut-husk burner owned by one of the young men—but I had the only table flat enough to use. As they ironed, they talked of who might be there, what they were going to do to attract the particular woman they wished would fight them.

All males who wish to engage in courtship will attempt to learn some spells or acquire some appropriate substance previously bespelled by another who is knowledgeable in this kind of magic. I remember reading a letter to a mother from her son who had recently gone to Rabaul to work. The letter urgently requested her to send him the bottle of shell magic, for he found he had taken by mistake the bottle of love magic, which he had no desire to use in Rabaul.

An important group of substances used in love magic are those that give off a fragrance: flowers, bark, leaves, oil, animal musk, and imported powder and perfume. Another group of objects are those of a nature to be shared between people: betel nuts and lime, tobacco and store cigarettes, which, when magically treated, will affect the consumer in ways not always desired.

Bamboo flutes and panpipes, if magically treated prior to playing one's own composition, will cause a lover to be attracted to the player. Finally, the bird called *sikul*, when magically entreated, will seek out the girl of one's choice and sing in such a way that the girl will follow it back to the waiting man. The purpose of all this magic is to affect an individual's mind (*mi*) so that he or she will find it impossible to resist engaging in courtship with the one who bespelled the objects.

While both males and females are said to know love magic and to perform it on their own behalf, and for others with appropriate payment, the majority of my information relates to males using it to coerce females, which is considered the appropriate action.

Another ploy males can use to entice females to attack them is contained in the performance of a particular masked dance, the *tubuan*.[1] The *tubuan* is a spirit which is "awakened" and called into a mask made of barkcloth stretched over a conical frame and painted with large round eyes. To awaken the spirit, fresh, new cockatoo plumes are fastened to the apex of the cone and iridescent fungi are "glued" to the plumes. Freshly cut pandanus leaves are fastened at the base of the cone, reaching from there to the ground. I was shown a mask frame as the spirit in it was being "awakened" and was told that this was not something females could see.

In the *tubuan* dance, young men don the identity-concealing mask and pandanus fronds, and throughout the night each tries to attract young females by the extraordinary, sexually provocative quality of their individual dance performances. The accomplished dancer sets the plumes, with the glowing mushroom eyes, swaying to and fro, emphasizing the provocative swaying of hips hidden under the pandanus

---

1. There is some evidence that this is an introduced dance. My informants claimed that their grandfathers knew of this dance and considered it one of their own dance forms.

fronds. An attracted female sometimes feels compelled to place her hand through the pandanus fronds and on his body underneath, perhaps on his genitals. Having done so, she is unable to be separated from him and will follow him wherever he goes. The spell may last for weeks or months, which may be an embarrassment for the male dancer, some of whom know of a counterspell to turn off the love magic when warranted. Such was the case when my two Angelek assistants went to a *tubuan* in a rather distant locale. They were followed home by two young women who hung around for weeks. They had tried to lose the young women on the way home by not following the normal track and bushwhacking through the forest, over mountains and through rivers, but the girls had no trouble following them. Nakling and Gaspat got quite worried, not only because the girls were eating up all their rations and wages with the nightly courting, but one of the girls had a very powerful father. The first week the boys seemed rather proud to have danced so well to have attracted such important and attractive girls, but at the end of the third week, Nakling got his mother to provide some "turn off" love magic and send the girls home. It worked.

Tok pilai, the joking aspect of courtship, is governed by the general rules: a woman should initiate and a man should follow. One should only *tok pilai* with those eligible for marriage, although there is an age factor here, as there is in the physical *ulal* courtship. Some freedom is allowed in *tok pilai*, but swearing obscenely or using obscene language (*tok nogud*) is not appropriate. *Tok nogud* spoken to someone of the same sex by either males or females will lead to a fight and/or payment. If the *tok nogud* is directed by one sex to the other, it is considered a very serious crime. It may be considered tantamount to rape if committed by a man against a woman, and in the past it resulted in death to the offender or a heavy fine paid to the victim. If a girl directs the insult to a man, he may be so shamed he may commit suicide or murder the girl or any unwary person.

Two courting girls directed *tok nogud* at one of my assistants in Umbi. He decided to leave immediately, going perhaps as far as Manus and "to stay until I am ready to die then I'll come home," he told me. Both his and the girls' relatives worked a compromise and within a few days he received a large payment in gold-lip pearl shells.

One of the more amusing episodes—to me, not to the participants—was when the *tultul* returned to Umbi one day with orders from the government. He tried to assemble the people to hear the message and called to some women to listen. Actually, he said either (a) get off your fat ass, or (b) get off your bloody ass. He said this in *tok pisin*, which few in Umbi understood. The *luluai* considered that the *tultul* had *tok nogud* to his wife and marched him up to my house for me to adjudicate the dispute with my supposedly superior knowledge of *tok pisin*. Then ensued a remarkable discussion of comparative obscene swearing in *tok pisin*, English, and Kaulong. Although both departed to seek the judgment of the *kiap* in Kandrian, they soon returned and decided to wait until the *kiap* made his annual patrol. When this occurred, this case was not mentioned.

Reversal of the expected roles in courtship is considered quite inappropriate. For a male to use physical aggression to initiate an affair with a female (unmarried or married) is a crime punishable by death, unless both are willing to be considered married. The girl's relatives (principally brothers, parents, and parents' siblings) have the right to enforce the sanctions: to force marriage on the male if the girl is willing, or to kill the man who committed the illegal act, and quite possibly the girl as well. A male's use of physical force in the initiation of a courtship relationship is referred to by the *tok pisin* term *pulim meri*, "to rape a woman." Informants told me that it was not the sexual act itself that constituted the crime, because intercourse may not have been carried out. The crime was, they said, the male's use of physical force in the initiation of the relationship. For example, should a female accuse a man of holding her against her will, then this was a clear intention of sexual assault, i.e., rape.

While marriage or death was the stated penalty for such rape, milder penalties were traditionally applied when dictated by relative status and other personality factors. I was told that a truly big man could not be accused of rape if the woman was from a group in his own sphere of influence. For within such a group he had enough personal power, often reenforced with knowledge of sorcery, to take any woman he wanted, or to have her killed if she refused. In a number of cases I was told about, the woman either attempted or succeeded in committing suicide. A big man who *pulim meri*, raped, a woman from another group had no such effective power to ensure his immunity from the wrath of the woman's relatives, and he was liable to be killed, often exacted in an all-out war between the two groups. If not war, then a heavy payment was asked for.

Under Australian law (prevailing in 1974), there can be no carrying out of the death penalty for rape, except that which is inflicted through such a covert practice as sorcery. In a number of local resolutions of accusations of rape that I have on record, the man was assessed a very heavy payment. Marriage could not be forced if a woman was unwilling, as she usually was in such cases.

It is worth noting that no cases of rape were brought to the government or to the church officials for adjudication while I was there. Separate conversations held with these officials give me a clue as to why they were not asked to intervene. The traditional behavior of the courting young women—running after the men and physically attacking them—did not go unnoticed by the European patrol officers or mission personnel. These officials thought it was all quite hilarious and quaint, and if some girls got raped, clearly they brought it all upon themselves!

It is equally calamitous if women reverse their expected roles in courtship. While love magic practiced by women (often through bespelled betel, lime, cigarettes, etc.) does not appear to be considered illegal, in that there are no penalties assigned or expected by those who practice the art, there are risks in using love magic and these appear to be greater for woman practitioners than for males. If a male can prove that he has been the victim of love magic it is considered a successful defense against the accusation of rape. It is, I believe, considered quite possible that no normal man (one in full control of his mind, self, and body) would ever rape a woman, considering the consequences—if not death by spearing, then death through female pollution—and thus such a rape is considered abnormal behavior induced by circumstances beyond his personal control. As one man said to me: *Wonpela samting tanim bel bilong mi long nait na mi go lon ol meri* ("Something worked on my belly in the night and I went to the woman"). If this defense can be seen to be a reasonable assumption no penalty is exacted, even if the girl accuses

him of holding her and loosening her skirt, or, indeed, of sexual intercourse. As might be expected with the present-day inability of the community to impose the death penalty, men are increasingly accusing
women of performing love magic on them as their defense of their
aggression in courtship. Under the protection of the government young
men were engaging young women in premarital sex, but this was best
done with women from a distant place, and more than one young man
told me he gave his "foreign" lover a false name and false address.

A woman who allegedly has caused herself to be raped by bespelling a man (who could not marry her) traditionally found herself
quite unmarriageable, and the shame of this, I was told, would often
result in her suicide. I was told of one case, occurring after pacification,
in which the resulting child of the rape was adopted by the woman's
own parents while the woman remained unmarriageable. If a man
attempted rape in the past and was successfully resisted by the
woman, he was also said to be so shamed that he would commit
suicide or resort to the male face-saving alternative—the murder of
anyone he could find.

Promiscuity (pre- and extramarital sexual relations) is becoming increasingly common. Extremely rare and causing great social upheaval
in the Umbi region, in Angelek it was quite frequent. Typically, in both
regions there was an attempt to marry the couple accused of sleeping
together, with threats of sorcery and economic and physical coercion.
If there was some reluctance on the part of the female, it was expected
that the marriage would not be a lasting one, for parents still allow the
female to make the choice to leave an uncongenial husband. Because
of this, marriage was not forced on the reluctant woman. The man was
given no say in the matter—his only recourse was to flee (if he could).

Traditionally there was no divorce. A woman was to marry only
once and for her lifetime and, indeed, for eternity, since she was strangled at her husband's death and buried with him, as we shall see
below.

It is not without significance that most of the sexual crimes re-
counted in mythology are those committed by women. They perpe-
trate their crime using a reversal of expected behavior and magic rather
than physical force to bespell their victim. The *esusu* are a class of

female spirits known to so affect males that men will follow them wherever they go, even to the extent of flying through the air with them. The spirits are themselves invisible, while the men following them remain visible to others but unresponsive to human conversation. I was told of an *esusu* who persuaded a man to kill his wife and cook her so they (*esusu* and her captive) could eat her. This act of cannibalism was evidently so abhorrent to the man that once he tasted his wife's flesh the spell was broken. When the man saw his wife's half-eaten body on the fire, he committed suicide. I believe this tale to be an ex post facto explanation for an historic event.

NANGIN/MARRIAGE

In Kaulong, the separation of the married from the unmarried is, I contend, greater than any separation or categorical distinction to be found between men and women. The significance is culturally marked in the rituals through which the transformation from virgin to sexually active is accomplished. This ritual follows the classic tripartite structure of a rite of passage first described by Van Gennep (1909), with an initial separation (by capture), a liminal transition, and an eventual reincorporation. Of all rites of passage among the Kaulong (marking birth, initiation, marriage, and death), it is marriage that is analytically the richest and culturally the most important, in my view.

As implied in the discussion of courtship, there was, at the time of my 1974 visit, some indication that significant changes in people's attitudes toward sexuality were occurring. What I discuss here is an analysis of data deriving from both Umbi and Angelek which I believe approximates a precontact attitude to sexuality.

One of my early titles for a paper concerned with Kaulong marriage was "When all males are brothers, what's a woman to do?" Indeed, it is appropriate that a girl select someone called "brother" to court and marry, but this brother should not be a "one-blood" brother (i.e., have the same father or the same father's father). In Umbi a man told me of his brother's son and daughter who had sex together. As they were incorrectly married, they ran away. Their father tracked them down to where they hid in the forest and killed them both. Interestingly, I was told the same story in Angelek, but in this version my informant said it had happened in mythological times. In both versions the "one-blood" sibling incest was behavior quite outside the range considered to be human, but in Umbi it was an historical fact, while in Angelek it was an ancient myth.

Parent and own-child incest was also considered to be a crime punishable by death, but I was told of no instances. I did learn of one case of a mother's brother marrying his one-blood sister's child. This raised only mild comment and raised eyebrows in some listeners as the genealogy was given to me. This couple eventually became the parents-in-law of one of my assistants, causing some interesting complications for the younger couple but nothing that could not be worked out.

Women who were already married were considered ineligible to form sexually active relationships with either married or unmarried men, and death to both the adulterous woman and the man was the traditional outcome. While a woman was traditionally a sexual partner of only one man throughout her life, and was strangled and buried with this man upon his death, a man could marry two or more women throughout his lifetime. In Umbi there was one polygamous man, and in Angelek, two. My genealogies show one, rarely two polygamous men in any given community. I knew of only two men who had as many as four wives. All of these were either recognized as *midan* or aspired to be one. My genealogies also show some men with no wives who were considered *midan*, men of reputation and managers of communities or hamlets.

No man should take a second wife without his first wife's agreement. And for the marriage to take place at all, the new wife must also have shown her agreement by choosing the already married man to be her husband.

Just as women are ideally, and largely in fact, the aggressors in courtship so they are also given complete choice in the eventual selection of the man they wish to marry. The woman desiring to marry a reluctant partner in courtship goes to her close kin, particularly her brothers, and asks them to help her trap the man in marriage. The aim is to lure the man into a house in which the woman is hidden, and then lock the door on the couple and stand watch outside in case the man tries to escape. If the reluctant man is unsuccessful in escaping and remains in the house with the woman overnight he and she are considered *nangin*, married. I was told that the brothers, who were often trading partners of their sister's boyfriend, would invite the innocent man to a singsing at their hamlet, promising pork or perhaps an opportunity for collection of a debt. The "setups" were often elaborate and frequently worked. But I also heard and witnessed some remarkable escapes, for example, a man breaking through the walls of the house.

Although in theory only one night together constituted proof of a marriage, there was always the chance that the man would escape after the fact and disappear for a very long time. Therefore, the woman's brothers stood watch outside the house for days ("for as long as necessary," I was told), until the man gave up any hope of escaping marriage (and all that it entailed) and paid shells to the guards to leave.

My assistant Ningbi was captured by Ihime one night when illness left him too weak to escape. Her brothers lured Ningbi into a village house built by Ihime's parents. The next morning I was told at breakfast time "Ningbi and Ihime are *nangin*." Ihime had been courting both of my assistants for months, sometimes with and sometimes without another young woman, Tihime. I was aware that things were getting serious as both young men told me often that they were going to leave and to live elsewhere, but I was not sure who was going to catch whom or when, and the marriage took me as much by surprise as it did Ningbi.

Much of the information that follows comes from my opportunity to examine closely the course of this marriage, from courtship through the significant first months of the newlyweds.

Immediately upon the mutual and public recognition that a marriage is a fact, the bride and groom cease all activity but that which is most essential to maintain physical life (they may go to the bush to relieve themselves and they may bathe in the river), and they cease nearly all social interaction aside from that with their closest primary kin and with each other. The cessation of all physical activity is considered essential, Ningbi told me, because "they are weak." They can do no household tasks, nor may they work in the garden. They will be given small amounts of cooked food to eat. Most of the time they sleep, I was told. This weakness may last a week or more, but gradually the pair regain their strength. At this point, a complex series of tabus affecting both bride and groom similarly severely restrict and restructure their interaction with all their own cognatic kin and that of their spouse, whether alive or dead, resident or nonresident.

The newly married man and woman may not use the name of any affine (other than that of the spouse), nor may they use the word from which the name was derived or words it resembles in sound or meaning. Since most names are derived from the common vocabulary, the effect of this tabu is that there is a major change in every married person's speech as they begin to substitute alternative words for those now singularly tabu to them. Kaulong call this form of speech *marid tok* (language of the married). At first I thought this to be a common language separating the married from the unmarried, but this turned out not to be the case as the choice of alternative words and the particular set of spouse's cognatic kindred (including both ancestral and contemporary persons) give each married person individual distinction in their speech. Alternative words are drawn from the total lexical pool of Whiteman languages (Kaulong, Sengseng, Miu, Karore), but may also include words from other languages that the newly married person might know. For example, Ningbi told me shortly after his marriage that he was speaking nothing but *tok pisin* and "Kimbe" (a place, not a language, on the north coast of New Britain where he had picked up some foreign vocabulary while working on a plantation). He was fairly sure that no one else (aside from me) knew enough *tok pisin* to have used it in naming any person, who might now be his affine.

Ihime, Ningbi's wife, came to me several weeks after the marriage and asked, "Where is 'Lukas'?" I had never heard of anyone by this name and asked her to repeat it. She said, "Lukas, Lukas, you know, the one who works for you." "Do you mean Ningbi?" I asked. "Yes, Lukas. I call him Lukas." I thought I understood that names of one's own spouse were outside the tabu and Ningbi that night agreed with me. "But she can't use the name of my deceased grandfather, who was also called Ningbi so she decided to call me Lukas." I was right that no one else was called Lukas, a safe choice. But *ningbi* also means "to cut the bush, to clear a garden or place," and Ihime used various circumlocutions to tell me where people had gone and what they were doing in the forest.

It takes rather a long period of time before each married person is set in their new lexicon, and when newly married and unsure of the extent and nature of the name/word tabus they tend to remain remarkably quiet and verbally hesitant. Ningbi and Ihime had a longer time than usual before each of their mutual kin were separated into affines and consanguines. Ihime's father was her mother's *wiheng* (mother's brother), a marriage which raised a few eyebrows but only that. However, because of this irregularity, the newly wed couple was unsure of which among their mutual cognates would now be considered an affinal, rather than remain consanguineal, kin. These decisions were not theirs to make. They told me that the big men would decide. Ningbi and Ihime had called each other brother and sister. Although descended from a remote brother-sister pair, their genealogies could not be separated as easily as would be possible had Ihime's parents married properly.

After a few weeks the newly married couple began to emerge from their almost total isolation in the house and to mingle once again with a few of the residents, but in their movements and in their speech they were considerably restrained.

A married person may not eat or drink in front of any affine (other than their spouse). Neither may they eat any food carried on an affine's head, or over an affine's body, alive or dead; nor walk over an affine's body, whether buried in a hamlet or sitting in front of them. Nor may a newly married person raise any part of their own body above that of an affine. With these tabus, neither bride nor groom may visit each other's natal *bi*, or any *bi* where affines are buried. They may not eat any food from an affine unless specially carried and prepared to meet the restrictions.

These affinal tabus serve immediately to separate the married from their married and unmarried kin, as well as from their affines. Typically, newly married couples move to a garden clearing and hut and reside there. Since males marry late in life, most have established gardens to which they may retire with their new bride. If necessary, because there is no garden at which they may be isolated, either the groom's kin or the bride's will allow immediate removal of some of the necessary restrictions so that the couple may reside with or close by one or the other affinal parent-couple. There is, however, a permanent, life-long restraint between affines to marginalize the married couple from too close or prolonged daily contact with either group of living affines and from their ancestral affines' place of burial. Married couples do not permanently reside in the *bi* with which they affiliate, but rather in their gardens isolated from unmarrieds and from other married couples.

Throughout the months following a marriage there is a carefully orchestrated exchange of shells between the consanguineal kin of one of the married pair and his/her affines. The timing of this exchange is in the hands of the affine and each exchange signals the removal of one of the behavioral restrictions in relation to that affine only. For example, when Ningbi and Ihime emerged from their initial isolation, one of Ningbi's consanguines gave him a shell and told him to give it to his mother-in-law. His mother-in-law accepted this shell, and I was told that he could now direct speech to her, but in a very quiet manner. He gave his father-in-law a similar shell. Then Ihime was given a shell by her mother to give to Ningbi's older brother, and another to his mother's sister. Shortly after this, shells were similarly exchanged as each walked behind a selected affine with a shell before presenting it to that person. Now the newly married person could physically place him/herself behind that affine. Shells placed on an affine's head removes the tabu of eating food carried on that person's head, and shells placed on the grave of an affine removes the tabu of complete avoidance of the affine's hamlet. The married person will always avoid walking over an affine's grave, as indeed a married person must never walk above or raise his arm over or threaten any affine in any way.

These nonaggression tabus are never erased, and the same is true of the tabu on calling the name of an affine or eating in front of an affine. To do any of these things is to cause great shame to the affine. Just as a brother-sister couple should never fight but should support each other in all endeavors, so should affines never fight and should work to support each other. The nonaggression between affines was overtly mentioned in many contexts. If a person was in a fight or a battle in which an affine was on the opposite side, neither person should enter into the fray. I was told the story of one man who continually brought trouble home to his brothers, who eventually grew weary of battling one of the groups their brother had enraged. So the brothers encouraged a sister from the other group to marry their aggressive brother so that he could no longer engage in fights with his in-laws, and peace between the two groups was reestablished.

One day several months into Ningbi and Ihime's marriage, Ningbi came stomping into my house and said he had divorced Ihime. Since in Umbi at that time, divorce was considered out of the question, I did not take him literally. Shortly after this, Ningbi's parents-in-law walked into Umbi and proceeded to take seats under my house, where I had my cooking fire. I whispered to Ningbi that they were there and he turned away from me, saying nothing. I went below to greet Sakhun and his wife and we all heard Ningbi stomping above. After a while Ningbi came down, and his parents-in-law told him that Ihime was at their hamlet; then they left. Having been carefully instructed in all the terrible consequences of breaking affinal tabus, I asked Ningbi how he could remain above and even stomp above his in-laws' heads. "Because I wanted them to know I was really angry," he replied.

Why one should not eat or drink in front of any affine is, I think, as much related to this nonaggression tabu as it might be to a sexual connotation. Eating, and to some extent drinking, involves showing and using one's teeth. In Kaulong, exposing one's teeth is a sign of animal-like aggression, hence the wearing of pig's tusks by *midan* and others when engaged in the most confrontational human activity—pork-exchange and fighting. Men have their own teeth artificially blackened, making them nearly invisible; while women's teeth become desirably dark through chewing betel. Even so, when laughing, one covers one's mouth to hide the teeth, I was told. And, finally, one man pointed out some human teeth among the many dog's teeth strung together in his decorative belt. He said that these were teeth of his consanguineal relatives, and when he danced at singsings, affines of these relatives would have to pay him when, in all innocence, they ate or drank in front of their affines' teeth.

Married people are marginalized in yet another manner, as the reference and address terms which have previously been used for them as single people are now altered to reflect the couple's reincorporation into the society at a very different level of participation. I remember the great puzzlement I had when Ihime's mother came to me one day and said, *"Inu ani?"* (Where is [my] mother?). I knew her mother was dead and mine was far away, and as I searched further in my genealogical memory I could come up with no one. *"Inu* who?" I asked, and she said, "That one who married your helper." "Do you mean Ihime?" "Yes," she replied. Then her husband arrived and asked for *Iok* ("father"). "Do you mean Ningbi?" "Yes."

Later that night Ningbi explained it all to me saying that now that they were married, Ihime's parents called them "mother" and "father" just as the younger couple used the same parental terms to refer to the older. These terms were now reciprocal, whereas when Ihime was unmarried she was called "daughter" (*eduk*) and Ningbi "son" (*widuk*) by her parents. When Ann Chowning told her own Sengseng informants about this, they said, knowing Ningbi and Ihime well, that this change in terminology comes when the couple first has sex. Ningbi did not volunteer this information to me. This does not seem unrealistic as I was told that a young couple were expected to be virgins at the time of marriage and that sometimes it would be weeks before they would speak to each other much less have sex. I suspect (but do not know) that Ningbi and Ihime were both virgins but that other marriages I witnessed in Angelek more likely took place after the first sexual intercourse.

A change in sibling terminology also occurs when a brother or sister marries. The same terms are used by both married and unmarried to refer to the married sibling. When the speaker is male he calls a married parallel same-sex sibling *widasuk,* and a married cross-sex sibling *pumu.* When the speaker is female, she calls a married parallel sibling *epa*, and a married cross-sex sibling *pala.*

FINAL EXCHANGES

The final ritual of marriage is often held six months to a year after the "capture" of the groom. A date is set and agreed upon at which relatives of the bride and of the groom gather and carry out the final exchanges. The exchanges I witnessed were all held at the groom's hamlet. Prior to the actual day, relatives of the groom speculated on whether the bride's kin would sacrifice a pig (an option) in exchange for the pig that was expected to be killed by the groom's kin. Days before the event shells were examined, polished, and refurbished with new decoration by both groups of relatives. The pig was killed early in the morning, and one of the first transactions was for each of the groom's kin individually to place one or two shells on the pig's body—totalling about twenty shells to go with the pig—which are not expected to be reciprocated. While shells form the basis of bride-payment, certain *midan* threatened to demand *mokmok* stones, although I never saw any paid in the five marriages in my records. In Angelek money was sometimes demanded when the offered shells were poor, and as employment cutting timber on the north coast increased, *tambu* shells available there were occasionally demanded as a part of the total package.

The rest of the event consists of *potupan*: the equal matching and exchanging of shells. Up to a dozen shells at a time are offered, one group defiantly placing (sometimes throwing) them on the ground in front of their adversaries, who can then choose whether or not to *potupan* and exchange shells with each individual. This can become quite competitive, and one group may be embarrassed by being unable to find shells of sufficient quality to match those of the other. This exchange may take hours. And, finally, shells are given by the bride and by the groom to any affines in attendance who have not previously been given shells in order to remove specific restrictions.

The shells placed on the pig, and the pig itself, are distributed to the bride's group. Those individuals who have played a significant part in the "growing up" of the bride, principally by feeding her taro and pork but also by offering specific services such as curing, receive the shells as payment for their services. Brothers, as mentioned above, do not receive any of the shells or any of the pork. They are not paid for their services because their services continue. Their final service would be to strangle their sister, and the twenty-shell payment on the pig is marked for this. So, should a sister not be strangled (as is the usual case today), these shells must be returned. Recall from chapter 6 that in the story of the three brothers, the man pays only his wife's mother and father; the girl's brother is not mentioned.

Marriage permanently marginalizes the couple in relation to the central clearing with which they affiliate. It is also true that married couples are placed in a medial position between hamlets. Typically, they live in their gardens, which may be some distance from the hamlet—from one to three hours' walk. Between their gardens and the hamlet are the gardens of the unmarried affiliates who frequently also sleep in the *mang* of the hamlet. Separated from the unmarried, the married are also separated from each other, being on the outer circle of affiliation surrounded by the forest. Sexual jealousy among married and unmarried is high and spatial separation is considered to be one way to control aggression. Married couples only come into the hamlet for collective affairs such as singsings and to trade with others who visit there.

While married life isolates both men and women from others, if the separation is too long, people begin to talk about the couple's too great attention to sex. Sexual intercourse is considered to be so inhuman as to preclude my getting any solid data concerning either sexual life or conception beliefs. This was true for Ann Chowning as well. I once saw what I thought was the ideal opportunity in Umbi to discuss these issues with three married women who were my very good friends and informants at a time when there was known to be no male within miles. There was great embarrassment as I asked them to "tell me how children are made." One woman, with eyes to the floor, said, "When we first have sex we put a shell on the man's thing." "Yes?" There was no more coming. I have never seen women so paralyzed and in such obvious pain from the questions I asked. I was placing them in an impossible position: although I am sure they wanted to answer, they could not verbalize the extremely sensitive and, I believe, also shameful topic. I went on to other matters, to the obvious relief of my friends.

Another opportunity presented itself while I was returning from a major singsing lasting more than thirty-six hours at a hamlet ten miles distant from Angelek. As we walked home through the forest together, a recently married young woman turned to me and asked, "Is it true that white people have medicine to stop babies?" I could not force myself to follow up on this. I was not only physically exhausted, but also hot and hungry, with many miles to go, and I knew I could not convince my mind to remember anything I heard at that moment. The woman left soon thereafter to join her husband in Wewak.

It is important to emphasize that while the tabu about speaking of sexual intercourse and conception applied equally to men and women, conversation about menstruation and childbirth frequently took place in mixed company. Even though these events are intensely polluting to men, I got almost as much information on these subjects from men as from women.

SIBLING RELATIONS AFTER MARRIAGE

A consanguineal brother maintains close contact with his married sister and, through her, with her children. In return for his attention and care, his sister and her children will visit frequently and contribute labor and goods to his enterprises. Older married sisters, as mentioned earlier, will frequently act as financial caretakers for younger brothers, for, unlike their brothers, sisters are not competitors and are considered to give the most helpful advice and to represent a very safe deposit for the young man's valuables.

A brother's obligation to his sister's children is greater than a father's obligation. A father, it is said, will care for his children if he desires and they in return will help their father if they wish. Competition between father and son is expected, and a son does not need to remain with his father. But a mother's brother must care for his sister's children. He can *pul* (entice) his sister's children to his *bi* and raise them there if he feels that they are not doing well living with their father. A mother's brother frequently works to attract his sister's son and may try to sponsor him in the tooth-blackening initiation rituals because the sponsor receives prestige through management of this important affair. A sister's daughter is often enticed to her mother's brother's place, where her uncle may encourage her to make a marriage choice among his young male affiliates, perhaps even his own son. In his relationship with his sister's children, a man thus comes in direct conflict and competition with the children's father. This conflict is not among equals, for the mother's brother has rights that can only be overridden by prior action by the child's father.

A brother's main obligation to his sister's children derives from his obligation to strangle his sister upon the death of her husband, so that she may be buried with him and continue the marriage in the afterworld. Although pacification brought with it a prohibition on strangulation of widows, my information on this practice comes from many personal accounts involving my male informants, who as brothers reported personally strangling a sister, or as sons had been forced to strangle their mother when their mother's brothers were not available. My latest firmly dated case occurred in 1959, five years prior to my hearing the story from the son. "When I hesitated, my mother stood up and spoke loudly so all could hear and said that the reason I hesitated was that I wished to have sex with her—she shamed me." There was no doubt that all my informants had found the obligation to be emotionally shattering and they expressed relief that now an external power had released them from this aspect of their brotherly obligation.

When a man was near death, word was sent to his wife's brothers, who immediately traveled to a place close to their sister. There they prepared a special knotted barkcloth and awaited final word. When they heard of the death of her husband they came quickly to their sister's side and looked after her while the grave was dug and her husband's body was placed within. The widow was given betel nut to chew, but no water or food, while she sat by her husband's grave through the night until dawn. At dawn she was strangled: her brothers took the knotted barkcloth; while one sat in her lap holding her down, another placed the cloth so that one knot pressed against her windpipe and the other two knots closed off the flow of blood to the brain. Death, my informants assured me, was easy and quick; the woman lost consciousness rapidly without struggle. The brothers then placed their sister's body in the grave with her husband and closed the grave.

Today, with such strangulation outside the law, brothers still rush to their sister's side when hearing of her husband's death. They fear in

A regional "big man" shows how pig tusks
should be worn to challenge someone.

Lipok, a "big woman" in Angelek, and her daughter-in-law

The very influential leader Maklun (*extreme right*)
discussing shells during a marriage exchange

A typical household scene includes women, children, and a pig

A very unusual mokmok, acquired by this man's grandfather
in trade for the region's first steel axe

A portrait of a "big man," showing dreadlocks colored with red ochre

Lemli, the albino headman of Angelek,
looking over his shells before making an offer

Men sing while drumming on shields and hour-glass drums.

Two young girls, dressed in their best skirts,
dance arm-in-arm at an all-night singsing.

During the night, with their spears and shields ready,
men from one group challenge another group.

The wife of the singsing host establishes peace
by carrying a glowing firestick between the opposing lines of men.

The morning after the singsing, the pig is speared.

At the conclusion of the singsing, a woman clowns
in front of a man who holds the pig's jaw.

some cases that the sister will hang herself out of shame, and so they will immediately pay her husband's kin for their sister's shame resulting from the implication that she will remain sexually active after her husband's death.

There were, of course, exceptions to such strangulation in precontact days, but they were rare and in almost every case involved either an exceptionally powerful man paying for the widow's shame and immediately marrying her; or mothers of exceptional children who were still nursing; or an exceptional woman herself, who dominated her own brothers and chose a second husband. I know of fewer than half a dozen such cases.

In Angelek and Umbi, one result of the cessation of strangulation of widows is an almost entirely new class of kin: grandmothers. True to the nature of Kaulong women, these largely postmenopausal women are playing a significant role as they work to support their sons. Some widowed women manage the daily affairs of their deceased husband's *bi*, scheduling the harvesting of the resources and often the singsings held there. And they are acknowledged to be skilled at raising grandchildren and pigs. Younger widows often remarry.

Children whose mother's brothers killed their mother were now bereft of both parents. Younger brothers of their deceased father were considered to have some responsibility for raising the new orphans. The youngest brother was supposed to remain unmarried (i.e., unaffected by female pollution) just for this role of caring for married brothers' children. However, the Kaulong considered a father's younger brother's interests to be inconsistent and divided. Today, when mothers are not strangled but often remarry, stepfathers are rarely considered to be interested in their stepchildren's welfare. It is when young children are orphaned that they are often removed from their father's place to their mother's brother's place and there come under his direct care and control. When the sister's children grow older and if they so desire, they can demand payment from their mother's brother for his part in strangling their mother and depriving them of her nourishing milk and maternal care.

When a mother's brother dies and his own young children become

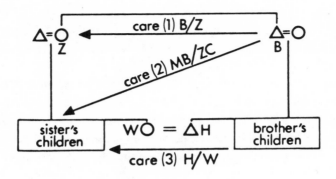

FIG. 6. Transfer of a brother's responsibility

orphaned, his resident sister's children may hold his wealth and valuables in trust for his own children. But since the sister's children are *da songon* ("of the skirt") to their mother's brother's children, the latter (as they come of age) regain their inheritance and also their slight dominance in the sibling relations as *da mulu* ("of the barkcloth") to their father's sister's children.

In a sense, the mother's brother's children replace their own father in his obligation to care for his sister's orphaned children, an obligation which underlies the dominant *da mulu* relationship involving care and control.

It is when obligatory care (of the brother for his sister and sister's children) translates into inherited care (of the brother's children over the sister's children) that sexual control and sexual desire among cross-siblings become somewhat ambiguous (and remember that the Kaulong always strive to achieve ambiguity). While there are a few cases of a mother's brother directly marrying his orphaned sister's daughter (in the case of Ihime's parents, for example), it is recognized as desirable for a sister's daughter to marry back to her mother's natal place, often choosing a son of her mother's brother. Thus, a consanguineal cross-sibling relationship (where intimacy, care, and obligation go with prohibited sexuality) is transformed into an affinal cross-sibling relationship where the same intimacy, care, and obligation lead to permitted sexuality.

The Reproduction of Siblings

In this concluding section I present what I believe to be the model of and for marriage among the Kaulong. Clearly, the Kaulong are extraordinary in their traditionally held view of sexuality/asexuality as a basic distinction informing their social world to the extent that individuals of both sexes are spatially, socially, and linguistically distinguished according to whether they are sexually active and married, or celibate and single. I believe that in Kaulong society it is more important whether one is married or single than whether one is male or female.

It is my understanding that the model of the Kaulong social and natural world is one that is basically asexual—one in which elements replace themselves through reproduction of substance. A plant metaphor for the human self is apparently valid for the Kaulong as it is characteristic of other Papua New Guinea societies (e.g., Panoff 1972, Herdt 1987, and others). Most tropical plant reproduction is viewed by Kaulong as asexual.

The Kaulong world presents a problem for Kaulong men: sexual reproduction of humans is animal-like, thus the Kaulong can either culturally deny the bisexual role in reproduction of persons (as in the Trobriands [Malinowski 1929] or on Malo [Rubinstein 1978]) and maintain the biological fiction that females alone reproduce the next generation or accommodate it and acknowledge bisexual reproduction as human behavior. The Kaulong resolution of this problem is to recognize the role of both sexes in the production of humans—as given in the common phrase: "When I am old and ready to die I will marry to have a child to bury me and replace me"—but to admit at the same time that this behavior is not only dangerous to male life but also shamefully inhuman. "They are behaving like dogs" is said of couples who are thought by others to be spending too much time together in sexual activity. "Too much sexual activity" is also the comment if a wife becomes pregnant too soon after the birth of a previous child. A woman is shamed to be pregnant if still nursing a two- or three-year-old child and usually kills (throws away) the infant upon birth. To refer to any sexual activity between husband and wife is considered an extremely shaming insult—as I had innocently done in the name of my science by questioning my friends about conception. The shame of sex between even husband and wife may derive both from its animal-like nature and from the similarity of the spouse cross-sibling relationship to consanguineal, "one-blood" cross-sibling relationship—thus making all intercourse incestuous, animal-like, and shameful.

In Kaulong the central justification for sexual activity seems to lie in reproduction alone. This is reflected in the change in kinship terminology used between parents and children when the child is known to be sexually active. After marriage, the term *inu* (mother) is used by the parents of both wife and husband for a married female child/daughter-in-law, while the term *iok* (father) is used similarly for a married child/son-in-law. These terms come into use not upon the successful capture of a husband by a courting wife, nor upon the birth of a child. These terms appear to be more appropriately considered as reflective of the referent person's engaging in reproductive activity rather than of parenting in an enculturative sense. To the Kaulong, the meaning of both "mothering" and "fathering" is *kuk*, "to give birth to," to reproduce one's self. Feeding, nurturance, cultivation, growth, and instruction, while characteristic of the mother or the father role, are not restricted to those roles nor are they distinctive to being a mother or father. Only a mother and her designated sexual partner for life may give birth to a replacement who replicates their substance.

I return now to the all-important model that siblings represent in the Kaulong world. Recall that in the origin stories of ancestrally placed cognatic kingroups there was either a pair of cross-sex siblings at the apex or cross-sex children of the founding male who subsequently either "fathered" (*kuk*) a line of descendants or "mothered" (*kuk*) an associated complementary line. From this reproductive activity comes the division of descendants according to whether they were reproduced by the sister, *da songon*, or by the brother, *da mulu*.

The model is one in which a set of cross-siblings reproduce themselves in each succeeding generation. Since the cross-sibling set cannot, like plants, do this by cloning, it must reproduce itself sexually and this incestuous, animal-like activity is shameful. I argue here that the self-reproduction of cross-sibling sets can be interpreted as a cultural *denial* that sexual activity is necessary for life, for immortality, or the regeneration of self. Likewise, the unisexual male view of the world is a similar denial. The ideal would seem to be to have males able to reproduce themselves without marriage, as they are able to reproduce all else of value in the world.

While I have emphasized the unisexual model of the Kaulong cultural world, I believe the model can be viewed more appropriately as an asexual one in which gender distinction is not important. In this asexual world the separateness of the male and female elements appears subordinate to the unity of the asexual sibling bond itself. Only in certain situations in which there is conflict over shared resources is the male, or that derived from the male (children of the brother), considered dominant over the female, or that derived from the female (children of the sister).

With the above concepts in mind I now turn to examine more closely the situation in which the reproductive resources of an ancestral place are themselves a major consideration. Marriage to someone who is not a "one-blood" brother may be seen as a resolution of conflict among one-blood brothers over the reproductive resource embodied in their one-blood sisters, which like all resources is to be shared. We must recall that a brother does not profit from his sister's marriage because, they say, it will affect her children in whom he has some interest. A husband, in paying for his wife, does so in order that she will remain with him in life and death and give him exclusive sexual access. He marries in order to reproduce himself ("when I am old and ready to die, I'll marry in order to have a child to replace me"), but it is also apparent that he does not have exclusive rights to her reproductive powers or products.

The expected conflict over a woman's reproductive ability is resolved differently when there is only a single child born than when there are multiple or no offspring. A single child is seen as a replacement for both the mother and father and conflict over this single replacement, a major resource, may be considerable. As in all such conflict over shared resources the dominance of a brother over a sister comes into the resolution. A mother's brother considers that he has greater claim over his sister's productivity than do her husband's brothers. Mother's brothers consider the single child to be their sister's replacement in their cross-sibling set and demand their sister's child to return permanently to his/her mother's natal place.

With multiple children, only one child (usually, but not necessarily, male) will be expected to replace the father in the father's place. It is important to have a replacement to bury the father and to maintain the replanting of the fruit and nut trees of the place. A second child (usually, but again not necessarily, female) is expected to replace the mother in her natal place, often marrying a male from that place, or if male, attaching himself to his mother's brother's establishment, whether married or single.

If a couple is unproductive or past reproductive age and childless through the death of offspring, then the husband and wife too are considered socially dead, for although they are married, their assumed sexuality is without meaning. I was told that sometimes the couple would commit suicide to make explicit what was implicit in their nonreproductive and therefore contradictory "married" relationship. Reproduction, like all else in Kaulong life, is an individual responsibility. While adoption does take place, it is usually not for replacement. I know of no case where the adoptee was considered the adopters' replacement; rather, the child was thought to be the birth-parents' replacement. It is for this reason that I consider that replacement for humans must involve transference of biogenetic materials to the young, the same process acknowledged in the regeneration of taro from the stalk or a coconut from its sprout, and a process typical of other tropical vegetation.

Individual children are expected to have considerable choice in their own placement as they gain adulthood. As discussed above, sister's children, when young and orphaned, frequently are taken to their mother's brother's place, where they are raised, nourished, and controlled. As these children become adults they share in the resources of their mother's place, but also are subordinated (born "of the skirt") to their mother's brother's children in regard to these resources. However, they are in a dominant position with regard to the resources of their father's place because they are "born of the male." It is this principle, that children of men have prior rights to resources, that apparently balances the dominant rights of a mother's brother over a sister's child. When the children make the choice of where to live, where to contribute their labor, they do so according to their personal judgment of where they may realize the maximum of self-potential. This is true of both males and females. Women, I was informed, choose their husbands based on their estimation of the man's political and economic potential, and men choose their residential affiliation according to where, as they say, "important things are made to occur." Men change their residential affiliation as frequently as necessary to achieve peace, power, and wealth.

In summary, then, the resulting model of Kaulong society is one in which individuals as well as sets of cross-siblings reproduce themselves by replacement of substance in a specific locality or *bi*. Substance is not gender specific. For the Kaulong, the brother-sister relationship is both an expression of reproduction and a denial of bisexual activity. A brother cannot engage in incestuous reproductive activity with a one-blood sister, so the sister is in effect sent away from the *bi* to be impregnated by another. It is as if the brother, like the male pigs and dogs of the place, chooses castration. Like the domestic sows and bitches, his sisters must leave to be impregnated by "other" (wild/inhuman?) men but are expected to return to the *bi* with their young. The brother, or his replacement, can marry the sister's daughter who returns to replace the sister in her natal hamlet.

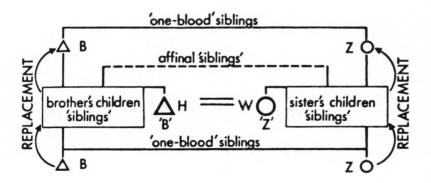

FIG. 7. Replacement of cross-sibling sets

The model then resolves itself into one in which sets of cross-siblings replace themselves through time, transforming the incestuous, one-blood sibling relationship into a controlled, affinal "sibling" relationship in order that each partner in the affinal set may reproduce the biogenetic substance of their respective natal places and associated one-blood siblings.

The fact that each affinal partner reproduces his or her own biogenetic substance derived from his or her own heritage, rather than each contributing, in a complementary way, to the formation of a new being is what distinguishes the Kaulong concept of self and reproduction of self. This concept appears to be derived from the model of the tropical vegetation rather than of the animals living in the forest surrounding them. Just as their human origins were in most cases trees or vines, which, through cloning, produced the ancestral sibling pair, so these sets of cross-siblings continue their existence by reproducing each component of the complementary "of the male" and "of the female" lines. By reproducing themselves they maintain the substance of their shared identity with each other, with the ancestral place, and with the first, one-blood sibling set.

8/ Singing in the Forest

In *Sound and Sentiment* (1982), Stephen Feld broke new ground in Melanesian ethnography by detailing the cultural significance of song and sound among the Kaluli of the forests of eastern New Guinea. Much of what he writes shows significant similarities with what I report for the Kaulong. Both the Kaulong and the Kaluli live in the deep forests and both have developed an appreciation of, and a symbolic system encompassing, the sounds of their world. I am not a linguist or ethnomusicologist, and I did not focus my field researches on Kaulong song and sound. However, it was impossible for me to live for a single day or night among the Kaulong and not recognize the cultural significance of song and sound, which is for them as deep and meaningful as it is for the Kaluli.

Music is everywhere in Kaulong. People sing in their houses, while leaving the village and walking along the forest paths, and as they approach a known clearing. Children learn to sing almost as they learn to form meaningful sounds in speech. Men and women sing the same songs and with the same tonality, so that it is often difficult to discern which gender is singing. Almost all extra-hamlet gatherings involve all-night singing. All-night singing with affiliates of only one hamlet is also frequent. In fact, it seems that when people gather in large groups, they sing first and transact business later. Singing is often competitive between groups and may supplant or precede physical violence and courtship.

While singing is the most important and diffusely significant musical event, instrumental music has its own place in the daily life of the Kaulong. I begin with a discussion of four instruments, three of which are made from bamboo: *lapulil*, flutes; *lawi*, panpipes; and *larasup*, bunched pipes. Drums (*lambu*), in the typical Melanesian hourglass shape, are an important accompaniment to the songs. Players make their own bamboo instruments, but the drums are imported.

INSTRUMENTAL MUSIC

Umbi women introduced me to flutes, but it was in Angelek that I encountered flutes and panpipes (of both varieties) in sufficient numbers that I had opportunity to appreciate fully the versatility of these instruments.

Bamboo (*kaut*) is used for both flutes and horizontally fixed panpipes. The flute is considered to be a woman's instrument. Some men practice and play it, but they are not considered to play it as well as women. My own observation verifies this. The horizontally fixed panpipe is a man's instrument (although some women learn to make and play one, they prefer the flute). The third bamboo instrument, the *larasup*, a bunched group of pipes, is exclusively an instrument of mature men although younger men will apprentice and practice.

Lapulil *(flute)*

Women make their own flutes, collecting bamboo on their way home from the garden and quickly drilling two holes near the distal solid end using a smouldering twig, and cutting or burning out the V in the mouth end. In blowing, the lower lip covers three-quarters of the hole and the air is expelled across the V. Breath control and fingering provide a range of notes of two to three octaves. Some women have perfected their playing of flutes, using air blown through their nostrils.

I attempted to learn the *lapulil* and after many months had mastered the scale and was having fun composing my own tunes. My friends then suggested that it was now time that I learn how to play the flute! What they meant, of course, was that I was still ignorant of how to produce meaningful music. Even though every player is expected to

FIG. 8. Flute (*lapulil*) (actual length: 24 inches)

Song of the *lapulil*

make up her own song, there are parameters to this composition, structures that I still had to learn.

Blowing the flute not only takes breath control, but it also takes considerable lung capacity, as long runs of notes without pause are considered commendable. In Angelek two women were noted as being superior in their ability to play their "tune and variations" lasting up to five minutes or more.

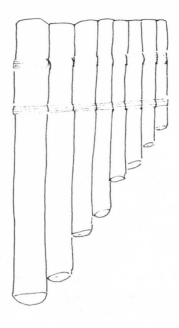

FIG. 9. Panpipes (*lawi*)

Song of the *lawi*

Lawi *(panpipes)*

For a two-month period in Angelek, the teenaged boys and young men went on a panpipe binge. Stimulated by the delight in being able to hear themselves play through my tape recorder, they cut and fashioned countless *lawi*, of every size and tonality. One lad, who was recuperating in my house from a severely cut foot, made a two-pipe *lawi*, on which he composed a "dance for my toes" in order to make his foot exercises more interesting. Most of the pipes have from six to eight tubes, carefully matched as to the bore of the pipe and then cut to provide the appropriate scale. The tunes are individually composed and show a variety of rhythm as well as tonality.

Big men said that if the young men blow *lawi*, they will increase their lung capacity and be able to walk long distances and sing strongly all night. I did not hear this said of women's flute playing, but the same would be true even if not emphasized culturally. Men also said that when they go along roads they play the *lawi* and it makes the "road short." More importantly, a traveler playing the *lawi* is announcing both his presence and his peaceful intent.

Both *lapulil* and *lawi* are capable of being bespelled with love magic. The tune then carries the magic and so bespells the hearer that he or she follows the tune to its source and cannot be turned away.

The *lawi* binge came to an abrupt end one day when a young boy cut his hand rather badly while collecting bamboo for yet another panpipe. The big men in the community banned any further cutting of bamboo for panpipes, "because *kaut* is angry at all the cutting"— another illustration of urging moderation and restraint when dealing with the forest. They went on to tell me that before they had steel knives they often made knives of split bamboo.

Larasup *(bunched pipes)*

Through all the recording of panpipes, the players kept saying that I must get Posin to play his *larasup*. They described it as another kind of panpipe. I was getting rather tired of panpipe compositions and did not press the matter, but one day Posin arrived "to play for me."

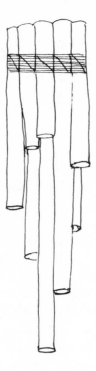

FIG. 10. Bunched pipes (*larasup*) (actual length: 16 inches)

The *larasup* is a collection of bamboo pipes of different lengths fastened in a circle around the longest pipe and held in place with two braided bands of pandanus. The player holds the bunch in one hand about six inches from his mouth, and while he blows a steady stream of air he moves the pipes around so that they pass through the stream of air in succession according to the desired sequence of notes. The resulting sound is one of whispered and somewhat blurred tones. Rhythm is achieved by moving the *larasup* through the air column, and a trilling effect is created by blowing through loose, fluttering lips. The versatility of the *larasup* is remarkable. The skilled player uses this range to convey a sound-picture of animals in the forest and of humans in the clearing.

It is with the *larasup* that old men tell stories in the men's house.

Typically, Kaulong stories involve characters speaking in song (see below), but in this case with the *larasup* imitating the speech of the characters.

STORY OF ASIS (GRASSHOPPER)

There were two women. They had no husband. They were unmarried. They went to the forest to cut firewood. They returned to their house and heaped the firewood inside. [Asis sings]

"What is that thing that cries inside the firewood?" one woman asked the other. They go to look and throw the firewood outside into the rain and look again and cannot see anything. [Asis sings again.]

The two women then threw the firewood to the other side of the house and looked at it again and cannot see anything. [Asis sings again.]

Then the women throw the firewood again. When they throw the piece with Asis in it, Asis sings again.

Then the two women grab their axes and break open this one piece of firewood and find Asis. "Sister, here is that one which sings," they exclaim together. The two women now marry Asis.—Posin

The trilling of the song of Asis is also found in the story of *Lapapimlo* the dragonfly, or again in *Asanga* the butterfly.

"Lapapimlo goes to the flower to drink"
(The *larasup* here imitates the dipping of the tail as the dragonfly drinks)

"Asanga flies away"
(Here the trilling of the *larasup* sound imitates the flutter of the wings as the butterfly flies away.)

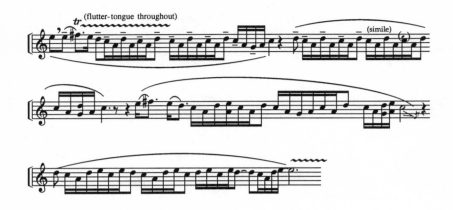

Song of the *larasup* (Song of Asanga)

SONG OF KAIYUGE'S WIDOW

"Kaiyuge dies and his widow wails beside his grave."
(The song of the *larasup* follows the typical woman's death
wailing, called *tinisli*.)

Song of Kaiyuge's Widow

SONG OF YUNGUL (FLYING FOX/FRUIT BAT)

"*Yungul* flies to a tree and sits there hanging upside down."
(The *larasup* rhythmically imitates the slow flight of this huge
bat and then, with a quickening beat, marks the bouncing up
and down as the bat settles down to sleep hanging
suspended from the branch of the tree.—Posin)

Song of Yungul

SONG OF KOKOMO (THE HORNBILL)
"*Kokomo* sits on the branch. He flies away."
(The slow whoosh made by the hornbill's wings as he flies
through the forest is imitated here, the pace of the flight
varying.—Posin)

Song of Kokomo

Posin's youngest son, Peiying, was learning the *larasup*, and when I
returned to Angelek in 1974 he played for me some of his original
compositions. He emphasized that he was just trying them out, that he
did not feel he had the sound quite right. One of them was about
Naiyong the inchworm:

"*Naiyong* was eating a tree and decided to go down to the ground."

Peiying explained that the Naiyong song was:

Naiyung, naiyung, naiyung
Nai a koli, nai a koli, nai a koli
Inchworm, Inchworm, Inchworm,
I go now, I go now, I go now.

Song of Naiyong (breath on every beat)

Listening to Peiying sing the words and play the *larasup* made me realize that an attempt was made to imitate speech as well as forest sounds.

The ability of the *larasup* to speak seems to have allowed the unspeakable—sex—to be expressed. For example: the words and sound rhythmically accented, "*wiak koli, wiak koli,*" was said to be *tok nogud*, "dirty talk." Peiying said, "You can't put this one in words, you must just think it." Mature men playing the *larasup* in the hamlet men's house may feel it possible to discuss sexual matters when the audience does not include women.

I feel I have just tapped the surface of the range of the *larasup* as an instrument in which humans can speak without words. Reproducing the multiple voices of the forest and human sounds of the clearing, players recreate these sounds, showing extraordinary sensitivity and appreciation for the least to the most important elements in their world.

The Drum (lambu)

The hourglass-shaped, hand-held wooden drum (*kundu* in *tok pisin*; *lambu* in Kaulong) is widely distributed in the Kaulong region and elsewhere in the interior of southern West New Britain. Most of those I saw were imports dating one or two generations back, and a few were new acquisitions made by men while working on plantations. While the drums were imports, they were newly fitted with lizard-skin heads in the bush. The drums and skins were important trade items.

I remember the day when my assistant Nakling was brought his deceased father's drum, which had been held for him by his mother's brother. No one had used the drum for the five years since the father's death. Nakling, full of pride, negotiated for a lizard skin and spent the day gluing the skin to the drum with tree sap and tying it securely with a narrow vine rope. When the sap had dried sufficiently he began tuning the drum by affixing pellets of beeswax arranged in the center of the drumhead. That night, partly in honor of the drum, but for additional reasons, Angelek held a singsing, a *dikaiyikngin*. Because it was a purely local event, only a dozen or more men beat drums as they circled the clearing and sang while women danced. The following morning, a man from a community about six miles distant came to Angelek and told everyone that he had heard the voice of the drum of Nakling's father for the first time in years and had come to find out who it was who had taken up this voice again.

To my untrained ear, one drum had sounded like any other except for variations in register. Clearly I was wrong; every drum has its own voice when properly tuned and played. And people know these voices, and know who is playing and singing and where, often many miles away from the origin of the song.

After I had taped countless song ceremonies with the accompanying drums, I asked my informants which of the tapes they thought to be the best. Without hesitation they referred to the small event in which Nakling had played his father's drum. "Why was it the best?" I asked. "Because you can hear the voices of the drums and the words of the songs—no crying babies or giggling women to cover these up." I had thought some of the large events with more than two hundred people singing were the best. Once again I was reminded that I was applying my own musical values.

I had taken with me tapes of music from around the world. Once I played the Yoruba drums of West Africa. Although Yoruba drumming is considered extremely complex and superb by many Westerners, the Kaulong simply commented, "They don't know how to play drums!"

Kaulong use their drums as percussion instruments in many different kinds of song performances. Where the singing is local only, with no "outsiders," only drums will be used; but in those events at which outsiders are expected, men take their spears and shields along and rhythmically beat one against the other to accompany the beat of drums and songs. A new sound has been introduced in places where there is access to tin cans. Flattened cans or lids are crimped around the end of the spear and when the spear is struck against the shield, the tin provides a rattling sound.

SONG AND SONG PERFORMANCE (SINGSING)

The human voice raised in song (lut), either solo or in chorus, is the prime musical instrument of the Kaulong. Everyone sings: men say they must sing well or be shamed; and all women sing, but the element of shame is not expressed as overtly or as often by them. Children learn to sing by attending lutngin (singsings) with their elders, by observing and listening, and by experimenting in play singsings about the hamlet. In their teens, they begin to participate with their elders. Often in preparation for an uncommon type of event, rehearsals will be held for days, if not weeks, in advance.

In Umbi I was able to attend a number of lutngin, at which I taped segments of the mandatory twelve-hour, dusk-to-dawn singing; however, most of my tapes were made while working in the Angelek region. I was also able to tape songs in my house both in Umbi and

Angelek, sung expressly for my tape recorder. The "live" recordings were of events that ranged from fewer than twenty-four participants to more than two hundred. In no case did I choose to record the entire twelve hours of the normal singing, rather I recorded segments, somewhat at random. Where there were several groups competitively singing, I moved from one to the other as they took turns singing, but when they tried to "out-sing" each other, my musical guides told me to stop recording as "it was no good singing." I learned to time my segments by the clock rather than by "song" and thus captured the significant pauses, the "tuning up" of voice and drum, as well as the discontinuous verses. However, in a number of cases where the form was unfamiliar to me, I neglected to capture a complete song, because I did not recognize until too late the nature of the continuities. My two assistants learned to operate my tape recorder, and I often gave it to them to carry as they participated in the singing; they, of course, emphasized what was important to them.

As I recorded these events, I had little opportunity to gather transcriptions and translations of the songs. However, I returned to Angelek for two months in 1972, expressly to work on transcriptions and translations.

Lutngin *(Song performances)*

Song *(lut)* is found in a number of contexts: as lullabies, in storytelling as a form of speech, and in song performances. It is the last form that I emphasize here. It is my belief that it is in the song performances that individuals display their knowledge in various categories, choosing what and how much to expose to challenge from others—and by so revealing their capabilities, to either gain or lose some degree of prestige and fame.

Some types of song performances are more competitive than others, particularly those called *lut a yu*, where pigs are displayed and killed and where people from two or more communities are involved. Indeed, in these most competitive events, outsiders arrive armed with shields and spears ready to fight: "We carry shields and spears to the singing to fight." Men do not often know of any specific cause for a fight before they arrive, but they expect arguments to break out between groups. The hosts try to keep everyone singing rather than fighting; therefore, the singing itself frequently turns into a challenge between groups. In spite of everything, a spear fight may break out in the early hours of sunlight.

There are four major types of song performances: (a) *dikaiyikngin* (singing around), (b) *lut a yu* (singing with pig), (c) *sasungin* (tooth blackening), (d) *sasokngin* (death). Other types include: (e) *laugnin* (with skull), (f) *tubuan* (masked figure); and two introduced forms, both from Arawe-speaking groups: (g) *sia* (a masked dance from Siassi), and (h) at a girl's puberty. In this chapter I will discuss the first two, *dikaiyikngin* and *lut a yu*, and also the *tubuan* and girl's puberty songs. In chapter 9, I focus on the death rituals and songs, the *sasokngin* and *laungin*.

A *dikaiyikngin* is a type of song performance that typically involves only those affiliates of the hamlet in which the performance is held. The hamlet leader must first agree to an affiliate's desire to hold a song performance. Soon after darkness falls, the singers (male and female) begin to walk slowly counterclockwise around the hamlet clearing, beating a drum or two and taking turns in leading the singing. Once begun, the song performance *must* continue until first light, approximately twelve hours hence. All members of the hamlet group take part; men and women lead the singing but younger members may try out the leadership role. Very young members sing along, and the infants fall asleep in their caretakers' arms, lulled by the rhythms of the song.

The role of song leader rotates among all men and women who desire to take it up. A song leader makes the decision as to which song to sing and hums and sings a line of chorus or so (what I called the "tuning up") until ready to begin. The leader then sings each new line while the others join in the chorus. In this way, the choice of new line is the leader's, and this is what makes the song his or her song.

In a *dikaiyikngin* there is no competition. This is where songs are learned, however, and participation by the nonleading singers is enthusiastic. I was told of only two people in the entire region who were said not to like to sing and who did not attend singsings. Although boys and girls both learn to sing and take leadership roles in the *dikaiyikngin*, boys say that it is important that they sing well or the girls would laugh at them. As I discuss below, in the larger *lut a yu*, men sing together while the women dance—a division of labor not found in the smaller events.

Hamlet leaders hold *dikaiyikngin* for a variety of domestic reasons:

1. To make things of the hamlet grow, i.e. coconuts, buoi, nut trees, and pigs and children.

2. To settle disputes among hamlet members.

3. As a payback.

4. As a *kapti* (*tok pisin*) celebration of comings and goings of a hamlet member.

5. As preliminary singing(s) to a major singing event, which may involve home hamlet members for up to five nights before the final competitive *lut a yu*, when a major tusker pig is to be sacrificed. These preliminary *dikaiyikngin* may also involve host hamlet members for months as they gather to prepare for the major event.

Making things of the hamlet grow through song performance involves singing special songs that focus on the development of coconuts, pigs, or children. Since the ancestors are also buried in the hamlet, I believe that there is some idea that the energy expended by the collected affiliates imbues the *bi* with song-sound—and proof of the continuity (immortality) of human existence there in the clearing.

Settlement of grievances through *dikaiyikngin*, rather than other competitive forms of song gatherings, seems to occur when the *midan* desires to reestablish peace within his domestic group or between his group and that of an important ally. Earlier I discussed the case of Mikail and his new wife Wiame, who had argued and injured each other while resident with Mikail's parents. Kamil, Mikail's father and the *midan* of Angelek, called a *dikaiyikngin* in Angelek that night and sent word to both Mikail's nonresident kin and Wiame's kin some distance away to come. Toward midnight, after five hours of singing by the locals, Mikail's kin arrived and joined the circling singers until dawn. Kamil then gave his daughter-in-law a number of shells to give to each of Mikail's attending kin in compensation for her action. When none of her kin showed up, Kamil asked for a second night of singing. They still did not arrive, and it was judged that they felt that the greater wrong was Wiame's and they would ask for no compensation.

Another instance was of a *dikaiyikngin* held to bring a young man to a hamlet where he was asked to pay the husband of a girl he had previously courted. He countered that the husband should pay him all the money and material goods he had given to the girl while she was courting him. In the conflict resolution following the singing, it was agreed that the husband was wrong to demand pay from the former suitor. Ningbi, who also had refused to pay Ihime's former boyfriends, said, "It's like poker—the winner doesn't pay back the losers."

I was indirectly responsible for a payback *dikaiyikngin*. Some of the Angelek young men heard news that there was to be a *dikaiyikngin* at Lapalam, a community with many affinal ties with Angelek but some ten miles distant. They went to Lapalam, arriving several hours after dark, and discovered everyone asleep and no ceremony. So they woke up some of the community, saying that they had come to sing. Then, I was told, the Lapalam group "had to get up and sing" with them. Months later, on the last night I was in Angelek, I finally fell into an exhausted sleep only to be awakened about midnight by visitors from Lapalam demanding that we get up and sing with them for the rest of the night. They explained that this was a payback. They also told us they expected a *kapti*, literally, "cup of tea," celebrating my departure. The fact that we had had a number of these in the preceding weeks did not impress them.

In these modern days people leave and return with greater frequency, involving greater distances, so *kapti* are held quite often, particularly in the good weather season. *Kapti* and *dikaiyikngin* are held whenever the *midan* wants to gather affiliates and kin from other hamlets. Getting everyone to the hamlet may precede a request for labor in building a new house or garden, or it may suffice as a fitting conclusion to such a task. It often seemed to me that a *dikaiyikngin* was a very efficient means of gathering large numbers of people to a hamlet for an extended period without having to provide beds or even to feed them.

Lut a yu *("Singsings with pigs")*

These singsings always involve members from different places, the hosts who provide the pig(s), and the visitors who will be presented

with portions of the pig(s) to take back to their own hamlets for distribution. Preparation for these events varies widely in time from a few
days to a year. The stated reasons for holding a *lut a yu* also vary, from
a simple individual decision to sacrifice a pig (e.g., "because I had a
dream last night"), to the elaborately planned affairs involving the
exhuming of the skull of a big man and those in which a tusker pig is
killed. Pigs are killed at singsings held to commemorate deaths, the
building of a new hamlet men's house, a child's full tooth eruption, the
final night of a tooth-blackening ritual, or any event that the *midan*
decides is important enough to so commemorate.

Prior to the *lut a yu*, the host group may hold many consecutive
dikaiyikngin as they make everything ready. Often at the final event,
the local singers are so hoarse from their singing that they can barely
talk. They say, however, that singing will make their voices strong
again, and, indeed, such seemed to be the case. During the day of the
final night, the pig(s) are brought to the *bi* clearing carried suspended
from their legs on stout poles. They are set down in a shady space, the
pole held on cross poles supporting their weight as they lie on their
backs in a slight hollow in the ground. Here the pigs lie throughout the
night.

Hosts begin singing at nightfall (approximately 6 P.M.). Women usually sing with the men during this early part of the affair. Invited
visitors are expected to appear a number of hours later, typically between 9 and 11 P.M. It is impolite to arrive too early. When it is known
that the visitors are nearby, the hosts regroup themselves in preparation. The visitors gather below the hamlet and put on their finery: the
dog-teeth belts, the pig-teeth ornaments, clean clothes, and sweet-
smelling powder and flowers for the young men, and the elaborate
fiber and flower skirts for the young women. When they enter the
hamlet, they do so in a massed form, singing loudly and in unison and
rattling their spears against their shields. They often shout hunting/
fighting cries in their song. The visiting group marches around the
clearing and then takes up its place on the edge opposite their hosts.
Visitors and hosts then alternate in song presentations, and, faced
with the competition, the host group sings with renewed energy.

A really large *lut a yu* may involve three or four visiting groups, and each group begins to compete with the other. First, the competition is in alternation of song and involves the women. Women and young girls, dressed in their finest fiber skirts, dance in twos and threes, arms over each other's shoulders and whistling shrilly through their teeth or fingers. They dance in the area between the men's singing groups, which are spaced around the edge of the clearing. As the singing becomes competitive, the women are seemingly drawn to the group currently singing, and they perform their hip-swaying dance in front of the men. The women come from several groups, and the men of one group become jealous of the men of other groups as each group in turn attracts all the women to dance in front of it.

In one very large singsing held at Dulago, the hosts and visitors began to advance on each other in alternation. First, the women carrying long, thin sticks danced up to the opposing group of men, who held their shields in a protective stance. The women danced threateningly in front of the opposing men while the men of their own group followed them, holding their spears "at the ready" at eye level and shifting their weight in a fighting dance. Then this group retreated, to be followed by the women of the opposing group and their men; and so it went, back and forth, for a while. Suddenly one group did not retreat, but turned to face the approaching women and men of the opposing group. They stared at each other with spears only inches away from each other's faces. The dancing women from both groups (with me among them) fell to the ground and scurried out of harm's way.

The fight did not escalate this time; the host's wife carried a firestick between the two groups to establish peace. It is also quite possible that fighting did not break out because Ann Chowning and I were both observers. This was the closest I saw the competition come to actual fighting. It seemed to me that the position of the women in the middle between the groups of men had the effect (if not the intent) of defusing the tension between groups, as women's clowning seems to do at other times of high tension, for example, during marriage transactions.

The singing continues until dawn. When it becomes light the pig is taken out and placed in the center of the clearing with a visitor usually being asked to kill it. Pigs should be killed only on the *bi* ground, where their blood may wash down on the bones of those buried there.

The pig is speared, and, as it squeals, the host group sings to drown out the pig's death cries. It is felt that someone might capture the pig's cry and make sorcery on it and so poison those who would eat its flesh.

During the cutting of the pig into the two major portions, the head and the body, women may clown, donning men's clothes and ornaments and making obscene jokes about the men. It is also during this time that the young men and women (not involved in the pork transactions) move away from the clearing and court each other. If fighting does break out in spite of all efforts by the hosts, it, too, must take place away from the clearing.

Pork is then presented to selected visitors who agree to pay for it later. This presentation may be enormously complex and take three or four hours, particularly when more than one pig is killed.

Visitors then leave around noon with their pork. If they come from far away, they will partially cook the pork on the way to preserve it. Major cooking and distribution take place at the pork receiver's hamlet.

The Songs of the Dikaiyikngin and Lut a yu

While the form of the performance is distinct, many of the songs of the *dikaiyikngin* and *lut a yu* are the same. All of these songs follow the same internal structure, so I am illustrating them together. Some comments concerning my methodology are in order.

As I began my serious work with the tapes, I first discovered that no one in Angelek would help transcribe and translate songs of the Umbi region because, they told me, these songs belonged to the singer— even when the "same" song was also sung in Angelek ceremonies. But because each singer has the right to sing the song his or her way, the songs become personally owned through specific performance in time and place. My Angelek translators would offer to sing the song "their" way, but would not "translate" the Umbi tapes.

During the two months I had available to me in 1974, I managed to transcribe and translate more than three hundred songs, with the help of many of the Angelek singers, but principally Mili, the aging former *luluai* of Angelek. I had initially sought the help of those fluent in *tok pisin*, but halfway through I discovered the well-known fact that to translate poetry one needs someone fluent in the language of the poetry! Mili was such a person: an elderly man whose physical and political power had significantly diminished, but whose intelligence and knowledge of the language had not. He was a very poor speaker of *tok pisin* (often ridiculed by young men), but he had the time and patience to attempt to convey the subtle distinctions of the poetic phrase by acting out the meaning for which he had no words. It fell to me to try to match these actions with English words. Translations that follow here are to be considered approximate. I hope, however, to convey a sense of the songs, poetry, and sounds. I do not attempt here a close analysis of meaning and metaphor.

It is in these songs that individuals display their knowledge in all categories: geography, geology, genealogy, botany, zoology, magic, pigs, people, and places. Young singers list only the most familiar names in each category, and often forget a name and substitute "la la la, etc." in place of a name. It was in analyzing the songs that I gained much of my understanding of the management of knowledge (chapter 2). Once when one of my singers was singing of places along a road in a distant place, a visitor from that region told me (after the singer had left) that "he didn't get it right, he hasn't been there," thus challenging the singer's personal experiential acquisition of this knowledge.

In the intergroup singsings, individuals (supported by members of their own group) compete with each other in the presentation of their knowledge in song. They literally try to out-sing others by overlapping their performance or never letting the other group take over the singsing with the presentation of a new song. In such competition each individual and each group has control over how much knowledge is displayed and the length of the song presentation. Clearly, the performance is as important as the content. The oldest singers sing songs listing far more names in the category than the youngest singers.

One of the most interesting categories to me was that of lists of important men or women, the *pomidan* and *polamit*. When he was about ten years old, one boy sang for my tape recorder the song of "big women." The list included his mother, sisters, and aunts. When I returned five years later, his list in the same song included women of neighboring communities, as well as those in his immediate family. These songs, then, illustrate the widening network of the singer's own social world. One should not, of course, include individuals not personally known. The same rules control the naming of places along roads, streams, and rivers. If one has not traveled those routes, one should not sing those names. It is important to keep in mind that in the song illustrations given below, I have chosen songs with short "listing" sections in the interests of space alone. Big men, knowledgeable men often sang songs listing many times the number of varieties I have used as illustrations here.

While there is some variation in the form and structure of the songs, most of the songs may be divided into four parts, to which I give the labels: listing, chorus, poetic ending, and final lines. My translators and I found it useful to use my labels since Kaulong do not use terms to refer to the separate elements.

Songs are recognized by their *chorus* line and category of subject matter. The *poetic endings* are two or more lines, which constitute what I call the nonvarying poetic element. The *final lines*, while nearly untranslatable, indicate the origin of the song, for the most part. For example:

"SPEARS RATTLE AGAINST THE SHIELDS"

In this song the *listing* is of types of palms used to make fighting spears, and the *chorus* refers to the sound made in singsings when the spear is used to strike against the shield to produce a rattling sound (*a klong mei*). The *chorus* usually begins and ends each separate listing.

NAME OF SONG

Le legi a klong mei
spear rattles (as it strikes the shield)

LISTING AND CHORUS

a klong mei li pali a klong mei
areca palm rattles

a klong mei li enghak a klong mei
? palm rattles
a klong mei li wili a klong mei
? palm rattles
a klong mei li no wetwet a klong mei
? palm rattles
a klong mei li nomal a klong mei
black palm rattles

POETIC ENDING

a klong mei miuk wo
rattles (at) fighting place
miuk wo yia keke
(at) fighting place fire ants
miuk wo wisu
(at) fighting place (the) sea eagle (maningula)

FINAL LINE

edowango
affine-mine

The *listing* usually goes from the smallest (or first) to the largest (or last) in each category. The sequence of names may vary according to the singer's desire, but the final name is usually the biggest, or generic, name for the category and should immediately precede the *poetic ending*. In the above song, the spear called *nomal* is made of black palm known to grow only in the Miu region of the far interior and is a widely sought-after trade item.

The final part, the *poetic ending*, does not (or should not) vary from singer to singer. One common feature of this segment is the balancing opposition of images as in the above: *miuk wo yia keke* (fighting place small biting fire ants) with *miuk wo wisu* (fighting place sea eagle, the largest of winged creatures which may eat people).

The *final line* is almost untranslatable. By pressing my informants, I was able to get some ideas as to the general meaning of final lines. I was told that these endings were the most traditional part of the song and often indicated the kind of occasion at which the song is sung and often the regional origin. I will return to a summary of these endings later.

In all I translated 154 songs that list things. In descending order of frequency they are: birds (55), big men (24), big women (15), rivers and streams (9), places (7), cassowary food (6), crotons (5), palms (5), bats (4), spears (4), lizards (4), pigs (2), fish (2), ginger (2), and one each of the following: dogs, bananas, coconuts, trees, snakes, housebeams and bedpoles, vines, taro, pepper leaf (*daka*), and reefs. Songs listing birds constitute the major category in my collection of songs. I believe that my collection is random enough for me to state that the dominance of birds is of cultural significance and not due to any bias in collecting. However, I cannot claim that I have an adequate sampling from which I can discuss the relative importance of the other categories. Since my sample contains songs sung "live" in song performances, as well as those sung expressly for taping in my house, I may well have a skewed sample. I have selected songs for variety and because they pleased me.

In giving examples of these "listing" songs below, I have omitted the repetitions and many "la la la" syllables.

1. "BIRDS CRY THE SPEAR (BLOWGUN DART) IS COMING"
The bird Truk cries the spear is coming
The bird Rau cries the spear is coming
The bird Pula cries the spear is coming
The bird Rau cries the spear is coming
(The singer repeated a name which is permissable but not admired.)

The bird Kadaruk cries the spear is coming
The bird Miling cries the spear is coming
The bird Wisu cries the spear is coming
[POETIC ENDING]
The spear is coming into the married house
The married house at Eloi
Eat until full, eat without noise
[FINAL LINE]
tom sail ailo, lail laililo

This is an ending from the coastal Arawe language group, early and traditional, but I could get no translation.

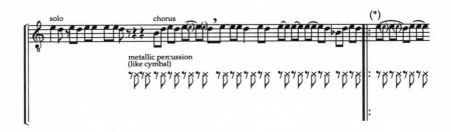

(*) On repeat, whistling indefinite, random
pitches on beat with upward glissando;
on later repetitions, whistling is varied
in rhythm, pitches remain random.

Song of the birds

In the above song, a number of "mistakes" were made. One should not have to repeat any bird's name; and in the case of all "bird" listings, four birds should finish the song: Rau, Kahok, Pula, and Wisu. Wisu, the sea eagle, is boss of all the birds. I find in my sampling of fifty-five bird songs that rarely were the four birds listed in a consistent order, only that in all of them, Wisu concludes the listing.

Without giving other examples in full, here I will demonstrate only the range of *chorus* variation in the bird category. For example: "birds cry (wail)"; "birds sing"; "birds drill a tree" (woodpeckers); "birds scratch the ground"; "birds slip and fall"; "birds are speared in the breast"; "birds laugh at you as you walk by"; "birds strike the tree branch"; "birds warn of a snake's presence"; "birds carry taro"; "birds talk about their food"; "birds commit suicide" (hanging of widow); "birds carry messages"; "birds rot in the grave"; "birds support each other"; "birds joke"; "birds travel a long way."

My informants say that sometimes the birds are *tamberans*, "deceased spirits." This would explain the humanlike activities of some of the bird listings, but, of course, other activities are characteristic of birds not humans. I discuss the human spirit after death in chapter 9.

The cassowary (*kukiung*) has his own song, naming the food that it prefers.

2. "THE CASSOWARY SINGS OF THE FOOD IT LOVES (*WAMINGO*)"
[listing followed by chorus]

I go (looking) for Warut, I love it
I go for pungil, I love it
I go for Eun (mango), I love it
I go for hus (passion fruit), I love it
I go for Eun, I love it
I go for Waho, I love it
I go for kili, I love it
I go for yiahop (malay apple), I love it
I go for Yihus, I love it best of all

[POETIC ENDING]

A spear thrown flies by me and stands up over there
A spear thrown comes and pierces me
(It) holds me and throws me down on the ground
Holds me and throws me down on the ground
Inside the grass of the graveyard at Mumbo
His legs surround me
His hands surround me
He holds me (I) fall down

[FINAL LINE]

yia si wok ho mihing, yia minmin e wamingo
Smoke spirals over cassowary, fire is cold, I love it.

The cassowary is a very special inhabitant of the forests, and it may not be considered a bird at all (although I did not formulate the essential question that would determine this). Cassowary is featured in a number of stories and is often referred to as *wiheng* (mother's brother); and like the mother's brother, it is someone who is called upon to help people (his sister's children) out of difficulties. However, sorcerers can take the shape of *kukiung*; when meeting the cassowary, one never knows whether it is truly a creature or a human being. In either form, the cassowary is considered dangerous.

Song of the Cassowary

3. "RIVERS SWIRL AROUND"

[this song begins with a paired opposition]

Thrèe men dance around each other

Three women dance around each other

[LISTING]

The river Silingi swirls around

The river Kalang swirls around

The river Uni swirls around

The river Apaon swirls around

[POETIC ENDING]

It carries with it a vine called Sihim

[a strong lawyer vine is strung across flooded rivers]

All hold it [the vine] at Selu
All hold it [the vine] at Wanu
What is it that goes on top, what is it?
The head of the river, the head, what is it?
The mouth of the river, the mouth, what is it?
[FINAL LINES]
Edowango imili
Affine of mine swirls around
Holul yia honehul
Listen the fire is out, the place is empty

This ending, from the inland forest regions, is old and traditional. The rivers and streams named here are all in the region in which the Kaulong language is spoken. The Apaon is the major river in this region and appropriately ends the listing.

4. "DOGS HOWL"

Dogs howl at Monio
Dogs howl at Dulu
Dogs howl because they dance
Dogs howl at Yangin
Dogs howl at Lingi
[POETIC ENDING]
Dogs howl on the grave
Dogs howl on the ground
Dogs howl on the rainbow
[FINAL LINES]
My affine, the Dog howls
Listen, there is no fire
(All places listed are *bi*, hamlet clearings where
    deceased affiliates are buried.)

The next two categories of song list big women (*polamit*) and big men (*pomidan*).

5. WOMEN BUNDLE FIREWOOD

Sister Molme bundles firewood
Sister Susun bundles firewood
Sister Paulme bundles firewood
Sister Belerope bundles firewood
Sister Lasinbo bundles firewood
Polamit bundles firewood

[POETIC ENDING]

Bundles firewood, she goes into the women's house
Into the women's house, into the men's house

[FINAL LINES]

Affine of mine, bundles firewood
Listen, there is no fire

All the women named here were resident in Angelek at the time of my
study. Lasinbo was the eldest and a true *polamit*.

6. "BANANAS, HALF-EATEN" (VARIETIES)

Half-eaten bananas there called a *bilil*
Half-eaten bananas there called *a sauip*
Half-eaten bananas there called *a siamen*
Half-eaten bananas there called *a noa*
Half-eaten bananas there called *a wisu*

[POETIC ENDING]

Half-eaten on the place cleared,
   [where ground is broken for garden]
Heap ground in basket, put leaf in basket

[FINAL LINES]

Affine mine *Ewikwik*
Listen, the fire is out

The *Ewikwik* is an insect that eats bananas, and the song belongs to
him. The heaping of ground and leaves put in the basket are said to be
the insects' food. It seems obvious that there is a metaphorical reference here. But I could get no further explanation.

7. "GINGER FRAGRANCES (YOU COME HERE)"

E hun your aroma come here

Sem your aroma come here

Nehuwi your aroma come here

Urong your aroma come here

Serem your aroma come here

[POETIC ENDING]

Your aroma catches the woman's breath,

It comes to a woman with upright breasts,

It comes to a woman whose breasts have fallen

[FINAL LINES]

sel dowango

Affine-mine aroma comes to you

Spears come together, spears come apart

(I am unsure of the translation of the last line here. It is an ending not heard very often and I received variable translations that were clearly guesses on my informants' part.)

Some songs outline a sequence of action in relation to a person, animal, or plant, as in the following example.

8. "TARO HARVESTING SEQUENCE"

Taro pulls up easily (dry soil filters back into hole)

Lift it out easily, it comes, you go get it

Lift it out strongly (hole remains open)

Comes out strongly you go get it

Pile up the taro, pile, pile

Scrape off the dirt, scrape, scrape

Mumu (cook) the taro, mumu, mumu

Pile up the taro, pile, pile

Mumu the taro, mumu, mumu

Uncover the mumu, uncover, uncover

Put the taro in the basket, put it, put it

Eat the taro, eat, eat

[FINAL LINE]

Sail, sail it goes, you go get it

The listing (naming) songs are the most common in my sample. But to show some of the variety of song, I give below songs from the *sasungin* and *tubuan* ceremonies and that of the girl's puberty ritual. The last is certainly imported and recent, the second probably imported but much earlier in time. The first is traditional to the region, but is rapidly becoming obsolete as young men move about outside the bush and realize that they are "different," with their jet black teeth acquired in their initiation rituals, at which *sasungin* are sung. Some men manage to scrape the coating off their teeth, while other young men object strenuously to having it applied. The songs, then, are becoming lost to many of the younger generation.

Sasungin, *Tooth-blackening Singing*

The *sasungin* takes place nightly while the young man lies in the men's house with the mineral manganese oxide (*egit*) plastered to the outside of his upper and lower teeth. Each evening the hosting group begins the singing and is joined later by selected outside groups, a different one each night. On the final night a pig is brought in and tied up and singers sing in front of it. The pig is killed in the morning, and the pork is distributed.

I attended only one *sasungin* held in Lapalam, at the outlying hamlet belonging to Maklun, the very powerful leader of the region. I went with some closely related kin of Maklun who had been invited for the next to last nightly singing. For weeks, Lengme, the mother of one of my assistants, herself from Maklun's hamlet, coached the men and women of Angelek in how to sing *sasungin*. The ritual had not been held in Angelek for some years. When we arrived in Lapalam we waited in a relative's house for the appropriate hour to go to the hamlet to sing. The young men and women were very hesitant and some never did go to the singing. They said the next day that they were shamed because they did not know the songs very well. I went with Lengme and her husband, and, as was my usual fashion on these slippery mountain paths, I fell en route. I gave it no thought, but my host considered it significant. Maklun asked us to stay for the final night's singing and the following morning presented the pig to me. He said he felt sorry for me, for I had fallen on the path and I had "sung" for two nights. Thus I entered into Maklun's pig network, providing desired cash, while my friends who went with me supplemented the payment with the required shells.

Women's clowning was also a part of the morning activity following the final night of *sasungin* singing. And there was a distribution of cloth to the clowns. Some of us received leaf packets of cold rice to eat before we returned home.

The *sasungin* singing is done while walking in a circle counterclockwise around the clearing, with men and women joining in together in singing the songs. The structure of the songs is distinct from that of both the *dikaiyikngin* and *lut a yu* discussed above, in that they do not have a chorus or list of names within a category of objects nor a concluding set of standard lines. Rather they consist of consecutive lines sung without repeats.

1. *"ELASI"* (A WIDOW WHO WILL BE HUNG)

[a widow not to be hung is called *wamoh*]

Sa kuhi por kang

The kuhi tree is toppled by the malais

Por kang e meouk

Malais is its name

Elasi Elaisak

The widow (who will be hung) named Laisak

Kerkerlau i me kus

(My) skin itches all over, I scratch

Elasi e Pomalngin

The widow waits at Pomalngin

Elasi eul lelwhal

The widow dances with her killer

Elasi epit mulul

The widow waits for her brother (who will kill her)

Esling e kwen kwen

The grass Esling makes a big noise

(I am not sure whether the last line belongs with those preceding because there was some interruption.)

2. "A MAN, *AIWUNG*, WALKS ABOUT"

Aiwung kineses Dawilo

Aiwong comes up to (knows) Dawilo (near Rabaul)

Na kuk kiok ewingo tobikok

"I must return home tomorrow"

Na wa wud to ka kiok tobikok

"I get a woman and we both will go home tomorrow"

Kisang ko yiang a sun poriru

Leaves fall in a heap

Ekak on song a sun mi yange

Pandanus grows in my mother's place.

Na ku kiok e Wihinu tobikok

I wish to go back to Wihinu tomorrow.

King wili ong sapot a Wihinu

A bird has killed something on the road to Wihinu

Sa Gimi balus sung Kaulung

Spears of Gimi meet the spears of Kaulong

King wili ong sapot i whalo

A bird killed something along the uncleared road

Na ko kiok Miange tobikok

I want to go back to Miange tomorrow

3. "THEY SHOOT ME"

Erioie Kumbunke ilio leloe-ol

Shoot me at Kumbunke and shields stand upright

Erioie Kumbunke ilio mulpas-ol

Shoot me at Kumbunke and shields move

Erioie Kumbunke yiama leluwi

Shoot me at Kumbunke and I die

Erioie Kumbunke susu le mori

Shoot me at Kumbunke my red blood flows and I die

(This song is not complete on my tape)

4. "THE TAMBERAN" (GHOST)

Ai Yungun sangkin li tingting tokin

The tamberan Yungun picks at his sore on his leg and he
sobs quietly

Daso marap lo bit enghik ko bit ko bit
   Aunti (FZ) looks at the blood that flowed
Daso marap lo bit engun pakikulu-kumu
   Aunti looks at the edible greens inside the lawyer leaf
   bundle
(repeat of last line)
Yungun sangkewin engul a linglingio
   Tamberan got his sore from edible greens
(repeat of first line)
(I have no other record of the tamberan Yungun that might
explain this song.)

5. "LITTLE CUCUMBER"

Ililua karim yiputsun
   Frighten him, little cucumber hanging there on the leg of
   its mother
Ililua o ililu karim mili ma li nuk
   Frighten him, frighten cucumber, he falls down and stops
   there
Ililua karim hwuk ma li nuk
   Frighten little cucumber, he stops there and stinks now
(One of the *larasup* stories concerns a little cucumber who
leaves its mother and gets lost. The little cucumber calls out,
"*na kuki, na kuki* [I am here, I am here"] No one ever
explained to me why cucumbers in particular are depicted in
story/song as leaving their mothers.)

Tubuan Singsings

I attended only one *tubuan* singing held at Pomima, an affiliated hamlet of Lapalam. The hamlet members had constructed a leaf shelter
with a couple of beds to "house" the visitors from Angelek. One of
my assistants invited me into the men's house where he was "getting
up the *tubuan*" by refurbishing the mask with newly obtained white
cockatoo plumes. On the plumes, disks of luminescent fungus was
attached, "the eyes of the *tubuan*." Finally, long streamers of pandanus were attached around the lower rim of the head-covering

mask, reaching to the ground. I was told that no woman should see this preparation.

The singing began as darkness fell, with first a *dikaiyikngin*, in which men and women sang together slowly, circling about the small clearing. After an hour or so, the singing abruptly stopped as someone said, "Listen, the *tubuan* comes." Distantly first, then becoming increasingly strong, we heard the characteristically rhythmic songs of the *tubuan* as he emerged from the forest and into the clearing. The *tubuan* walked in such a way that the plumes and the pandanus swayed vigorously as "he" beat the drum and sang his song and danced with a hip-swaying step. He was followed by the young men and then joined by the women and men waiting in the clearing. They all took up his song and with a swaying gait circled the clearing counterclockwise. After a while, the *tubuan* retreated to the forest, reemerging shortly to continue the singing. It is thus that the young men take turns in putting on the mask and becoming the *tubuan*, leading the songs, and, it is hoped, attracting the young girls to them by their skill of song and dance performance. Girls who are attracted hold onto the pandanus streamers, or are so overcome by "love" for the *tubuan* that they place their hand through the streamers, perhaps on the young man's genitals.

At Pomima, a single *tubuan* was "got up," but I heard of others where two *tubuan*s are "got up" and sing competitively. At one of these, one group was so successful in attracting women, that they forced the other group to depart "early" (by six hours), shamed by their ineffective performance.

I taped only a sampling of *tubuan* songs. Because I was unfamiliar with the format, I missed some verses of the songs because they were so discontinuous in elapsed time that I was unaware of the connection. When I was able to transcribe and translate them later I realized my error.

1. *Malis pai sungun*
   A Malis (fish) twirls (her) skirt (while dancing)
Li Malis pai ang glas
   Malis flashes its light (in its middle)
Naiyoh uluoh Enumo
   Naiyoh (insect) scares (children) in men's house

Malira iglu Rabal

    Love magic calls them all to Rabaul

Malira iglu anemu

    Love magic calls them with anemu (red leafed croton)

Sakalngin lilil ma mangin whang karagut

    Talk no good makes me shamed, hurts me too much

Wudwala Kaulung hi hak

    Woman of Kaulong pulls the canoe

Inu kukngo lungunan

    Mother who bore me, a rubbish man

Inu kukngo kaualang misan

    Mother who bore me, (with) birth blood only

Esulu lingin tobi bimiku

    Torches light the place too dark

2. AIRPLANE

Gimo lo lore o e kung katim—oh

    Gimo seduces him (*tubuan*). She takes his breath away

Engin balusio, Gimo, lo lore engin balusio

    Engines of plane, Gimo sends love magic to engines of plane

Por engin balusio, Gimo, lo lore por engin balusio

    Four-engine plane, Gimo sends her magic, four-engine plane

Gimo lo lore galasium balusio, Gimo lo lore galasium Balusio

    Gimo (sends) magic through binoculars (repeated)

Por engin por daun, Gimo lo lore por engin por daun

    Four-engine (plane) falls down, Gimo sends magic, four-engine plane fall down

Gimo lo lore

    Gimo sends love magic

3. LUNGA, THE *TUBUAN*

Wo e Lunga, Lunga kai wori

E Lunga E Lunga oh e Lunga Lunga kai wori

E Lunga, Lunga mulpasi limlut

Wo e Lunga, Lunga kruk sail

Oh e lo e lore, Oh e lo e lore, wini lawi oh oh
sa hik i oh, sa hik oh, a i li sa hik i oh
Ine mulpas io, E loi i loi ah?
Oh Lunga, all come to be happy with you
Oh Lunga, this dance makes you happy
Oh Lunga, Oh Lunga, Oh Lunga, this dance makes you
   happy
Oh Lunga, Lunga lift up your pandanus skirt
Oh Lunga, Lunga raise your feather plumes
Oh send your love magic, send your love magic,
blow your panpipes;
The spear breaks, the spear breaks
Mother raise your skirt, you go where
(I was told that this song comes from the north coast of West
New Britain, Talasea and/or Kimbe; however, some of the
phrases are in Kaulong or Miu.)

4. EUROPEANS

Pora li lain oh
li laina Portmosbi
Portmosbi, pora li lain oh
Li lain oh Morobe
Pora li lain oh
Li lain oh haus wailis.
Whiteskins go to live there
Live in Port Moresby
Port Moresby, whiteskins go to live there
Go to live in Morobe
Whiteskins go to live there
Go to live in radio station

Although my sample is extremely small for this type of song, it seems obvious that the *tubuan* is largely of recent origin for the Kaulong in spite of the insistence of older informants that they have "always had this singing." But then the participants are the young men, the ones most likely to have had out of region work experiences and to have come in contact with other performances of *tubuan*. It is also likely that the songs can and are made up to reflect the experiences of the singers, giving the set I recorded a "modern" flavor.

Christmas 1968 saw the first Catholic Mass held in the bush away from the mission at Turuk. Various communities joined together to put on three simultaneous singsings to follow the singing of Christmas hymns (in Latin) during the midnight Mass. Angelek and its neighbors were asked to sing *sia*, a dance from the Siassi region (the extreme western tip of New Britain, across the Vitiaz Straits and including the Finschhafen area of mainland New Guinea). For weeks men who had learned the dance while working in this Siassi region schooled Angelek and others in the songs, and they prepared the distinctive masks. The actual event turned into an all-night intensive rehearsal rather than a solid performance. The other two groups performed the *tubuan* and *dikaiyikngin*. While I recorded the Christmas *sia*, I did not attempt to get the tapes transcribed or translated, considering others more important to my researches.

As the *sia* is being introduced, so too is a girls' puberty singing (I have no name for it). I saw three such singsings, two attached to a *lut a yu* and following the killing and distribution of pork. The third singing was held separate from any other singing: the girl's father was shamed that he did not have a pig to kill for his daughter's ceremony and was going to ignore the event, but was persuaded to carry it out so that everyone would know his daughter was now a menstruating woman.

The songs—and ritual—all come from the coastal Arawe language, and I received only partial translations. The singers are predominantly women, but at least one older man joined in the singing. As they sing, the women take the men's dog-teeth and tambu-shell waistbands and swing them against the girl's buttocks.

1. TYPES OF SKIRT MATERIALS

Skirt Paingin come
Skirt Rupio come
Skirt Minmin come
Mountain Porikbi goes down
Mountain Selmus goes down

Mountain Mimlo goes down
All go around the mountain, it goes down
All goes around a mountain, it goes down
Oh shell come
It comes
Skirt Minmin come
Skirt Paingin come
Skirt Rupio come
(During the singing, some older women don men's clothes
and ornaments and clown.)

I leave until the final chapter the discussion of the most serious of *lutngin*: song performances of the *laungin* and *sasokngin*, those having to do with death. I have tried here to give some indication of the importance of sound and song for the Kaulong (and indeed for all those in this region). Singing is seen as an alternative to fighting. In the competitive singing with pigs, hosts try to maintain the peace during the night of singing and prevent an outbreak of fighting at dawn so that they may distribute their pork. In a number of ways the attending hamlet groups collectively can demonstrate their superior knowledge of song and strength of body (wind and voice) by out-singing other groups, rendering them almost songless as these groups try to break into the performance of a more dominant group and begin a song of their own. Dominance in such competitive singing is measured by volume of sound (the number and vocal condition of singers/fighters) and length of song (i.e., the number of verses and/or consecutive songs a group may be able to sing without a pause). I was told that some hamlet groups are so shamed they leave in the middle of the night.

The relationship of song to peace is also seen in the staging of sing-sings by a hamlet leader in order to resolve or allay conflict. Playing flutes and panpipes and, indeed, vocalizing while traveling through the forest also signal a peaceful intent. The acuity of hearing and discrimination of sound in the forest and clearing are, to the untrained ear of the European, remarkable. All sounds are meaningful; some belong to the forest and some to the clearing, and they all have names.

What is also apparent is that formal education of the young in the taxonomies of the physical and social environment is to a large extent encoded in the songs, which both list and describe features of the natural world such as the growth stages of the coconut, rivers in flood, travels between known places, etc. By learning to sing at a very early age the young men and women begin to acquire important knowledge of their world. And as their world expands, so does their participation in the *lutngin* song performances.

The emotional pull of song is significant. Those who had gone away to school or to work said what they missed most were the *lutngin*. And those who had tried to go to school in Kandrian said that once they heard the drums and songs, they had to come home. If they were to get schooling, they said, they would have to go to Rabaul, far away from the songs. Song for the Kaulong is a major component of being human.

9/ "Listen, There Is No Fire": Songs of Ghosts

THE ORIGIN OF CUSTOM AND SONG

There were three ghosts (*iwun*) who were named Akong, Aumbi and Aimngin (Homngin). They were snakelike in form and traveled underground along a road made by the sharp nose of Homngin. They came to surface inside a house where they found a man and his wife both dead. The two were left sitting upright on the bed to rot and their four-year-old son, Malangin, was keeping watch over them. The three *iwun* told Malangin that they wanted to "eat their bananas"—it was improper to use the words "human flesh." The ghosts told the boy that they would take away the two bodies and after they had eaten, they would bring the bones back. This they did. When they returned with the bones they taught the boy the songs called *sasokngin*. They also told him that henceforth all dead people should be buried in the ground, because the flesh belonged to ghosts, but that after the flesh had gone people should take up the bones and sing with them and kill pigs and then bury the bones again.

The song that the *iwun* taught the boy, as sung by Molio (Angelek), follows:

> *Mulu da mopola, mulu*
> You go outside quickly
> (chorus) *a oh, a oh, a oh, a ai*

You go . . .

Mulua yei, palupo Setlatu (chorus)

You go gather together at Setlatu

Da Wasum lo (chorus)

You gather at Wasum (on the coast)

Da Wasum lo palupo Aiwo (chorus)

At Wasum go gather together at Aiwo

Da Wasum lo palupo Aiwo (chorus) [line repeated]

At Wasum go gather together at Aiwo

Da Aiwo, palupo Kumrum oh (chorus)

At Aiwo, gather together at Kumrum

Da Kumrum, palupo a Wewep (chorus)

At Kumrum, gather together at Wewep

Da Wewep, palupo a Liklo (chorus)

At Wewep, gather together at Liklo

Da Liklo, palupo a Yangsin (chorus)

At Liklo, gather together at Yangsin

Da Yangsin, palupo a Ukur (chorus)

At Yangsin, gather together at Ukur

Da Ukur, palupo a Soplo (chorus)

At Ukur, gather together at Soplo

Da Soplo, palupo a Yiallal (chorus)

At Soplo, gather together at A Yiallal

Da Yiallal, palupo a Miung (chorus)

At Yiallal, gather together at Miung

Da Miung, palupo a Didi, palupo a Yumiel (chorus)

At Miung gather at Didi, gather at Yumiello [Kandrian]

Da Yumiel palupo a Kamlo, palupo a Pui (chorus)

At Yumiello, gather at Kamlo, gather at a Pui

[Apugi is one of the offshore islands at Kandrian]

Da Pui palupo a Keklep, palupo a Nukur (chorus)

At Pui, gather at Keklep, gather at Nukur

Da Nukur, palupo a Palik, palupo a Punu (chorus)

At Nukur gather at (river) Palik, gather at Punu

Da Punu palupo a Kinum, palupo a Kiwong (chorus)

At Punu gather at a Kinum, gather at Kiwong (chorus)

Da Kiwong, palupo a Walan (chorus)

At Kiwong, gather at Walan, you go

Da Walan, palupo a Auwo (chorus)

At Walan gather together at Auwo (the boy's hamlet)

Auwa ka suk kung (chorus)

Auwa becomes frightfully dark (with smoke)

Auwa ka suk kung, Auwa ka sa kan (chorus)

Auwa becomes frightfully dark, Auwa becomes light and
clear

[FINAL LINE]

Lingri yia si wok, yia si wok song ka wi, oh Akong (chorus)

I am hungry, fire spirals up, fire cools, Oh Akong
(name of Death), you go

DEATH AND BURIAL

The final line of Akong's song is common for many of the *sasokngin* songs I recorded, and indicates a song whose origin is in the Arawe-speaking country on the coast, referred to as "the beach" by inland Kaulong-speakers. Molio of Angelek sang this song for my tape recorder and told the story of the three ghosts (*iwun*), coming to teach the boy how to bury his parents. Some of the *bi* can be identified. Wasum is on the coast to the west of Kandrian in the Gimi region and near the mouth of the river Anu. The song then lists places eastward and along the coast as far as Sengseng country at Kinum. Akong was said by Molio to be the "boss" of the *iwun*; the song itself falls into the "listing" category of songs, and the places named were those where people gathered to hold *sasokngin*.

While the burial customs and ceremonial singing seem well-established in Kaulong, Umbi, Angelek, and Sengseng, it is strongly suggested by this story and by the song of Akong that some of these customs and songs have been introduced from the Arawe-speakers who are spread along the coast. Interesting but unsubstantiated support for a change in burial custom following the introduction of the present customs from the coast to the inland comes from an early patrol report for the interior region to the east of the Karore people.

The patrol came upon a recent death and found the body left unburied in the hamlet men's house. The people said it was not their custom in the bush to bury their dead.

Death may come prematurely, through accident or violence, or may be considered natural. The Kaulong say that every person has a preordained span of life. Old age is a period of life when the physical health and strength of the body diminishes naturally, permitting less activity relating to the input of knowledge/experience (and growth of self). At the same time, there is apt to be a greater expenditure of knowledge (and depletion of the self). The result of this imbalance may be seen in the gradual wrinkling of the skin, and later in the dullness of the eyes. Some few men and women manage to outlive their "time" and are universally respected by all who know their name for their unusual capacity and control of body, self, and mind, but sooner or later they too will die. Death is determined when the breath is gone.

All burials take place in the main hamlet house, the *mang* or men's house. Most elderly people are married and thus live in garden huts some distance from the hamlet. If death is felt to be imminent, the elderly people may move to the hamlet or be carried there by their close relatives. When death occurs outside of the hamlet, the body is carried to the clearing. As the bearers proceed, they may rest awhile and put the body down on the ground. These body-resting places are known as *pohonungin*, "something associated with death." For a considerable time following the burial, travelers passing by these "body-resting places" put a leaf or twig on the spot saying, "Here is something for you," naming a food item or material possession which they symbolically give to the ghost to forestall its taking the real object. The carriers are usually related males of another hamlet; however, a woman may not be carried by a brother or husband. A number of songs of the type found in the commemorative *sasokngin* skull cycles (see pp. 234–35) are said to be songs composed by the ghost, telling of events leading to his or her death and naming the places where she or he rested while traveling from the place of death to the place of burial in the hamlet. These songs are transmitted to and sung by a living descendant.

My assistant Nakling was taught a song by the ghost of Umul, his

mother's brother (who "grew him up"). Umul's ghost gave the song to
his sister's son in a dream and told him what had happened to him
after he died.

UMUL'S JOURNEY TO THE GRAVE

Sakalgnin me whango
   Talk comes and kills me
Nga dungdung li mau
   On the name of Dungdung (a *midan*) I swear it's true
Nga sisak li mau
   I swear it's true
Ngaiyen a li komen
   Alone, I go now
Saihi'ngin me whango
   Sickness attacks me
Whiwhingo li ko mok
   Attacks me, I go to the *mok* (married house)
Whiwhingo ko mang
   Attacks me (I) go to the *mang* (men's house)
Wer kama na wulwul
   Under the betel called *wulwul* (a small variety)
Ngai sil bi momruk
   I walk in the true (virgin) forest
Poi suk da Enopua
   Into the garden called Enopua
Si e su Elilis
   at the bottom of Elilis (a hamlet)
Poi nihing din Asa
   They gather strength at Asa (a hamlet)
Wilingo nihingome
   My arms become strong
Keiwhingo nihingome
   My legs become strong
Tok a li bi mon iok
   We two go down from the hill

Wird pana kap da gnin
  Under breadfruit that I nurtured
Tok a li Eyihime
  We two go to Eyihime
Wet lingep mordpongin
  Under the almond tree called mordpongin
Po pilil a Selu
  All come to the grass (clearing) at Selu
Mara suk ung wonu Elwul
  The three carriers see the graveyard at Elwul
Miuk kari da li nuk
  They put (me) down to stay
Miuk kilpi e lo men
  They (3) dig over there
Miuk delpi elo yiang
  They (3) dig throwing the ground outside
Miuk kari do lo nuk
  They (3) put (me) inside to stay
Miuk wuapi mulupon
  They cover with ground
Miuk yiangyiang miuk lu men
  They (3) go outside, they go over there
Marango po miuk
  I (the ghost) look at the three
Ngai yen muk ed tirinis
  I look there and she wails
Ai iwong me lukwhal
  The ghosts come calling together
Li hehuwhal wha yunggu
  Together they pull the stinking logs (all come to eat the
  stinking flesh of the dead body)
Sirenu kinesio
  My mother recognizes me
Sirenu tinis i oh
  My mother wails

Edohang Aiya Lanis

Name of my affine

[FINAL LINE]

Holul, yia honehul

Listen, the fire is finished

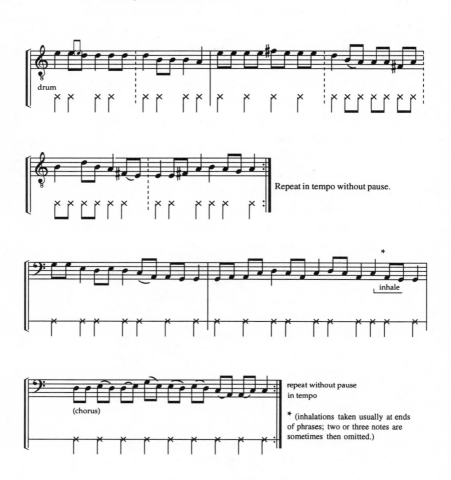

Songs of Umul's ghost

While a grave is dug in the floor of the main hamlet house, the body is laid on the bed. An incident that occurred in a hamlet near Umbi haunted me for years. The body of the deceased on the bed suddenly sat up! I asked a woman who was there, "What did you do?" She said that after the initial shock had passed, they had buried the body anyway. This evidently was an unusual occurrence; no one present had ever seen it before. Much conversation about possible explanations produced several: "The spirit had a hard time leaving," "Someone startled the ghost." With enough explanations, finding final cause is not necessary. They continued with the burial. Many years later I learned that the onset of rigor mortis sometimes causes this violent body spasm. I had thought that perhaps they had buried a person not yet dead.

News of a death is sent first to the kin of the deceased who are within a day's walk. They and the deceased's trade-network partners living close by attempt to arrive before the final burial takes place. One of the deceased's pigs (or one belonging to a close kin) is speared. Upon their arrival, all nonresident hamlet affiliates and visitors place a pearl-shell (euk) valuable on the pig's body as payment for the care given by the resident affiliates to the deceased in his or her old age, and later they give additional shells to those who labored in carrying the deceased and in digging the grave. The pig will be cooked and eaten by all but the close kin of the deceased and the pig's owner(s).

A shallow grave of one or two meters is dug. Bones from earlier burials dislodged in the excavation process are stuck back into the walls of the grave with little care to keep any natural association between the several bones. The body is placed in the grave on its side, with ankles and wrists tied together. The eyes, if open, are not closed, and a coconut-leaf basket may be placed over the head. The basket is to keep dirt out of the open eyes, for it is felt that the deceased's soul (enu) is keeping watch for its killer if the death was considered to be premature.

If the deceased was a married man, his wife was (before pacification) strangled by her closest male kin (brother, father, or son) and buried in the same grave. The widow sat by the open grave throughout the night and was given no food or water, but only betel to chew. In the morning her kin would strangle her so that she would journey with her husband to the mountain land of the dead. I heard of grieving men trying to strangle themselves in order to accompany their deceased wives to the mountain. Parents, or sometimes only the mother, might commit suicide to accompany a very young child who had died, in order that the child not lose the way to the place of ghosts.

Before pacification altered the tradition of strangling a widow upon her husband's death, the first all-night song ceremony was held while the grave remained open waiting for the widow to join her husband in the morning. Today, during this first singsing, pork is cooked and some of the flesh is burned in the fire beside the grave and later buried with the body. The singing is a local affair and the cooked pork (and taro that always accompanies cooked meat) belonging to the deceased is distributed and eaten by singers and visiting kin.

The grave is closed in the morning, and a fire is built on top to hasten the "drying" of the body. Close kin sleep near the grave during the ensuing period of time, known as the "time of the ghost," in order to keep the fire lit, to care for the deceased soul, and to keep pigs from uprooting the body (one of the reasons for burial inside the hamlet *mang*). They do not sleep inside the *mang*, but in one of the hamlet *moks*. Children are told that this is the time of ghosts and to remain quiet and not run about. Everyone uses soft speech tones. These precautions last for a week or ten days. Eventually the *mang* will be closed and locked until final rituals are held many months later, after the "stink" of the flesh has gone entirely.

The liminal period for the *iwun* may last for only a week or for as long as three months, depending on age, gender, and the fame of the deceased. It is brief for small children and longer for important men and women. During this time the soul (*enu*) of the deceased detaches itself from the body and wanders about, collecting itself from those objects that the person has made by putting his or her efficacy (or self) into them.

Close kin of a deceased person will choose to tabu eating either taro or pork (and eel, considered to be the pork of *iwun*) for this period of time following a death. These tabus are self-imposed, but may be lifted only when a shell is given by another member of the hamlet. Some may also tabu particular taro grown on stalks planted by the deceased person. This tabu may last a lifetime.

Many *enu*s of recently deceased individuals have been sighted by living people, recognized, and avoided if possible. These wandering souls may be extremely dangerous, attacking humans and eating them. New ghosts are considered to be extremely hot and aggressive, while old ghosts are considered cold, friendly, and often supportive of their living descendants.

Once when camped with a small group of Umbi residents who were hiding in the forest from an evil spirit that was causing an epidemic in the region, one of my assistants went back to Umbi to spit ginger (bespelled by one of our local sorcerers) in front of all the houses, to protect them from the sickness and from other sorcerers as well. On his way back to our forest fortress (a giant ficus tree), he was attacked by three ghosts. They grabbed his arms and he dropped the flashlight I'd loaned him. Then they grabbed his legs, and he fell to the ground and continued to fight with them. Finally he managed to escape and arrived in our camp in a state of near collapse and shock. It took him an hour before he could speak, when he told his tale. He had long scratches on his back and around his thighs and ankles, which he attributed to his attackers. "Did he recognize them?" "No," he replied, but one had a basket on his head and was a *midan*. There were three of them traveling together. It was some time later that we heard of three deaths (from the dysentery epidemic) in another community, one of them a *midan* buried with a basket covering his eyes. After hearing his story everyone agreed that Ningbi had met up with these three ghosts traveling together.

A man told me that he had met the ghost of his father with a pig on the path as he was moving through the forest. He returned to the hamlet to find that his father had just died and a pig had been killed.

Seeing ghosts is extremely common but always upsetting for those who do so. I was told by one Angelek informant that the ghost goes first to the sea to wash out the dirt from its eyes so that it can see clearly. It then eats a round stone called the "pig of ghosts" and calls "um, um, um" to the fish, who make a bridge for it to cross over the large river named Alimbit. Once on the other side, it climbs toward the mountains until it reaches a mountain named Aurop Iwindine where all ghosts live. When there is no road but only a stone wall, it stops. A large callophyllum tree on top of the cliff lets down a branch, and the ghost climbs the branch and reaches the top of the tree where it finds other ghosts, and where it will remain.

A number of the *sasokngin* songs, sung by the living, are those "sung" in the name of the ghost and describe its journey after the liminal period. In the following song, titled *Emon Sikali*, the listed birds (who here are considered to be *iwun*) sing.

> Bird Kahuwon sings, Bird Lambo sings, Bird Keleng
>   sings, Bird Sopo sings, Bird Rau sings, Bird Kahuok
>   sings, Bird Pula sings
> Bird Wisu (sea eagle) sings
> Bird Sea Eagle cries and dawn breaks
> Bird Kahuok cries and dawn comes up
> The callophyllum near the water
> The callophyllum bends under the water
> The lowest branches bend under the water
> The top branches bend over the water
> Fire smolders, Bird Wisu calls
> Dawn comes up

Related to this may be the fact that in many origin myths, the ancestral founders of hamlets emerge from the trunk or branch of a tree, although some others are said to have emerged from holes in the ground and/or underground rivers. While the cycle of life and death certainly begins and ends in the forest wilderness, it is less certain whether it goes from "tree to tree."

Another *sasokngin* that has a coastal origin tells of the journey of a ghost. The chorus and title of the song is "Reefs that reject me"; the explanation given: the listed reefs are dangerous spirits, and they try to kill the man and put him under the reef.

> Reef reject him, Death, he goes,
> Oh death he goes to Pangiwo, Pangiwo rejects him
> He goes to Bepleswo, rejects him, he goes
> He goes to Kumulo, rejects him, he goes
> He goes to Blekwo, rejects him, he goes

[listing of 11 more]
Rejects him, swallows him
Swallows him inside Enum
Inside Enum called Bipiwo
Bipiwo, the place is empty
Yia si wok aral, o Urung
Fire dies at Aral. Oh Death

While there is variation in the song collection for the place of the dead, questioning the living did not produce any consistent response. People of both Umbi and Angelek were quite clearly not concerned with ghosts when they reached whatever place they found to stay. They were concerned only with the journeying *iwun*, who were clearly dangerous. In fact, I was told that ancestors were not important; they could not be called upon to aid the living, in spite of the message of a cargo cult leader Koriam (later a Member of the House of Assembly), who promised that the ancestors would bring all good cargo to the living if the living supported him, Koriam, the cult leader. Unlike some of the Sengseng, who did support Koriam, the Kaulong thought the whole message nonsense, for they told me, the "dead were only bones and couldn't do anything—and besides, no one ever helps us." But bones are important, as I shall shortly show.

However, I was told of the ghost of a mother's brother coming back and helping a sister's son who had no father in order to show him things, but this type of encounter with an *iwun* was nowhere near as common as the sighting of ghosts of the recently deceased. But it is also true that some knowledge and songs are passed on from ghosts to the living—in dreams, they say. I finally decided that this ambiguity concerning ghosts was necessarily not resolved, as is so much else in Kaulong life.

SONG CYCLES

When the "time of the ghost" is over and the soul believed to be safely away from the world of the living, the major cycle of commemorative *sasokngin* song ceremonies begins. First, the bones must be prepared.

My data on skull and bone preparation are from informants only, as the Australian administration as late as 1974 still declared exhumation to be "illegal" (however, see below). I am not clear whether all deceased adult men and women were so treated, but suspect that only the skulls of *midan* and perhaps those of big women were commemorated by full *sasokngin* ritual cycles.

A specialist is called in to exhume and prepare the bones. The skull and jaw bones are certainly removed and sometimes also the long bones of the arm, the scapula and collarbones, and the breastbone. (I believe it to be significant that these bones are the same as those in the butchered head portion of a pig). During the preparation, which involves cleaning and painting the bones with red ochre, the specialist may not touch with his hands any food that he or others eat. Instead, he uses a stick to carry food to his mouth. Periodically he washes his hands and rubs a sticky sap on them and then holds a very hot roasted taro in both hands. Dropping the taro he clenches his fists, and if his hands are still hot, the "stink" of the dead remains and he must continue his treatment. When his clenched hands are cold after this test, the bone preparation is complete. He will be paid for this task with shells given by the mother's brother(s) and son(s) of the deceased.

During the preparation period, the bones are hung on a forked branch, with long bones tied on, together with the deceased's shells, stone valuables, dog-tooth belt, and pig-tusk ornament. The branch, with its decorations, is placed in a special house, where a big fire is kept burning and in which small portions of pork and perhaps (if the deceased was male and married) a bit of fiber from a wife's skirt are also burned, so that the fragrance of these items will waft over the bones. This last action only makes sense if the widow is not killed and buried with her husband. The shells, stone valuables, dog-tooth belt, and pig-tusk ornament will all be inherited by various children of the deceased.

The painting of the skull, jaw, and bones is done at least three times, with perhaps a week in between each painting. At the time of each painting, a song ceremony called *laungin* is held, beginning uncharacteristically in the heat of the day and continuing all night for several nights in a row. Each night, different sets of visitors from various hamlets attend. The skull and bones are carried by a woman of the hamlet in a basket, hidden from view during the singing. No one should see the skull, but the skull may be taken out of the basket and held facing the crowd; and should the skull see its killer in the group, I was told, it will strike him dead on the spot. No fire should burn during these singsings, no light should shine.

The specialist paints the skull and bones with red ochre (*emi*), which is considered to be cold. Thus, the painting may be seen as a process of cooling the skull and bones, making them less dangerous. The painter paints everything except the eyes. At the final painting, he places a small stone valuable in each eye socket and "shoots" red ochre through the center hole of the stone valuable and into the eye sockets of the skull. The eyes are now "closed" and the skull "cold," and with the preparation finished, the first of the skull song-cycles (*sasokngin*) takes place.

This home-hamlet song ceremony is one in which a tusker or other major pig belonging to the deceased is killed. Guests are invited from hamlets where pork-trading partners and other kin are located, particularly those who are close "brothers" or "mother's brothers" of the deceased. Only closely related people attend this first song ceremony because it is felt that the deceased may still have the power to cause death through poisoning the flesh of his pig(s), and the pork distributed at this time is presented only to these close kin. Even with this precaution to reduce potential conflict at the singsing, there will be considerable tension between hosts and visitors when the cause and manner of death is still unresolved, or when there are conflicting claims on the dead person's remaining property. As most of the deceased's pigs and taro have been sacrificed and distributed during the earlier singsing, only his shell and stone valuables remain.

At this home singsing, a major portion of the principal pig will be offered to a pork-partner of the deceased who agrees to kill a tusker at a stated time within the next year or two. This person will receive the skull and bones of the deceased along with the head (preferably) or ribs of the pig. When he in turn kills his tusker at the next event in the cycle, he distributes the pork "in the name of the skull" to the next person in the deceased's pork-network, and he hands over the skull and other bones as well. In this fashion the skull makes its final journey along the "road" between previous pork-partners, distributing pork in its own name. At each stop during the journey, the skull and bones are kept in the hamlet house hidden in a basket or box with shells covering it, safe from casual view. While it is in temporary residence, the skull's eyes protect the house, its contents, and the hamlet inhabitants from harm.

Pork trading networks are closed to any pork trade upon the death of one of its links. This final journey of the skull repairs the network, which has been broken. When the skull finally reaches its own hamlet, after a journey of from six to ten or more years, the rebuilding of the broken pork road is complete and may be reopened to trade. The skull is reburied in the home hamlet house by a descendant, who may then be considered as the deceased's replacement in the trading network when he reburies the skull, kills a pig, and trades pork to a partner under his own name.

Although the Australian government had outlawed this practice, in 1974 on the eve of independence, my Kaulong friends openly acknowledged it to be a continuing custom; and eventually (after I had attended the big skull-cycle singsing), I heard the following story.

When Puha died, he was buried in the administratively designated graveyard for his community. Puha had four wives, three of whom had predeceased him. His surviving wife was not strangled on his death, but her brothers had given payment to Puha's kin to pay for the *mangin*, the shame of her remaining alive.

Puha was a pork-trading "brother" of Maklun, the very powerful *midan* of Lapalam. Maklun decided that his friend and trading partner should not remain buried in the official graveyard. He passed the word that his bones should be exhumed, saying words to the effect that "who among his close kin is man enough to gather the bones?" Some men from Uresu, kin of Puha, took up the challenge and raided the graveyard one night, carrying the bones to Paduor, Puha's hamlet.

I heard much talk in Angelek about a coming song ceremony and was told that it was a "big one." I decided to make the ten-mile trip together with those in Angelek who were related to people from Uresu, the group we were to join. Not liking to negotiate slippery mountain paths in the dark, I set off in late morning with three trusted companions and guides, a young woman and two young men.

Vivid is my memory of a necessary negotiation of a single log bridge over a raging stream fifteen to twenty feet below. The woman and one young man went across first, carrying my tape recorder and camera. They turned at the other bank and tried to provide tension on the lawyer vine. As I, hand in hand with the remaining young man, began to inch my way over the slippery, muddy log, the rope broke and all four of us fell off. At our end we fell on the rocky bank before it dropped off into the water. We couldn't see the others. It took all my courage to get back on the log, with blind determination not to be the cause of my companions' death as well as my own, and to make it to the other bank. There we found the other two, bruised but intact; the woman, holding up my bag of equipment, told me proudly that she hadn't let it touch the ground! She also remarked that had she not been wearing her very full dance-skirt, she would have broken her back-side. The thick skirt had padded her fall.

As we approached Paduor, we heard some singing; but as it was still daylight and we were not supposed to be there yet, we hid ourselves in the bush and prepared for a long wait until the rest of the Uresu people would arrive, well after dark. Much to our dismay, we saw a man come into the bush to relieve himself. We were in a quandary, for to let him shame himself in front of women was nearly as bad behavior as announcing our too-early presence. In desperation we did the latter, calling out to him and then fleeing to another hiding place before we could be recognized. The man ran away in the opposite direction and never did return to the singsing.

Together with people from Uresu and Angelek we entered the hamlet several hours after dark. We did not carry shields and spears because we were to join the local group at Paduor. The home group is always unarmed for it is they who wish to promote a peaceful ceremony. As the men of the home group had been singing for days, they barely had voice to greet us. They assured us that once others had arrived and they began to sing in earnest their voices would return. Now augmented, the home group numbered about fifty men.

Shortly after us came the Lapalam group. Their spears crimped with tin and striking against their shields, the men charged the clearing and sang with strength and spirit. Their song (see pp. 207–8) was answered with a song from the Paduor group, and so they alternated for an hour or so. Then a group from Iumielo on the coast joined the celebration, also carrying spears and shields. They, too, sang in alternation with the other two groups. As each group sang, the women from all the groups danced in the center of the clearing, arm in arm with two or three similar-sized women; they whistled through their teeth in counterbeat to the drums and shields and danced with a skirt-swaying step. The women went to dance in front of each group of men in alternation, as the singing shifted. I estimated a total number of participants at about two hundred men, women, and children.

The songs were similar to songs found in *lut a yu*, in which names of things in the natural world and names of big men and women are listed. After four or five hours, the singing became much more competitive, with overlapping songs, and I was told not to waste my tape on such "bad singing."

Although I could not distinguish any change, a type of song called *tomasang* was sung close to dawn. These songs are sung as though the ghost is singing. It is clear that the image of the ghost here is that of a bird, named Sakul (a specific and rather small bird), which appears to represent the soul of the deceased. Examples that follow were given to me later in my house and in all of them, places familiar to the deceased are named. "We two" refers to the deceased husband and wife pair.

1. TOMASANG

In the rain time strong downpours
River rises, comes inside house
Charred firewood [dead body?] floats away
Bumps against the hamlet Emaningo
We two go to Elemdun
We two go to Elaiiko

To the bank of the river, Segit
Under the Aila [*Inocarpus fagiferus*], Apilpal [a variety with
    large fruit]
A man, Naul places a croton where body rested
At Epluk, a red ground

The bird vomits the spear—it hits his son
Elumaya, marks a white tree
Under the ancient Lumlum tree
Sakul (the bird) sits down
On top of the breadfruit tree, Anggelme
He goes down below the breadfruit
He goes on top of the breadfruit
I, father, stay here in this house
The house called Elewa
House of women, house of men
Paki kahauk kulalwhal
At the edge where the bush and clearing meet
Holul yia honehul
Listen, the fire is finished

2. *TOMASANG*

I curl up to sleep
I attack the place Angelek
I go now, I go, now I return
Raise up my tail, raise up my head
[These first four lines are a chorus repeated after each place
   listed below]
Under the breadfruit Merak
We two go to Dingding
We two go to Minielem
We two go to Salokmum
We two go to Nalop
We two go to the source of the water Nambula
We two go to source of Yungul War
We two go to the river Posungin Ehukuk
I see the mountain
I see the mountain Asake
I see the base of the mountain
I see the top of the mountain
Where the two roads come together
At the base of the bamboo Alilis

I go around the bamboo
Sikul flies up and sits on the breadfruit and sings
He goes down below to sing
He goes on top to sing
I, father, go to the *mok* [married house]
The house called Egiwol
This house belongs to women
This house belongs to men
Where the forest and clearing meet
Listen, fire is finished

Toward dawn, at the first light, the Lapalam group withdrew into the forest, only to reappear with threatening cries as they charged the clearing. As an outside group, they were reacting to possible accusations that they had caused the death. This is a customary action on the part of visitors.

When full light came, the very large tusker pig was carried out from its resting place. With the pole supported by four men, Maklun took the proffered spear and thrust it into the heart of the pig. As the pig cried, men from Paduor took up a special song, *kalalangin*, in which they named people who have killed pigs at Paduor in the past. The purpose of this song is to drown out the cries of the pig, lest someone capture the squeal and make sorcery on it, causing the flesh of the pig to poison those who ate it. The squeal is also captured on croton leaves that are planted in the hamlet to promote pig growth.

It was then that I noticed a woman wandering about on the edge of the singing men, wailing in typical fashion and holding a basket above her head. When I asked why she did that, I was informed that inside the basket was the skull of Puha. His widow was holding it up so it could indicate if its assassin was among the crowd. Until that time, I had no idea that the bones of Puha had been exhumed.

The pig finally died and was butchered into head and body portions. The head was offered to Maklun, who said he would prefer the body portion because plenty of people at his hamlet were hungry. Maklun took the pork and the skull of Puha to his hamlet outside Lapalam. The Iumielo group took the head, and Uresu/Angelek returned home without pork, which was appropriate since we were part of the hosting group.

About four months later, Maklun held a singsing at his hamlet outside Lapalam, and he passed the skull together with the head of the pig to a man at Uresu. I left the field before any subsequent link in the skull's journey could be made.

THE SONG ENDINGS

In discussing ceremonies, I have stressed the songs and the performance of competitive singing. In my attempts to gain a better understanding of the content of these songs, I found the most difficult part to be obtaining a translation of the concluding one or two lines. My informants had a very difficult time with these lines, too; as I remarked above, I came to consider them as "amens"—endings whose translations are not essential to the meaning. I persisted, however, and obtained the following classification of songs and endings, thus arriving at a better—though still tentative—understanding.

The following types of song do not have endings: *sasungin* (tooth-blackening), *tubuan* (masked figure), *ewit* (coconut-growing songs), *kalalangin* (a type of song sung to bring dawn).

Singsings with pig, *a yu* or *a sun* (an alternate word for pig), have three endings: some of these are said to be old bush (Kaulong) endings (*aiyik*) or old beach endings (*a murmur*). The first is old for both groups: *holul yia honehul* ("Listen, the fire is finished"); the second is old for the bush (Kaulong): *To miuk selsel edowang edowang, holul yia honehul* ("We three, my affine, my affine, listen, fire is finished"); the third is *nak maran*, which indicates a new, not traditional, song: *angli supangin supangin* ("Stand at the edge of the clearing, come on top").

Songs accompanying *sasokngin* ceremonies, where the skull of the deceased is present, have four endings: *lingiri yia si wok, yio minmin* ("I am hungry, fire spirals up, fire cools"); *yia si wok, wio minmin* ("Fire spirals up, fire is cold"); *paki kahauk kulalwhal* ("Where clearing meets forest"); and *holul yia honehul* ("Listen, the fire is finished"). Most of these endings indicate a hamlet place that is abandoned, empty of both persons and fire, a prime symbol of humanity.

Tomasang songs (sung near dawn for both *a yu* and *sasokngin* sing-sings) carry the corresponding endings given above. *Dikaiyikngin* songs carry the traditional ending (for both bush and beach): *Tom sail a ilu* (never satisfactorily translated).

Lausang songs are sung after *a yu* are finished (usually after midnight). The bush and beach endings are the same and are traditional: *edowang kaiyungan, sail a milim, sail a yok* ("Affine, your fragrance, spears come together, spears come apart"); or variants *Sel dowango* [name], *sel a milin, lai ya yiok* and *Lai a miling ko lai ai yiok*.

RITUALS AND SONGS OF DEATH

The rituals and songs of death emphasize Kaulong concepts concerning humanity and inhumanity. The living human being is composed of mind, bones, flesh, and a permeating soul or self. After death only the self and bones are significantly human. The flesh belongs to snakelike spirits of the forest who take the body away from the hamlet clearing, consume the raw flesh, and return the bones. I was told that human bones buried in the hamlet men's house make everything in the hamlet grow and flourish. If a place has no food and its people are hungry, they must dig up the bones and dance and sing with them during the day and night. Then food will return, and the people will become strong. In telling me about the rituals of death, people said that the *lausang* rituals involve singing during the daylight and night hours with the skull of the man who died. It seems possible to infer that with the death of a hamlet leader it is necessary to reinfuse the *bi* with productive energy or human efficacy (*enu*).

Snakelike spirits who consume human flesh in the forest return the bones to the clearing. Snakes that are killed in the forest and garden are eaten by humans in the clearing, and their bones must be returned to the garden. This is said to make the taro strong. Some snakes and certain worms and caterpillars found in a taro garden are not killed, for they are regarded as important intermediaries between gardeners and the major spirits who control the presence or absence of taro corms growing under the replanted taro stalks. These same snakes, worms, and caterpillars may also act as protectors of the growing corms.

Human bones that remain after death and the self or soul that departs after death, both powerful, are distinguishable in death as they were separable in life. In life, the self is the embodiment of the social identity of the person, directly reflective of the social activities that are classed as human, constructive, and productive. The body (*wo*, flesh and bones) is merely the container and, directed by the mind (*mi*), it engages in both human and nonhuman activities during the course of a lifetime. In death there is a reversal of roles and meaning of the *social* self and the *personal* bones. The social self (*enu*) eventually separates from the body, leaves the clearing permanently, and becomes an asocial self (*iwun*) in the forested mountain wilderness; while the skull and bones become a permanent fixture in the hamlet clearing and are the sole embodiment of the social identity of the person.

A person's name stands for his or her social identity. Throughout life individuals work to "get a name," that is, to make their name known near and far. When the skull and bones are buried or reburied in the hamlet, the name of the individual and his or her social identity are permanently placed in the hamlet for as long as the hamlet clearing is maintained.

The songs associated with death and burial are often those of the *iwun*, either traveling to the hamlet for burial or standing on the edge of the clearing where the forest begins. The endings emphasize the importance of fire in the hamlet, which symbolizes human occupation, and the loneliness of the *iwun*, which abandons the hamlet and travels to the mountains. It was only when I understood this transformation of social identity from *enu* to *iwun* and the shifting of the personal identity ("name") from body to bones that I came to appreciate the ambiguity of ghosts, who are both in the hamlet and yet never there but rather in the mountains.

10/ Of Pigs and Humans:
Where Forest and Clearing Meet

The task I set for myself in writing this book was to convey the complexity and meaning of the symbols with which the Kaulong communicate to each other the essence of meaningful, human life in the forests and the clearings of their world.

In this final chapter I reexamine those meaningful symbols of humanity to show how ideas about the nature and development of the social and physical identity of a human person are symbolized in pigs, teeth, bones, sex, song, and fire. I argue that these seemingly unrelated symbols are all, in fact, centrally related to the definitions of individual humanness and humanity in their world view. These key symbols, individually and collectively, in daily life and in ritual expression, serve to remind Kaulong that the "humanness" of the person is an achieved, not a given, condition of life. This message is transmitted by each symbol in variable combinations or alone during much of the daily activity of men and women. But the message is most explicit and forceful in the funeral rituals for individuals who have clearly achieved a high degree of "humanity"—the big men and big women of "renown."

OF PIGS AND HUMANS

As frequently reported for nearly every Melanesian society, pigs are an important item for transaction. They have also been discussed ecologically (Rappaport 1967; Vayda 1961), economically and politically (Rubel and Rosman 1978; Strathern 1971), and symbolically (Kahn 1986). But as Rathje (1978:170) points out: "Social anthropologists concerned with economic models have struggled valiantly to wrestle pig production and big-man ceremonies into place. They have measured calories, salt-intake, eating habits, and garden to pig ratios: . . . [but] the pig complex still does not seem to make 'economic' sense."

Other items involved in ritual and in exchange in Melanesia are human heads and other body parts. Although this exchange was seriously interrupted by colonialism, there are related data to examine, in myths and burial customs, where treatment of the human body helps inform us about concepts of the person, self, and social identity encoded in the various body parts (see Fortune 1935; Zegwaard 1959; Van Baal 1966; M. Panoff 1966; McKinley 1976; Herdt 1980). When these parts are also found as exchange or ritual objects, then we may assume that they are also saying something about the exchange relationship itself.

In Kaulong, pigs and humans are—not so curiously—compared and contrasted in nearly every possible way. They are the same, and yet they differ. I contend that the Kaulong consider pigs and humans to occupy a single continuum of existence in the world of forest and clearing. At the extremes of the continuum, pigs and humans are completely contrasted (as in the story, below), yet most of the time they move together through the activities that define them as either "human" or "inhuman."

THE STORY OF YUMIHIN

Yumihin (*yu mihin*, pig head) lived on top of a mountain. He looked like the butchered portion of pork called the "head," with the skin detached from the body but left attached to the skull. The skin was like a cloak and included his forelegs. Yumihin was a monster. In the morning the big men and women left the hamlet and went to their gardens to work. The children remained in the clearing to play. Yumihin came to the edge of the clearing and lured the children to him. Suddenly he trapped the children, wrapping them in his skin, and carried them away to his mountain where he ate them. When the big men and women returned, they found the clearing empty and wondered where all the children went.

The following day in another hamlet, the big men and women went to their gardens to work and the children remained to play. Yumihin came to the edge of the hamlet and again lured the children to come close to him and he wrapped them in his skin and carried them away to the mountain to eat. In hamlet after hamlet, Yumihin carried the children away and the big men and women wondered where all their children had gone.

One day a man decided to remain behind with the children in the clearing. As before, Yumihin came to the edge of the clearing. The man told the children not to go too close, but to lure Yumihin into the house where he would hide with a spear. When Yumihin entered the man threw his spear and impaled the monster and fastened him by his skin to the floor. The man then told the children to build a large fire and to heat some stones. When they had done this, he told them to put the stones on the skin of Yumihin. Yumihin died. The people roasted Yumihin on the hot stones and ate him and the children no longer disappeared from the hamlets.

The first of a number of important distinctions between pigs and humans in this tale are: pigs eat raw human flesh in the forest, while humans eat roasted pork in the clearing. Other creatures of the forest (for example, demons, local spirits, new ghosts, and people possessed by forest spirits) also eat human flesh. The Kaulong consider cannibalism practiced by other peoples (in the past) to be distinctly inhuman and expressed this view with a shudder of revulsion when I questioned them. I told earlier of the humanity-testing of the twins born in Umbi by giving them some pork fat to eat at the very tender age of a few weeks. When one refused, he was thought to be inhuman.

OF TUSKS AND TEETH

An important set of pig/human distinctions is that drawn between "teeth" and "tusks," between "black" and "white," and between the "invisible" and the "visible." This set not only distinguishes between pig and man as animal and human, but also between "child" and "adult" and between "man of anger" and "man of peace."

No one should mention the teeth of an infant until the first full set has erupted, lest the child die. When the set of baby teeth has come through, a pig is killed and the child's head is rubbed with the blood of the pig. A child's teeth are white, as are the teeth of pigs and other nonhumans. Fully adult teeth are black. Children, like pigs, are ambiguously human and nonhuman.

Adult males, and some women, have their teeth permanently blackened with *egit* (manganese oxide), an event ritualized with *sasungin* singing. When the manganese oxide is applied, a curved pig's tusk is pulled against the young man's teeth to test the strength of the application. All adults who chew betel nut acquire very heavily stained teeth.

Teeth should be invisible. One should cover the mouth while laughing, and in the presence of affines one should never drink or eat (i.e, expose one's teeth). Black teeth are nearly invisible.

White, visible teeth signify aggression. Pigs' tusks are white and very visible as they protrude from the lower jaw. When the tusks are made into ornaments, men clench these between their own teeth so that the curved white tusks appear to come from their own mouths as they challenge others in battle and song and when transacting pork. I was told that a man must kill another to validate his wearing of the pig's tusk ornament.

Dogs' teeth, also white, are strung on the wide belts worn by men. Dogs, like pigs, are found wild in the forests but may be domesticated to the clearing. Monsters of the forest all have white teeth and are known to eat humans.

Pigs (and dogs to a lesser extent), however, are also an important element of the hamlet where they are raised and cared for. They eventually become the center attraction of all-night singing ceremonies, before they are sacrificed and distributed to pork-partners of the ones who cared for them. Hamlet pigs are not usually aggressive; they do not eat humans (unless they are uncared for and become feral).

The same could be said of humans. The Kaulong distinguish between a "man of anger" and a "man of talk." The first is a fighter, a breaker of social relationships, a man who is unconcerned with building a network of social relationships through transactions in pork and shells. The second is a peacemaker, a builder of social relationships, one who raises and kills many pigs at his own *bi* and who travels to other places to receive pork in return. Of the two, the "man of talk" achieves greater respect; he is of the hamlet, while the fighter is of the forest.

The essential ambiguity of both men and pigs lies on a continuum of peaceful (human) to aggressive (inhuman) behavior. Pigs may behave more or less like humans, and humans may behave more or less like pigs. Both are found in the clearing of the hamlet and in the forest. Both may act as solitary nonsocial and nonhuman individuals, roaming the forests, impregnating females, and attacking gardens and hamlets in a destructive manner, much in the style of forest demons. The similarity of pigs and humans can be seen in their both having souls in which the essence of social being is to be found; the soul, however, must be continuously nurtured and nourished throughout life. The development and display of both human and pig "self" takes place during rituals held in the hamlet clearing. And when a human dies a pig is sacrificed in the rituals of the hamlet. In certain cases, the skull of the man and the head of the pig travel together in the individually constructed social network that had previously been symbolized by shells and pork.

THE IMPORTANCE OF FIRE

Pigs eat the same food as human beings do, but they eat it raw, while humans must cook it. Fire as a symbol of humanity has considerable significance in Kaulong life. Fire symbolizes the hamlet clearing. Oaths are sworn on fire. If an oath is falsely made, fire will not cook the liar's food and he will die. Fire is also a way for humans to control aggression directed at them by animals or by people. A glowing or dead firestick carried or planted between fighting individuals or groups should be respected by the combatants; if not, fire will not cook their food and they will die.

OF SEX (FOREST) AND SONG (CLEARING)

The forest is controlled by spirits and wild things, while the hamlet clearing is entirely human-made and maintained. The forest is an unpredictable place; it can be dangerous, filled with white-fanged human flesh-eaters or it can be beautiful. The forest is where a person can be alone, in peace and silence. Finally, the forest is for sexual reproduction; it represents mortality and abandonment of fellow human beings.

In contrast, the hamlet clearing is where all activity that defines humanness takes place: display of self, sacrifice of pigs, and social transactions with others. It is a place where pork is eaten, where self-development takes place, where one strives for immortality through replacement, where the concerns of the affiliates outweigh those of the individual. It is also a place where song, rather than conflict, is expected.

The central dilemma for Kaulong men is to maintain the continuity of life in the hamlet through replacement of themselves without having to meet the requirements of biological reproduction through sexual intercourse, which is always in the forest, as is birth and the menstrual hut. Humans solve this for their pig counterparts. They castrate the boars and send the sows into the forest to mate with wild boars, and then work to entice the sow to return with her young to the hamlet to maintain continuity there through replacement.

Forest (Spirits control)	Clearing (Humans control)
inhumanity	humanity
human eaters	pork eaters
white teeth	black teeth
individual/"me"	society/"we"
peace/silence	conflict/song
mortality/abandonment	immortality/work
sexual reproduction	self-development

FIG. 11. The contrasting domains and activities in which pigs and people define themselves in the world order.

Men of the hamlet—brothers, as we have seen—"send" their sisters out of the hamlet to mate, and then entice them to return any children to their natal hamlet to "replace" themselves and perhaps their brothers as well. Or a sister herself can be enticed to return with her children. A brother cannot marry his own sister, but he can marry his sister's daughter, or, more commonly, attract the sister's daughter to his hamlet to mate with one of his children.

Men's fear that they will die without anyone to bury them is a fear that they will not be replaced in the hamlet. If not replaced, there will be no song and the fire will die, the forest will overtake the abandoned place, and the man's name will be forgotten. Burial and replacement ensure a degree of immortality since pigs will be sacrificed and their blood will wash over a man's bones and he will be remembered by name. I believe that a woman's desire for immortality through replacement is the same, but does not constitute such a challenge. A woman does not have the same fear of marriage and sexual intercourse that a man does, and therefore does not try to avoid biological reproduction. However, marriage does mean death for the woman as much as for the man when she is strangled to share her husband's grave. A woman does share the same concern with her brother in maintaining their *bi*, the hamlet clearing and its human and nonhuman resources.

The contrast between the forest and the clearing can be fully understood only if one accepts the Kaulong idea that being nonhuman (animal-like) is the natural state of people. Hunting in the forest is clearly preferred to gardening; fighting is easier than talking; being alone is easier than trying to live with others; ambiguity is preferable to finding (and acting on) a final cause. The Kaulong truly love the forest; it is full of an abundance of food found in and under the deep shade of trees and in cool streams. Men and women both hunt and travel alone for long distances between hamlets. Only during the height of the rainy season must they curtail their excursions into the forest. The forest is a peaceful place albeit dangerous at times; its song is the familiar one of birds and other creatures, not the challenging song of humans.

The hamlet clearing is special. What takes place there is always social, sometimes involving many people and often involving strangers from distant places. It is a place where humans make shell transactions, where they acquire and display their personal and entirely human self through production, trade, and ritual. While there is always an emotional attachment to the hamlet, it is not one of repose; rather, it represents human conflict as well as achievement of both contemporary and ancestral human beings. But the clearing is not where humans live for the most part. The forest together with the garden—also surrounded by deep forest and far removed (usually) from the hamlet clearing—are the usual surroundings for all.

While gardens are economically and politically extremely important spaces, they are not equal to the forest and clearing as key symbols (Ortner 1973). Rather, the forest is only temporarily cleared and rapidly reverts to a forest when abandoned. No important activities, other than the production of food, take place in gardens.

Song and instrumental music seem to be the mediator between forest and clearing. Birds and men sing; birds belong to the forest, while men sing in the clearing. But singing is opposed to physical conflict: birds do not sing in the forest if danger is about, and men sing in the clearing, competing with words and sounds, rather than doing battle with spears. If fighting does take place, it must be in the forest beyond the edges of the clearing, and the singing is stopped.

Knowing the language of forest-dwellers makes the domain a friendly not strange place. In the clearing one's knowledge is challenged in song.

To achieve humanity requires one to go against nature. It requires one to carve out clearings from the forest for hamlets and to work hard raising taro and pigs. It requires one to travel, transact, negotiate, and compromise; to attract and not repel people; to acquire and display knowledge, opening one's very self to challenge and ridicule. It is very hard to be human. But without the struggle, when the ghost "stands where the forest and clearing meet" he will "listen and hear no song, and see that there is no fire," and he will know that humanity has lost.

Bibliography

Allen, Michael R.

1967   *Male Cults and Secret Initiations in Melanesia.* Melbourne, Australia: Melbourne University Press.

Barth, Frederik

1975   *Ritual and Knowledge among the Baktaman of New Guinea.* New Haven: Yale University Press.

Bateson, Gregory

1931–32   "Further Notes on a Snake Dance of the Baining," *Oceania*, vol. 2.

1958   *Naven: A Survey of the Problems Suggested by a Composite Picture of a Culture of a New Guinea Tribe, Drawn from Three Points of View.* Stanford: Stanford University Press. (Originally published in 1938.)

Battaglia, Debbora

1983a   "Projecting Personhood in Melanesia: The Dialectics of Artefact Symbolism on Sabari Island," *Man* (n.s.) 18 (2).

1983b   "Syndromes of Ceremonial Exchange in the Eastern Calvados: The View from Sabari Island." In *The Kula: New Perspectives on Massim Exchange,* ed. E. R. Leach and J. W. Leach, pp. 445–65. Cambridge, England: Cambridge University Press.

Berndt, Ronald

1962   *Excess and Restraint.* Chicago: Chicago University Press.

Brown, Paula, and Georgeda Buchbinder, eds.

1976   *Man and Woman in the New Guinea Highlands.* Washington, D.C.: American Anthropological Association Spec. Pub. 8.

Capell, A.

1954   *A Linguistic Survey of the South-Western Pacific.* South Pa-

cific Commission Technical Paper, no. 70. Nouméa, New
Caledonia.

1962   "Oceanic Linguistics Today," *Current Anthropology* 3(4):
        371–428.

Chinas, Beverly

1973   *The Isthmus Zapotecs: Women's Roles in Cultural Content.*
        New York: Holt, Rinehart and Winston.

1976   "Non-formal Roles: First Steps toward a Systematic Ap-
        proach." Paper presented at the American Anthropologi-
        cal Association meeting, Washington, D.C.

Chinnery, E. W. P.

1925   "Notes on the Natives of Certain Villages of the Mandated
        Territory of New Guinea." Territory of New Guinea An-
        thropological Report, no. 1. Melbourne, Australia: Govern-
        ment Printer.

1928   "Certain Natives of South New Britain and Dampier
        Straits." Territory of New Guinea Anthropological Report,
        no. 3. Melbourne, Australia: Government Printer.

Chowning, Ann

1958   "Lakalai Society," Ph.D. dissertation, University of Penn-
        sylvania, Philadelphia.

1961   "Amok and Aggression in the D'Entrecasteaux." In *Proceed-
        ings* of the 1961 Spring meeting of the American Ethnologi-
        cal Society, Seattle.

1966   "The Languages of Southwest New Britain." Paper read at
        the Eleventh Pacific Science Congress, Tokyo.

1969a   "Recent Acculturation between Tribes in Papua New
        Guinea," *Journal of Pacific History* 4:27–40.

1969b   "The Austronesian Languages of New Britain," *Pacific Lin-
        guistics* A-21:17–45.

1974   "Disputing in Two West New Britain Societies: Similarities
        and Differences." In *Contention and Dispute: Aspects of Law
        and Social Control in Melanesia*, ed. A. L. Epstein, pp. 152–
        97. Canberra: Australian National University Press.

1978   "Changes in West New Britain Trading Systems in the
        Twentieth Century," *Mankind* 11:296–307.

1984 "Culture and Biology among the Sengseng of New Britain," *Journal of the Polynesian Society* 89(1):7–31.

1985 "Rapid Lexical Change and Aberrant Melanesian Languages: Sengseng and Its Neighbors." In *Austronesian Linguistics*, ed. Andrew Pawley and Lois Carrington, pp. 169–98. Fifteenth Pacific Science Congress, Wellington, New Zealand.

Chowning, Ann, and Jane C. Goodale

1965 "The Passismanua Census Division, West New Britain Open Electorate." In *The Papua New Guinea Elections, 1964*, ed. D. G. Bettison, C. A. Hughes, and P. W. van de Veur, pp. 264–78. Canberra: Australian National University Press.

1966 "A Flint Industry from Southwest New Britain, Territory of Papua New Guinea," *Asian Perspectives* 9:150–53.

1971 "The Contaminating Women." Paper presented at the American Anthropological Association meeting, Washington, D.C.

Counts, Dorothy A.

1990 "Introduction" and "Conclusion." In *Domestic Violence in the Pacific*. Special issue of *Pacific Studies* 13(3):225–54.

Counts, Dorothy A., and David R. Counts, eds.

1985 *Aging and Its Transformations: Moving toward Death in the Pacific Islands*. Pittsburgh: University of Pittsburgh Press.

Deacon, A. B.

1934 *Malekula: A Vanishing People in the New Hebrides*. London: G. Routledge and Sons Ltd.

Epstein, A. L.

1969 *Matupit, Land, Politics, and Change among the Tolai of New Britain*. Canberra: Australian National University Press.

Epstein, T. S.

1968 *Capitalism, Primitive and Modern*. East Lansing: Michigan State University Press.

Errington, Frederick R.

1974 *Karavar: Masks and Power in a Melanesian Ritual*. Ithaca, N.Y.: Cornell University Press.

Evans-Pritchard, E. E.

1940   *The Nuer: A Description of the Modes of Livelihood and Political Institutions of a Nilotic People*. New York: Oxford University Press.

Faithorn, Elizabeth

1976   "Women as Persons: Aspects of Female Life and Male-Female Relations among the Kafe." In *Man and Woman in the New Guinea Highlands*, ed. P. Brown and G. Buchbinder. Washington, D.C.: American Anthropological Association Spec. Pub. 8.

Feld, Stephen

1982   *Sound and Sentiment: Birds, Weeping, Poetics, and Song in Kaluli Expression*. Philadelphia: University of Pennsylvania Press.

Forge, Anthony

1965   "Art and Environment in the Sepik." In *Art and Aesthetics in Primitive Societies*, ed. Carol Jopling, pp. 290–314. New York: E. P. Dutton and Co.

1972   "The Golden Fleece," *Man* (n.s.) 7:527–40.

Fortune, Reo

1932   *Sorcerers of Dobu*. New York: Dutton.

1935   *Manus Religion*. Memoirs of the American Philosophical Society, vol. 3. Philadelphia.

Geertz, Clifford

1973a   *Interpretation of Cultures*. New York: Basic Books.

1973b   "Thick Description: Toward an Interpretive Theory of Culture." Chapter 1 in Geertz's *Interpretation of Cultures*, pp. 3–30. New York: Basic Books.

Gilliard, E. Thomas

1961   "Exploring New Britain's Land of Fire," *National Geographic Magazine* 19(2).

Gillison, Gillian

1980   "Images of Nature in Gimi Thought." In *Nature, Culture and Gender*, ed. C. MacCormack and M. Strathern, pp. 143–73. Cambridge, England: Cambridge University Press.

Goodale, Jane C.

1966a   "Blowgun Hunters of the South Pacific," *National Geographic Magazine* 129(6):793–817.

1966b   "Imlohe and the Mysteries of the Passismanua, Southwest New Britain," *Expedition* 8(3):20–31. Philadelphia: University Museum, University of Pennsylvania.

1971   *Tiwi Wives: A Study of the Women of Melville Island, North Australia.* Seattle: University of Washington Press.

1973a   "The Kaulong Gender." Paper presented at the Association of Social Anthropology in Oceania meeting, Orcas Island, Wash.

1973b   "The Rape of the Men and Seduction of Women among the Kaulong and Sengseng of New Britain." Paper presented at the Association of Social Anthropology in Oceania annual meeting, Orcas Island, Wash.

1976   "Big-Men and Big-Women: The Elite in Melanesian Society." Paper presented at the American Anthropological Association meeting, Washington, D.C.

1977   "The Management of Knowledge among the Kaulong." Paper presented at the Association of Social Anthropology in Oceania meeting, Monterey, Calif.

1978   "Saying It with Shells in Southwest New Britain." Paper presented at the American Anthropological Association meeting, Los Angeles, Calif.

1980   "Gender, Sexuality and Marriage: A Kaulong Model of Nature and Culture." In *Nature, Culture, and Gender,* ed. Carol MacCormack and Marilyn Strathern, pp. 119–42. Cambridge, England: Cambridge University Press.

1981   "Siblings as Spouses: The Reproduction and Replacement of Kaulong Society." In *Siblingship in Oceania: Studies in the Meaning of Kin Relations,* ed. Mac Marshall, pp. 228–44. Ann Arbor: University of Michigan Press.

1985   "Pig's Teeth and Skull Cycles: Both Sides of the Face of Humanity," *American Ethnologist* 12(2):228–44.

n.d.   "The Two-Party Line: Conversations in the Field." Unpublished manuscript.

Harding, Thomas G.

1967   *Voyagers of the Vitiaz Strait: A Study of a New Guinea Trade System.* Seattle: University of Washington Press.

Healey, Christopher

1990   *Maring Hunters and Traders: Production and Exchange in the Papua New Guinea Highlands.* Berkeley: University of California Press.

Herdt, Gilbert H.

1980   *Guardians of the Flutes.* Berkeley: University of California Press.

1987   *The Sambia: Ritual and Gender in New Guinea.* New York: Holt, Rinehart and Winston.

Huntsman, Judith, and Anthony Hooper

1975   "Male and Female in Tokelau Culture," *Journal of the Polynesian Society* 84:415–30.

Kahn, Miriam

1986   *Always Hungry, Never Greedy: Food and the Expression of Gender in a Melanesian Society.* Cambridge, England: Cambridge University Press.

Kelly, R. C.

1988   "Etoro Suidology: A Reassessment of the Pig's Role in the Prehistory and Comparative Ethnology of New Guinea." In *Mountain Papuans: Historical and Comparative Perspectives from New Guinea Fringe Highlands Societies,* ed. J. F. Weiner. Ann Arbor: University of Michigan Press.

Layard, J.

1942   *The Stone Men of Malekula Vao.* London: Chatto and Windus.

Leach, E. R., and J. W. Leach, eds.

1983   *The Kula: New Perspectives on Massim Exchange.* Cambridge, England: Cambridge University Press.

Lewis, A. B.

1945   *Ethnology of Melanesia.* Chicago Natural History Museum Guide, part 5, 2d edition.

McKinley, Robert

1976   "Human and Proud of It! A Structural Treatment of Headhunting Rites and the Social Definition of Enemies." In *Stud-*

ies in Borneo Societies: Social Process and Anthropological Explanation, ed. George N. Appell. Special Report no. 12, Center for Southeast Asian Studies, Northern Illinois University.

Malinowski, Bronislaw

1929   *Sexual Life of the Savages.* London: Routledge Kegan Paul.

1961   *Coral Gardens and Their Magic.* London: George Allen and Unwin, Ltd. (Originally published in 1935.)

1984   *Argonauts of the Western Pacific.* Prospect Heights, Ill.: Waveland Press. (Originally published in 1922.)

Mead, Margaret

1930   *Growing Up in New Guinea.* New York: William Morrow.

1935   *Sex and Temperament in Three Primitive Tribes.* London: George Routledge and Sons.

1938   *The Mountain Arapesh*, vol. 1: *An Importing Culture.* Anthropological Paper 30 (3). New York: American Museum of Natural History.

Meggitt, Mervyn J.

1964   "Male-Female Relationships," *American Anthropologist* 66 (4):204–24.

Meigs, Anna S.

1984   *Food, Sex and Pollution: A New Guinea Religion.* New Brunswick, N.J.: Rutgers University Press.

Munn, Nancy

1982   "Gawan Kula: Spatio-Temporal Control and the Symbolism of Influence." In *The Kula: New Perspectives on Massim Exchange*, ed. E. R. Leach and J. W. Leach, pp. 277–308. Cambridge, England: Cambridge University Press.

Oliver, Douglas

1955   *A Solomon Island Society.* Boston: Beacon.

Ortner, Sherry B.

1973   "On Key Symbols," *American Anthropologist* 75:1338–48.

1974   "Is Female to Male as Nature Is to Culture?" In *Women, Culture, and Society*, ed. Michelle Z. Rosaldo and Louise Lamphere, pp. 67–88. Stanford: Stanford University Press.

Ortner, Sherry B., and Harriot Whitehead, eds.

1981   *Sexual Meanings.* Cambridge: Cambridge University Press.

Panoff, Françoise

 1972 "Maenge Taro and Cordyline: Elements of a Melanesian Key," *Journal of the Polynesian Society* 81:375–90.

Panoff, Michael

 1966 "The Notion of the Double-Self among the Maenge," *Journal of the Polynesian Society* 77:275–95.

Parkinson, R.

 1907 *Dreissig Jahre in der Sudsee.* Patrol Reports, Kandrian 7/57–88, Stuttgart.

Pavlides, Christina

 1993 "New Archaeological Research at Yombon, West New Britain, Papua New Guinea," *Archaeology in Oceania* 28:55–59.

Pavlides, Christina, and Chris Gosden

 n.d. "35,000-Year-Old Sites in the Rainforests of West New Britain, Papua New Guinea." Manuscript.

Pomponio, Alice

 1991 *Seagulls Don't Fly into the Bush: Cultural Identity and Development in Melanesia.* Belmont, California: Wadsworth.

Poole, Fitz John Porter

 1981 "Transforming 'Natural' Woman: Female Ritual Leaders and Gender Ideology among Bimin-Kuskusmin." In *Sexual Meanings,* ed. S. Ortner and H. Whitehead, pp. 100–154. Cambridge, England: Cambridge University Press.

 1982 "The Ritual Forging of Identity: Aspects of Person and Self in the Bimin-Kuskusmin Male Initiation." In *Rituals of Manhood,* ed. G. H. Herdt, pp. 99–154. Berkeley: University of California Press.

Powdermaker, Hortense

 1933 *Life in Lesu.* London: Williams and Norgate.

Powell, W.

 1883 *Wanderings in a Wild Country.* London: Sampson Low.

Rappaport, Roy

 1967 *Pigs for the Ancestors: Ritual in the Ecology of a New Guinea People.* New Haven: Yale University Press.

Rathje, W. J.

 1978 "Melanesian and Australian Exchange Systems: A View

from Mesoamerica." In *Trade and Exchange in Oceania and Australia*, ed. James Specht and J. Peter White. *Mankind* 11(3):165–76.

Read, Kenneth E.

1965   *The High Valley*. Berkeley: University of California Press.

Reay, Marie

1959   *The Kuma: Freedom and Conformity in the New Guinea Highlands*. Melbourne, Australia: Melbourne University Press.

1966   "Women in Transitional Society." In *New Guinea on the Threshold*, ed. E. K. Fisk. Canberra: Australian National University Press.

Rubel, Paula, and Abe Rosman

1978   *Your Own Pigs You May Not Eat: A Comparative Study of New Guinea Societies*. Chicago: University of Chicago Press.

Rubinstein, Robert

1978   "Placing the Self in Malo: An Account of the Culture of Malo Island, New Hebrides." Ph.D. dissertation, Bryn Mawr College.

1981   "Knowledge and Political Process in Malo." In *Vanuatu: Politics, Economics and Ritual in Island Melanesia*, ed. M. R. Allen. Sydney, Australia: Academic Press.

Salisbury, Richard

1962   *From Stone to Steel: Economic Consequences of a Technological Change in New Guinea*. Melbourne: Melbourne University Press.

1970   *Vunamami: Economic Transformations in a Traditional Society*. Berkeley: University of California Press.

Schieffelin, Edward L.

1976   *The Sorrow of the Lonely and the Burning of the Dancers*. New York: St. Martin's Press.

Sexton, Lorraine

1986   *Mothers of Money, Daughters of Coffee: The Wok Meri Movement*. Ann Arbor, Mich.: UMI Research Press.

Sheehy, Gail

1976   "The Mentor Connection: The Secret Link in the Successful Woman's Life," *New York*, April 5, pp. 33–39.

Shore, Brad

1978   "Ghosts and Government: A Structural Analysis of Alter-
        native Institutions for Conflict Management in Samoa,"
        Man (n.s.) 13:175–99.

Specht, J., I. Lilley, and J. Normu

1981   "Radiocarbon Dates from West New Britain, Papua New
        Guinea," *Australian Archaeology* 12:13–15.

1983   "More on Radiocarbon Dates from West New Britain, Papua
        New Guinea," *Australian Archaeology* 16:92–95.

Strathern, Andrew

1971   *The Rope of Moka: Big Men and Ceremonial Exchange in Mount
        Hagen.* Cambridge: Cambridge University Press.

1972   *One Father, One Blood: Descent and Group Structure among the
        Melpa.* Canberra: Australian National University Press.

1984   *A Line of Power.* London: Tavistock.

Strathern, Marilyn

1972   *Women in Between.* London: Seminar Press.

1981   "No Nature, No Culture." In *Nature, Culture and Gender,*
        ed. C. MacCormack and M. Strathern, pp. 174–222. Cam-
        bridge: Cambridge University Press.

1988   *The Gender of the Gift: Problems with Women and Problems
        with Society in Melanesia.* Berkeley: University of California
        Press.

Todd, J. A.

1934–35 "Report on Research Work in S. W. New Britain, Territory
        of New Guinea," *Oceania* 5:193–213.
        "Native Offenses and European Law in S. W. New Brit-
        ain," *Oceania* 5:437–61.

1935–36 "Redress of Wrongs in S. W. New Britain," *Oceania* 6:401–
        40.

Tuzin, Donald

1978   "Yam Symbolism in the Sepik: An Interpretive Account,"
        Southwest Journal of Anthropology 78:230–54.

Valentine, Charles A.

1961   *Masks and Men in Melanesian Society.* Lawrence: University
        of Kansas Press.

Van Baal, Jan

1966   *Dema: Description and Analysis of Marind-Anim Culture*. The Hague: Martinus Nijhoff.

Vayda, A. P., Anthony Leeds, and D. Smith

1961   "The Place of Pigs in Melanesian Subsistence." In *Proceedings*, American Ethnological Society. Seattle: University of Washington Press.

Wagner, Roy

1967   *The Curse of Souw*. Chicago: University of Chicago Press.

Weiner, Annette B.

1976   *Women of Value, Men of Renown*. Austin: University of Texas Press.

1979   "Trobriand Kinship from Another Point of View: The Reproductive Powers of Women and Men," *Man* (n.s.) 14:328–48.

1988   *The Trobrianders of Papua New Guinea*. New York: Holt, Rinehart and Winston.

Weiner, Annette B., and Jane Schneider, eds.

1991   *Cloth and Human Experience*. Washington, D.C.: Smithsonian Institution Press.

Whiting, John

1946   *Becoming a Kuoma*. New Haven: Yale University Press.

Young, Michael W.

1971   *Fighting with Food: Leadership, Values and Social Control in a Massim Society*. Cambridge, England: Cambridge University Press.

Zegwaard, G. A.

1959   "Headhunting Practices of the Asmat of West New Guinea," *American Anthropologist* 61:1020–41.

Index

Accidents, 41–42; prevention of, 43
Adultery, 144, 166
Aka, New Britain, 8, 9
Alimbit River, 6, 100, 233
American Council of Learned Societies, xvi
Ancestors, 112–14, 134–35, 142, 145, 235
Andru River, 6
Angelek, New Britain: description of, 28–34 passim
Anu River, 226
Apoan River. *See* Ason River
Arawe Islands, 6, 87, 89, 153; language of, 154, 226
Arihi, New Britain, 10
Ason River, 5, 6, 12, 15, 16–17, 100
Association of Social Anthropologists in Oceania, xv
Austronesian languages. *See* Languages, Austronesian
Australian Administration. *See* Department of Native Affairs

Barkcloth, 87, 145, 176. *See also* Clothing
Bats, cave, 71
Behavior: predictability of, 48, 52; elite, 125–33 passim; continuum of, 250
Bi. See Hamlet (*bi*)
Big man (*pomidan*), xii, 14, 31–32, 34, 54, 70, 89–90, 110–11, 115–16, 125, 128–29; as headman, 106, 204, 207, 211
Big woman (*polamit*), xii, 31, 54, 109–11, 115–16, 125–28, 204, 207, 211–12
Birds, 3–5, 61–62, 150, 207–9, 241
Birth, 117–18, 137, 150, 153–56, 175, 180; -order, 141–42; of twins, 155–56

Blowgun, x, 7, 24, 71, 207. *See also* Hunting
Body (*wo*), xi, 37–38, 47, 54–55, 57, 244–45
Bones, xii, 53, 65, 114–15, 117, 236–38, 244–45. *See also* Skull, human
Burial, 103, 114, 115, 117, 176, 226–27, 229–38 passim

Calendar, 67–68
Cannibalism, 47–48, 165, 248
Cargo cult, 65, 235
Cassowary, 31, 69, 71, 72, 207, 209; as mother's brother, 210
Castration: of pigs, 70, 83, 183; of dogs, 70
Catholic Church, 7, 8, 10, 16, 17, 39; at Turuk, 30, 33
Children, 70, 86, 118, 142–43, 149, 177–78, 181–82; as parents' replacements, 109, 117; and sharing, 119–20
Chinnery, E. W. P., 30
Chowning, Ann, ix, 6, 9–14, 17, 26, 44, 106
Christianity, 33, 55. *See also* Catholic Church; Church of England
Church of England, 7, 10, 16, 17, 30
Clothing: and accessories, 101, 159; male, 70–71, 84, 101, 145, 149; female, 101, 136, 145, 149, 153, 155, 201
Clowning, 111, 118, 133, 154, 156, 201, 203
Competition: in exchange, 99, 129, 137, 142, 144–46
Conception, 154, 180
Conflict, xi, 137–41, 149, 161, 163, 185, 197–99, 202–3; affinal nonagression, 171